Outside the Lines of

Gilded Age Baseball

The Origins of the 1890 Players League

Also by Rob Bauer

Nonfiction
Outside the Lines of Gilded Age Baseball: Alcohol, Fitness, and Cheating in 1880s Baseball

Outside the Lines of Gilded Age Baseball: Gambling, Umpires, and Racism in 1880s Baseball

Outside the Lines of Gilded Age Baseball: The Finances of 1880s Baseball

Fiction
My Australian Adventure

The World Traveler

The Buffalo Soldier

Darkness in Dixie

The Long Way Home

Outside the Lines of Gilded Age Baseball

The Origins of the 1890 Players League

Rob Bauer

Copyright © 2018 Robert A. Bauer
All rights reserved.
ISBN-13: 978-1-948478-10-6

No part of this book may be reproduced in any form or by any electronic or mechanical means, including information storage and retrieval systems, without written permission from the author, except for the use of brief quotations in a book review.

For any inquiries regarding this book, please contact Rob at robbauerbooks@gmail.com.

For Ron, Pearl, Eric, Owen, Aaron, & Isaak

Still my best friends.

Contents

Introduction	1
1. The State of the Game in 1885	4
2. The Cast: The Owners	16
3. The Cast: The Players	38
4. Reaction to the Brotherhood of Professional Baseball Players	48
5. The Brotherhood and the Salary Limit Plan	62
6. The Winter of 1886-1887	75
7. The Winter of 1887-1888	97
8. The Brotherhood Grows in Stature	115
9. The Brotherhood and Player Contracts, 1887-1888	130
10. Spalding's Tour and the Rowe-White Affair	154
11. The Brotherhood and the Brush Plan	179
12. The Beginning of the End of the American Association I	206
13. The Beginning of the End of the American Association II	223
14. The Storm Gathers	243
15. The Storm Breaks	259
Notes on Statistics	286
Terminology of the 1880s	290
Bibliography	293
Index	297
About the Author	310
Acknowledgments	311

Introduction

ALL THE OTHER VOLUMES IN MY SERIES on 1880s baseball occasionally refer to how, in 1890, the players of the National League seceded from the National League and formed their own organization, known to baseball history as the Players League, although some contemporaries also called it the Brotherhood League. I have not hesitated to call it the greatest disaster afflicting baseball in the 1800s, no small claim considering the gambling scandals of the 1870s, the syndicated ownership issues of the 1890s, or the banning of African Americans from the game after 1884. All these other events can make a respectable case for the title of baseball's worst disaster of the nineteenth century.

When I use the term disaster to refer to what happened in 1890, however, I do not mean it was a disaster in the sense that all the decisions leading to the Brotherhood's revolt were bad ones and everyone in baseball should have seen it coming. The events building through the 1880s to their culmination in 1890 were not, therefore, like those in my home state of Montana in the 1880s. In that disaster, ranchers overstocked the grassland with cattle, sheep, and other animals to the point where everyone who acknowledged reality knew a crash would happen sooner or later. Instead, I use the term disaster in the sense that the outcomes were bad for baseball as a sport, at least many of them, even the outcomes unforeseen when the players made their move. In making such a grandiose claim, it is only right to explain why the National League players decided to set out on a new path of their own in 1890. This book explains the entire story of why they did so.

Like most major events, the Players League was the culmination of a series of decisions that led toward a certain outcome. That means it was not inevitable, and had certain people acted differently at important times or had different personalities been involved, it may never have happened. This is, by itself, a very good reason for writing a history of the causes of the Brotherhood War of 1890. Those of us who care about baseball deserve to know how something so important to the first century of the game came about. We need research about the decisions people made and the personalities of the men making those decisions. Without this knowledge, it is tempting to see the Players League of 1890 as a minor blip in baseball's history, an experimental league lasting just one season and therefore deserving of minor recognition, if any, in our view of baseball's history.

Part of the reason this is the wrong way to look at things is because had the Players League succeeded, and it almost did, the entire history of baseball might have been different. By different, I do not mean different in the way that Red Sox history would have been different if Boston had never sold Babe Ruth to the Yankees or had Bill Buckner fielded that ground ball cleanly in the 1986 World Series. I am not writing about the fate of one or two franchises. Instead, had the Players League proved successful, the entire ownership structure of baseball might have turned out different, the reserve clause might have disappeared after 1890, and who knows what that would have led to down the road?

Even though it failed, the Players League of 1890 produced, or contributed to, important changes in baseball's history. Its demise helped the National League eliminate the American Association and gain a monopoly over major league baseball that lasted for a decade.

Introduction

Although baseball historians sometimes misunderstand the role of the Players League in that sequence of events, as chapters twelve and thirteen demonstrate, it played a role. The defeat of the Players League also destroyed the concept of unionism in baseball for the foreseeable future, affecting the financial operations of the game significantly. Finally, the Players League, while short-lived, initiated the important practice of putting two umpires on the field at the same time rather than one, greatly improving baseball thereby.

Those are just the major consequences, to go with a host of minor ones. Clearly, then, the Players League is important to nineteenth-century baseball history, indeed, to baseball history generally. It stands to reason that something so important should have a multitude of causes, and complex causes at that, rather than one or two simple ones. This book, along with the three others in my comprehensive series *Outside the Lines of Gilded Age Baseball*, lays out those causes for all to see. If you, the reader, find yourself wondering about anything mentioned here that I have not described to your full satisfaction, the answer you are looking for is probably in one of the other three books in my series.

Whenever possible, I've described events in the words of those who participated in them. The story includes some memorable characters, too, although some are easier to identify and sympathize with than others. Whichever ones turn out to be your favorites, however, I have done my best to make them human by describing their good qualities along with their questionable ones. Except for Arthur Soden in Boston. After reading six years of weekly sporting newspapers, I am still waiting for his good qualities to appear.

In any case, you have in front of you as complete a description of the origins of the Players League as I can write. I hope you enjoy it.

Chapter 1

The State of the Game in 1885

AMONG THE GREATEST IRONIES OF 1880S BASEBALL is that the most disastrous season of the nineteenth century, 1890, followed on the heels of an 1889 pennant race that was probably the most exciting in baseball's history to that point. To most of the sixteen major league baseball franchises, the future of the game must have looked bright indeed when the 1889 season closed. The National League concluded its fourteenth campaign with a monumental contest between the New York Giants and Boston Beaneaters. Both teams fielded lineups flush with future Hall of Fame players. On October 1, Boston defeated the Cleveland Spiders while the Giants stumbled against the mediocre Pittsburgh Alleghenys, leaving the Beaneaters a single game ahead with four to play. The Giants recovered, however, beating Pittsburgh the next day, then sweeping Cleveland in three games to close their season. The Beaneaters, meanwhile, lost the concluding game of their series with Cleveland on October 2, dropping them into a tie with the Giants. They won the first two games of their next series with Pittsburgh, meaning the race remained deadlocked until the last day of the season, October 5. On that fateful day, the Beaneaters fell 6-1, giving New York the championship. It was the second straight pennant for the Giants after several years of frustrating failures and near misses that had New York fans wondering if their costly collection of star players would ever triumph and win first place in the National League.

Baseball's other major league, the American Association, boasted a championship race almost as dramatic. The Association's eighth season featured a thrilling campaign culminating with the Brooklyn Bridegrooms barely outdistancing the St. Louis Browns, giving a team besides St. Louis the Association pennant for the first time in five years. Things seemed secure enough for the Bridegrooms as late as September 15, when they held a five-game lead in the standings with just nineteen games to go. The Browns refused to go quietly, however, winning fifteen of their next seventeen games, including twelve in a row, so that by October 10, Brooklyn's lead was a mere two games.[1] After winning four consecutive Association pennants, Browns team captain Charlie Comiskey would not allow his team to go down without a good fight. The Bridegrooms did hold on, finishing two games up, but St. Louis's finishing flourish ensured the outcome remained uncertain until the season's final two days. In fact, the Bridegrooms were not secure in their possession of the championship until a few days after the regular season ended, for reasons discussed later.

---

[1] In 1889, the schedules of the respective leagues did not finish simultaneously as they do in the twenty-first century. This is because the two leagues, while not exactly at war in the sense of each actively trying to eliminate the other, were two separate organizations, each with its own league offices and league president. They were competitors in the business of baseball, rather than partners like the American and National leagues are today. Thus, although both had a 140-game schedule, the leagues finished play about a week apart. In addition, teams did not always make up games lost to rain or darkness, so even teams in the same league did not always finish with the same number of games played. In 1889, the Giants completed 126 of their 140 scheduled games, going 83-43, while their World Series opponent, the Bridegrooms, played 137 times, winning 93.

Outside the Lines of Gilded Age Baseball

Along with the terrific drama on the field, this nerve-wracking ending meant, above all else, three things to major league baseball. First, for the quartet of cities involved in the pennant race, it meant lots of money. Thousands of fans streamed to ballparks to watch these teams during September and early October, and the dramatic final week heightened enthusiasm for the World Series that followed the championship season. As a result, 1889 set a new season attendance record. In addition, the drama distracted the attention of most baseball observers, fans and the press alike, from the most important off-field event of the nineteenth century, the decision of the Brotherhood of Professional Baseball Players (BPBP) to part ways with the National League and start its own league for the 1890 season. While the Brotherhood had not made its decision public as of early October, this possibility hovered in the background, like a nightmare waiting to spring from the shadows. In late September and early October, however, most people ignored this issue, entranced by the drama in New York, Brooklyn, St. Louis, and Boston. Finally, the American Association race highlighted an important personal rivalry shaping the destiny of baseball, that between St. Louis president Chris Von der Ahe and Brooklyn president Charles Byrne.

All three of these issues—the unceasing search of baseball teams and their owners for more money, the relationship of the players to the teams employing them, and rivalries between the teams themselves—have deep roots and important consequences. They rate among the central forces shaping baseball in the 1880s. To comprehend why this is true, we must understand how each of these threads developed during the 1880s and then wound together in 1889 to produce the rebellion of the Brotherhood of Professional Baseball Players. Let us begin with some of the relevant pieces of baseball history prior to 1885.

Ideas about how to run the game of baseball as a business evolve continually, but even though the sport was still relatively new in the mid-1880s, a few fundamentals seemed clear. As a group, baseball's owners took many of the practices so popular in their other business pursuits and began adapting them to baseball. They tried to limit competition and create monopolies, control as large a market share as possible, keep labor under control, and the like. For example, in the first half of the 1880s, the two major leagues fielded teams in competition with each other in some cities, namely New York, Philadelphia, and St. Louis. By 1889, this pesky competition was nearly a thing of the past, with major league baseball boasting sixteen teams operating in fifteen different cities. (New York and Brooklyn were separate entities until 1898, when Gotham absorbed the City of Churches.) Philadelphia was the only city in which the leagues continued competing directly.

This effort to increase stability through limiting competition was quite important to team owners because team turnover was a chronic problem. Of the eight founding franchises of the National League in 1876, only two, Boston and Chicago, remained in 1889. No fewer than twenty-two clubs had occupied the other six slots in the league. The American Association, with its shorter history, had done a bit better, but franchise instability was certainly on the minds of baseball's magnates.[2] Collectively, they decided that limiting the competition for fans within cities would aid their search for greater profits and greater continuity.

A second issue for owners was their perceived need to tighten control over the labor of their players. Toward that end, major league baseball owners had two primary measures at their disposal by the

---

[2] Had the owners had a chance to see into the future, they would have known this problem was nearly over. Of the eight National League franchises competing in 1889, five (Boston, Chicago, Philadelphia, Pittsburgh, and New York) are still members of the National League, although Boston is now the Atlanta Braves and the New York Giants now play in San Francisco. Two other members of today's National League, the Cincinnati Reds and the Brooklyn (now Los Angeles) Dodgers were in place by 1890, so seven of the eight teams in the NL before the expansion of 1962 were members by that year. The remaining team of the eight, the St. Louis Browns (now Cardinals), arrived in 1892 following the dissolution of the American Association after the 1891 season.

middle of the 1880s. The first of these, the reserve clause, had existed since 1879 and, over the subsequent decade, baseball owners slowly realized the various ways they might use this instrument to depress player salaries and limit player mobility. New to their toolbox in 1885 was a salary limit plan that the owners hoped would limit the pay players received, allowing the owners to keep a greater share of baseball's growing pie.[3]

Baseball's barons had discussed such a plan on and off for several years. Prior to deciding on the salary limit plan of 1885, for example, they discussed a graduated plan for player salaries to try to reduce salaries and "to protect their own interests by mutual agreements and concessions." Proponents, worried that only clubs in larger cities could turn a profit under existing conditions, professed their hope that a graduated salary scale would provide incentives for players to improve their play and move up the scale, although the "record, habits, & co" of the player would also factor into their salary rating. Technically, the clubs did agree to a simplified version of this scheme, capping salaries at $2,000 for all players, but from the outset, it proved unworkable because there were no penalties for circumventing the rule. Understandably, however, this plan caused significant unease amongst players. Other owners called for a simple blanket on top salaries and arbitrary salary reductions of 20-40%, but because they were not in concert regarding what to do in 1885, they settled on their unsuccessful salary limit plan.[4]

---

[3] Peter Levine, *AG Spalding and the Rise of Baseball: The Promise of American Sport* (New York: Oxford University Press): 58, and John Thorn, *Baseball in the Garden of Eden: The Secret History of the Early Game* (New York: Simon & Schuster, 2011): 227-228, 232-233.

[4] M. C. D., "From Providence," *The Sporting Life*, August 26, 1885, 1; Olympic, "Graded Salaries," *The Sporting Life*, August 26, 1885, 1; "Conferees to Meet Monday," *The Sporting Life*, August 26, 1885, 1. The salary limit approved in the winter of 1885-1886 technically remained in force even when the National League adopted the Brush Plan for 1889. However, because there were no penalties attached for violating the provisions of the 1885 rule, adherence to the measure was almost nonexistent, and players often earned money outside their

The State of the Game in 1885

Whatever National League owners tried to do to maximize their profits and limit player independence, the one owner at the bottom of any plan was Al Spalding of the Chicago White Stockings. From 1885 onward, he schemed ways to help owners get the upper hand over their players. Throughout the summer of 1887, when Spalding promoted a potential scheme for uniting the two major leagues into one, his hometown newspaper, the *Chicago Daily Tribune*, described him as "endeavoring to create a baseball trust," while *The Sporting News* accused him of plans for "one great stock company" and being a "one-league monopolist."[5] While these plans, first unveiled in 1886, did not come to fruition right away, "President Spalding, of the Chicago Club, is still working on his one-association scheme for next season . . . The exposure of the scheme has killed whatever chance of success it had for next season, but Mr. Spalding is not easily discouraged, and he will stick to his pet theory till the last."[6] Spalding later saw his wish fulfilled after the demise of the Players League in 1890 and the American Association in 1891.

The Sporting News proved correct in its assessment that Spalding would not give up easily. Some baseball historians believe it was Spalding, not Indianapolis owner John Brush, who was the true author of the Brush Classification Plan adopted in November of 1888 to limit player salaries, discussed in detail in later chapters.[7] Likewise, in 1889 Spalding proposed a new plan to codify the financial structure of all of baseball. In July, he wrote a letter to Nick

---

official salary by various unofficial means. Still, it was a concern to ballplayers throughout this era because should management ever enforce this rule consistently, it would drastically reduce salaries for some players. "The Base Ball Compact," *The Sporting Life*, October 28, 1885, 1. Also, we should note that in the 1880s baseball sportswriters did not always sign their articles with their names. Some used aliases or initials, and some did not sign their work at all, so we do not always know the identity of each author with certainty.
[5] Levine, *AG Spalding and the Rise of Baseball*, 56-57.
[6] "Caught on the Fly," *The Sporting News*, September 13, 1886, 5.
[7] Thorn, *Baseball in the Garden of Eden*, 232-233.

Young, president of the National League, proposing a system wherein all baseball leagues, major and minor, would enter into an arrangement featuring the two major leagues at the top and all minor leagues organized into a four-tier structure below. Few other than the sixteen owners of major league teams endorsed Spalding's plan, however, citing its tendency to enrich a small group at the expense of the rest of organized baseball. The *Chicago Herald* denounced it as a plan for a "baseball trust" and a "scheme for the monopoly of the business."[8] The fact that Spalding was the originator of many such plans, however, not only makes him a more likely suspect for authorship of the Brush Plan, but also shows that few people in baseball spent more time thinking about how owners might take tighter control of the sport.

The other central pillar in the financial structure of major league baseball was the reserve clause. When it came to issues directly affecting individual players, nothing outranked the reserve clause in importance. When a player signed a contract with a major league team, the team signed the player for that year but also had the option of retaining the player's services for the following season. If the team exercised its option and brought the player back, when the player signed the next season, again, the team reserved the option to bring him back the following season. In other words, every contract was essentially a one-year contract with a team option for the next season. The player, by contrast, had no ability to opt out of the contract at any time, save by retiring or deciding to play in a low-level minor league that did not observe the reserve rule. A player might get his team to release him, but once he signed with another major league team, he fell under the umbrella of the reserve clause once again.

---

[8] Levine, *AG Spalding and the Rise of Baseball*, 57-58. The plan also garnered criticism from writers Frank Brunell and Harry Palmer of *The Sporting Life*, among others. F. H. Brunell, "Brunell's Budget," *The Sporting Life*, July 24, 1889, 8; Harry Palmer, "Chicago Gleanings," *The Sporting Life*, July 24, 1889, 8.

The State of the Game in 1885

The imbalance of this situation was clear to all by 1885. When major league teams first started enforcing the reserve rule in 1879, only five players per team fell under its control. The players not reserved retained the freedom to sign with the team of their choosing the following year. As the years passed, however, teams applied the reserve rule to more players each year. Baseball owners extended it to cover eleven players in 1884, twelve in 1886, and fourteen players for 1887, which in the 1880s was the entire roster of most teams. This situation chafed worse than anything else with the players. It did not matter how poorly their teams treated them, how much money they might earn playing somewhere else, or how much service time they had provided to their ball club. If the team wanted to reserve a man for the next year, he had no recourse save complaining, sulking, and hoping his team had a change of heart. For the players, the idea of being unable to work where they wanted seemed to contradict American values about freedom. Although players did not say explicitly they thought they were slaves in the way African Americans had been before 1865, many players considered the reserve rule akin to a sports version of slavery.

Financial considerations were not the only issue between players and owners. However harsh the reserve rule was, players also did things that hurt their own cause, and nothing frustrated team owners more than players' excessive drinking. The list of 1880s ballplayers who sabotaged their careers through alcoholism is a lengthy one. Baseball may have begun as a gentleman's game played by club teams, but by the 1880s, many, perhaps most, of its players came from Eastern cities and were working-class in background. They often behaved accordingly, and, sadly, drinking was rampant. It would have been one thing if the players confined their drinking to the off-season, but all too often, they continued imbibing during the season, too, sometimes even arriving at the ballpark too drunk to play. This hurt their play on the field, no doubt. It also caused a chronic shortage of money for some players who never should have been in a shaky financial situation. Alcoholism was the biggest problem in 1880s baseball, and many team owners and sportswriters obsessed on how to limit or prevent player drinking.

Lushing by players was not the only issue, however. Fitness and training also mattered. Unlike drinking, players were not necessarily negligent in this regard. Many worked to stay in shape during the off-season, so they could play their best baseball the following year. In the process, they provided a strong counter to one of the arguments put forward to limit their salaries: the notion that they only worked six or seven months of the year. Some performed physical fitness exercises, some played other sports, and some worked at physical jobs, but one way or another, many ballplayers tried to stay in top form during the winter.

One reason these two things, alcohol and fitness, were so important was that most owners believed that baseball fans wanted to see the game played "scientifically" by sober, athletic men. Owners worried that if players appeared drunk, or fat, or both, fans might turn up their noses and stay away from the ballpark. Less attendance meant less money, so it was important that players appear healthy specimens of manliness. To use the phrasing of the day, teams wanted men "in the pink of condition," not "ice wagons."

This desire for healthy, athletic players also manifested itself in other ways. Peruse any book discussing the rule changes in baseball from year to year, and one will note that the 1880s were a time of great experimentation. Some of these experiments were to the core rules of the game, such as how many balls a player needed for a walk or strikes needed for a pitcher to record a strikeout. Part of the reason owners experimented so much was to please the fans, and in the 1880s owners believed the fans wanted to see games full of action. Spectators wanted to see batters hit the ball, fielders chase it, and baserunners take chances. In short, they expected a game of motion. The fans did not want to sit through an endless wait for batters to swing or watch overweight men who could not steal bases or get to balls in the field. Knowing this, owners constantly tinkered with the rules to encourage the things fans liked, and this would only work if their players were in shape and healthy.

Some of the game's most critical issues involved player behavior, but not all of them. Some situations neither players nor owners directly controlled, such as the performance of umpires. The identity of the umpire rarely causes much concern in baseball today, but in the 1880s, finding qualified umpires was one of baseball's biggest challenges, mainly because just one officiated at a time. This sole umpire had to call balls and strikes, judge plays on the base paths and in the field which were over one hundred feet away in many cases, watch all the players to be sure they were not cheating or fighting each other, and generally make sure the games moved along so that fans would not complain about the action moving too slowly. It was next to impossible to find a single person who could do all these things competently at once, but rather than put a second umpire on the field to make the job something mere mortals could handle, baseball owners continued casting about for superhumans who could do everything necessary simultaneously.

Another reason the lone umpire was so critical, besides having games decided by the merits of the players, was that when umpires failed to do their job well, players, and sometimes even fans, took to the field to argue and cause fights. Each time they did so, middle-class patrons lost patience with baseball, and some stopped going to games. Baseball owners took note of this money-losing trend and realized that if they wanted to court middle-class people and convert them to steadfast baseball fans, they needed games that ran smoothly.

In addition, the threat of gambling posed problems. Gambling reared its ugly head many times in the 1870s, marring the game and threatening to ruin the confidence of the spectators in its integrity. The National League banned a handful of players and one umpire for life because of their proven gambling connections. Baseball's leaders claimed they had eliminated the problem by the mid-1880s, and for the most part they were right, but the issue lurked in the background, threatening to wreck the public's confidence in the game with some new scandal.

A handful of other issues arose by 1885 that seemed less pressing to baseball's magnates but merited at least modest consideration. For instance, should teams sell beer at their games? Doing so made money in the short run, but, just like when players drank, too many drunken fans, with their rowdy behavior, might discourage middle-class spectators from attending in the future. Some clubs, worried about public perception, tried various strategies to lure women to baseball games, hoping that might have a moderating effect on male fans' behavior. The Sunday baseball issue was much like the selling beer issue. Should teams play on the Sabbath? Doing so meant more working-class fans and more money, but it might hurt in the long run by offending the sensibilities of religious patrons.

Finally, racism in baseball was an important issue in this decade. After the 1884 season, the last team in major league baseball to employ African Americans, the Toledo Blue Stockings, left the American Association. When it did, no other team picked up either of Toledo's black players, Moses Walker and his brother Welday. As a result, 1884 was the last time African Americans appeared in major league baseball until 1947. Minor leagues followed suit and drew their own color lines over the next few years. What is curious about this, and unfortunate, is that the sporting newspapers of the 1880s very rarely commented upon this injustice. At least in print, sportswriters took no notice at all of the absence of black players. Even though baseball fans today regard baseball's color line as a grave mistake, contemporaries hardly even thought about the issue. It is another example, it seems, of just how far African Americans fell in the perception of white America by the 1880s.[9]

---

[9] For a complete description of all these issues in baseball in the 1880s, see the other books in my series on 1880s baseball: *Outside the Lines of Gilded Age Baseball: Alcohol, Fitness, and Cheating in 1880s Baseball*; *Outside the Lines*

The State of the Game in 1885

This is what the baseball world looked like in 1885. Everyone in the game knew baseball's popularity was growing. The question was how to manage the growth, encourage more of it, and address the many salient issues described in this chapter. By the end of the decade, baseball's barons had not solved any of their problems fully, although they certainly made progress in some respects. More important by far, however, was when National League players decided to leave the National League and form their own league for the 1890 season. This event overshadowed all other issues during that year. This is the story of why those players took such a momentous step.

---

of Gilded Age Baseball: Gambling, Umpires, and Racism in 1880s Baseball; and *Outside the Lines of Gilded Age Baseball: The Finances of 1880s Baseball.*

Chapter 2

The Cast: The Owners

IF WHAT HAPPENED IN MAJOR LEAGUE BASEBALL IN 1890 was a tragedy for everyone involved, or nearly everyone, we must spend a moment describing the cast acting out the tragedy. Like all great tragedies, there are both heroes and villains, several twists of plot, and plenty of hubris, betrayal, and acts of bravery. Authors should not play favorites with the characters in their story; it is enough to describe each person's actions along with analyzing the consequences of those actions. So perhaps, instead of referring to certain individuals as a hero or villain, a protagonist or antagonist, we should content ourselves with showing some characters as worthy of greater sympathy than others. After all, another aspect of great tragedy is that good and evil are not absolute. Heroes can fall from grace, while villains always have a chance at redemption.

On the side of baseball's owners, no figure looms larger than the man we met in chapter one—Al Spalding, owner of the Chicago White Stockings. Because he was one of the prime movers in baseball, Spalding's background merits detailed description. His rise to influence in baseball mirrors that of several of his capitalist

The Cast: The Owners

brethren in late-nineteenth century America, the main difference being in the details rather than the generalities. Like most of the men known alternately as "captains of industry" or "robber barons," Spalding's story was hardly rags to riches, however much he pretended that it was. It is more accurate to describe his life with a slight modification of an oft-quoted baseball saying: "He was born on third base and went through life thinking he hit a home run." This is not to imply that Spalding merely lived off an inheritance or coat-tailed his way to wealth. In fact, he was quite intelligent and possessed a fair measure of business savvy. He also, however, began the race of life with quite a head start over most of his contemporaries.

Spalding grew up amongst the mahogany furniture and gold-banded china of his parents' home in Byron, Illinois. For Spalding's father, James, "managing his investments and buying and training his horses seem to have occupied his working hours." Spalding's mother, Harriet, who contributed a large inheritance herself to the family finances from a previous marriage, described James as a man who "took life leisurely, and was prosperous in every way."[1] Far from being rags to riches, then, the real story behind Spalding's rise in the business world is worthy of the financial elite of which he was a well-established member by 1889.

The rise began in true robber baron fashion, by disregarding one contract for another, more lucrative, one. By the conclusion of the 1875 season, baseball observers regarded Spalding as the premier pitcher in the game based on his record of 54 wins against 5 losses for the Boston Red Stockings, a team so dominant it won 71 games that year against just 8 defeats, including winning all 37 of its home games. Besides Spalding, the Red Stockings lineup featured three other Hall of Fame players, Jim O'Rourke, George Wright, and Deacon White, not to mention Cal McVey and Ross Barnes, both considered superb hitters. The club was a member of the National

---

[1] Levine, *AG Spalding and the Rise of Baseball*, 3.

Association, the predecessor of the National League that dissolved following the 1875 campaign.

The National Association had both Eastern and Western teams, but the Eastern teams dominated the standings, much to the chagrin of Chicago coal magnate William Hulbert, a man described as "rugged, self-willed, blunt and determined, but possessed of great executive ability and unflagging energy." Believing Western clubs could succeed both on the field and in the account books, Hulbert made overtures to Spalding about returning to his native Illinois for a yearly salary of $2,000 (although longtime baseball observer Henry Chadwick claimed it was $4,000), further sweetened by the positions of team captain and field manager, plus 25% of the team's gate receipts. Despite his association with the Boston Club and the National Association's prohibition on engaging players already under contract to other clubs, Spalding accepted.[2]

When Spalding reached Chicago, he was not alone. With him were three of his Boston teammates, McVey, White, and Barnes. This was part of Hulbert's plan as well. In his communications with Spalding, Hulbert wrote, "Bring with you to Chicago the pick of the Eastern club talent, or as much of it as you can induce to come, and I shall be in a position to offer you such inducements as I think will be more than satisfactory to yourself, and fully so to the players you bring with you." Spalding also netted two of the top players of the

---

[2] Levine, *AG Spalding and the Rise of Baseball*, 22-23; Harry Palmer, "From Chicago," *The Sporting Life*, February 2, 1887, 2; Harry Palmer, "America's National Game," *Outing*, July 1888, 353-354; Henry Chadwick, "Chadwick's Chat," *The Sporting Life*, February 9, 1887, 2. It is also worth noting that in the early years of the game, the position of field manager was quite different from what it is in the twenty-first century. The team captain typically performed the duties of today's manager. The manager of the 1870s was essentially a business manager, sometimes the owner of the team, who oversaw ticket receipts, corresponded with other managers to set up exhibition and regular games, kept track of the team's finances, and the like. For more, see Chris Jaffe, *Evaluating Baseball's Managers: A History and Analysis of Performance in the Major Leagues, 1876-2008* (Jefferson, North Carolina: McFarland & Company, 2010), 65-66.

Philadelphia Athletics for his new employer in the Windy City, Ezra Sutton and Adrian "Cap" Anson, although Sutton later had second thoughts and returned to the Athletics.[3] This was, without a doubt, one of the greatest transfers of talent in the entire nineteenth century, ranking with the exodus of Louisville's entire corps of quality players to Pittsburgh after the 1899 season, or the move of Buffalo's "Big Four" to Detroit for 1886.[4]

The deal went down in, at best, a quasi-legal fashion that was emblematic of the business world of Gilded Age America, although the exact details of what really did go down depend on which baseball writer the reader credits. According to Chicagoan Harry Palmer (who was, admittedly, Spalding's mouthpiece in the press at times), Hulbert was angry over losing out on a third baseman and shortstop named Davy Force. In the days of the National Association, Force was, true to his last name, a force when at bat, and he also enjoyed a reputation as a nice defensive player. Hulbert wanted to bring Force to Chicago very badly and believed he had signed "Wee Davy" (his official playing measurements were a height of five-foot-four and a weight of 130 pounds) to a contract for 1875. However, at that point Hulbert was, in his eyes at least,

---

[3] Palmer, "America's National Game," 354.
[4] The difference is that in both the Louisville and Buffalo cases, the team was about to disband. With Louisville, the owner of the team, Barney Dreyfuss, also had bought into ownership of the Pittsburgh Pirates and served that club as its president. With Louisville set to disband, he transferred most of the best players to Pittsburgh, including Fred Clarke and Honus Wagner, easily the best player of the first decade of the 20th century. This situation, of one man owning shares in more than one franchise, was quite common in the 1890s, just like in the corporate world, where single individuals sat on the board of directors of countless corporations. According to Harold Seymour's research, by the year 1900 every owner of a National League franchise owned shares in more than one franchise. The consequences of this for competitive balance, or the lack thereof, are not hard to imagine. In the Buffalo case, one team, the Detroit Wolverines, purchased the entire Buffalo franchise to obtain the quartet of Dan Brouthers, Hardy Richardson, Jack Rowe, and Deacon White. However, Buffalo continued to exist as a franchise, fielding a replacement team of marginal players. Harold Seymour, *Baseball: The Early Years* (New York: Oxford University Press, 1960), 170, 303-304.

cheated out of getting his man when the Philadelphia Athletics swooped in and signed Force to a contract fraudulently dated before the Chicago deal. When he took his complaint to the National Association's annual meeting, Hulbert discovered that Philadelphia had packed the meeting against him. His anger, according to longtime baseball observer Harry Wright, was volcanic: "Hulbert was a sight to look upon that day. He was simply one magnificent spectacle of rage and wrathful indignation—a thunder cloud of suppressed fury that it did me good to look upon."[5]

The Solon of baseball writers, Henry Chadwick, recalled things a bit differently than Palmer, however. In Chadwick's recollection, it was Chicago, not Philadelphia, which had tried the nefarious trick of antedating its contract with Force; it was the fact that he had failed to sign Force legally, not the rage over Philadelphia cheating him, which fueled Hulbert's anger throughout 1875. Bill James sides with Palmer, however. He asserts that Chicago had indeed signed Force first, but that when a Philadelphia Athletics executive became the head of the National Association, he called another meeting at which the Judiciary Committee reversed its old decision.[6] Al Spalding also claimed that Philadelphia had acted out of line, not Chicago, although as an interested party, his words require several grains of salt.[7] Whatever the truth, it is safe to say that Hulbert's ambition led to what happened next.

Chicago's coal baron plotted revenge over this "outrage." He started a correspondence with Spalding to try to get the star pitcher to sign a deal and come to the Windy City in 1876. The two men exchanged letters through the early months of 1875, and in June, during the playing season and therefore in violation of the prohibition on negotiating with players already under contract, Hulbert made his move. He traveled to Boston to meet Spalding in

---

[5] Harry Palmer, "From Chicago," *The Sporting Life*, February 2, 1887, 2.
[6] Bill James, *The New Bill James Historical Baseball Abstract: The Classic, Completely Revised* (New York: The Free Press, 2001): 33.
[7] Harry Palmer, "From Chicago," *The Sporting Life*, February 16, 1887, 2.

secret, hoping to lure him back to the West. Hulbert got to the Hub City at 10 p.m. and traveled straight to his hotel, meeting Spalding by appointment there. They talked all through the night, until 4 a.m., at which time Spalding agreed to sign a Chicago contract for 1876. The next morning, Hulbert inked Ross Barnes to a Chicago pact by 9 a.m., Cal McVey by 10, and Deacon White by 11. Later that same day, Boston management discovered in the Boston morning papers that Hulbert was in their city and immediately located the Chicagoan, wining and dining him for two days in hopes of keeping him away from their players. Harry Palmer described the drama by writing, "For two days they never left him; invited him to dinner, to breakfast and to supper; took him to the theatre, slept with him, and froze to him tighter'n a brother."[8]

It was not enough. At the end of the two days, Hulbert and Spalding were to meet at the Old Colony rail depot and catch a train for Philadelphia where they could meet with Anson and Sutton and complete the talent heist. Anson and Sutton did not enamor Hulbert as much as the Boston quartet, but getting even with Philadelphia for Force by swiping two of its best players in return seemed fitting revenge. At first, things did not go according to plan. When Hulbert arrived to meet Spalding at the depot, Boston's team president and secretary were still with him. Spalding hid in a baggage car until the train made it out of Boston, then returned to coach and located Hulbert, who was shaking in fear that Spalding had changed his mind. Reunited, the pair proceeded southward and signed their men in Philadelphia, with the understanding that everyone would keep the negotiations secret.[9]

The secret lasted all of two weeks. Because all these events transpired in the middle of the 1875 season, fan reaction in Beantown was unmerciful toward the "secessionists," while Boston management hatched all kinds of schemes to try to get Spalding and

---

[8] Ibid.
[9] Ibid.

friends back into the fold. Boston's owners also took heat from their fans over not paying their star players enough to keep them from deserting. None of the schemes worked, although after Ezra Sutton decided to return to Philadelphia, Cap Anson wavered and nearly decided to join him.[10]

On the field, Hulbert's move bore fruit immediately. When the 1876 season ended, Chicago dominated the new National League with a 52-14 record and, despite the significant cash outlay to draw the "Big Four" plus Anson to the shores of Lake Michigan, the team turned a profit during the nation's centennial.

Because he was the one player who, in 1890, stood most firmly with the National League against the Brotherhood, we should also introduce Cap Anson and describe his story in some detail. Although Anson was just twenty-three at the time of the 1876 move to Chicago, his connection with Spalding was already well established. Back in 1870, when Spalding pitched for the Rockford Forest City team, Rockford played an exhibition series in Anson's hometown of Marshalltown, Iowa. Anson played so well that Rockford offered him a contract for the following season, which he accepted rather than continue his on-again, off-again efforts at attending the state college in Iowa City, today the University of Iowa. He thus embarked on a professional career in which he played regularly for twenty-seven seasons, not retiring until after the 1897 campaign. Anson's association with Spalding strengthened further in 1874 when Spalding, by then with Boston, and Anson, by then with Philadelphia, participated in an exhibition of baseball in the British Isles. Boston's manager, Harry Wright, was born in Sheffield, and wanted to prove the superiority of the American game over cricket to his former country and perhaps his father Sam as well, who was president of New York's St. George Cricket Club.[11]

---

[10] Ibid.
[11] Levine, *AG Spalding and the Rise of Baseball*, 18-19; also see Anson's biography at the Society for American Baseball Research's website, http://sabr.org/bioproj/person/9b42f875, accessed January 14, 2014. The

The Cast: The Owners

The tour of the British Isles took Spalding's Boston club and Anson's Philadelphia nine to Liverpool, Manchester, Sheffield, London, Nottingham, Dublin, Glasgow, and other stops in Great Britain: "The object of the voyage is to give Englishmen a practical illustration of the beauties claimed for the American game." The Brits proved gracious hosts, and a few commented favorably on the "scientific" nature of baseball, but they remained largely unconvinced of baseball's future in Britain, preferring the "dignity, manliness, and system" of their own native sport. The tour failed to wean the British from their allegiance to cricket, but Anson's friendship with Spalding proved enduring, and Anson became the field manager of the Chicago White Stockings by 1879 and eventually owned a small share of the team's stock.[12]

Besides his longevity and excellence on the field, baseball historians today associate Anson with two other rather unseemly things during his career. His ability to belittle and berate opposing players and umpires was legendary. Although most baseball records give his nickname as "Cap" for captain, or sometimes "Pop" because he managed to play to such an advanced age, many in the 1880s nicknamed him "the Baby" because he whined and kicked so energetically against umpires. Because he was successful as a captain, other teams copied his practices, and a few even took them to a level Anson never reached. St. Louis Browns captain and future Chicago White Sox owner Charles Comiskey excelled at this practice as well, and Comiskey's teams likewise had great success on the field. The result was that during the 1880s and 1890s, the game on the field was rowdy in the extreme, featuring foul play, foul language, dishonest tactics, and frequent on-field violence against opponents and umpires. Observers of the day recognized the change,

---

England tour's history appears in "The Trip to England in 1874," *Spalding's Official Base Ball Guide, 1889* (Chicago and New York: A.G. Spalding & Bros, 1889): 91-93.

[12] "The United States," *The London Times*, August 4, 1874, 3; Levine, *AG Spalding and the Rise of Baseball*, 18-19.

and many did not like it. As early as June 24, 1883, *The Sporting Life* criticized a Philadelphia writer for disparaging umpires in print, thus serving to encourage rowdyism, and that same day *The Sporting Life* also drew attention to managers removing their teams from the field of play and refusing to continue the game when they felt particularly aggrieved by an umpire's decision.[13]

The second black mark on Anson's record is his leading role in establishing segregation in major league baseball. In 1883, he nearly refused to play the Toledo club, set to join the American Association the following year, in an exhibition because the Blue Stockings featured an African American, Moses Walker, as their catcher. Anson's club played that day when threatened with the loss of gate revenue if they refused, but Anson would not play against teams with black players in the future, and thus, after 1884, the color line became part of major league baseball for more than six decades. Within a few more years, it was part of minor league baseball as well. While Anson was not alone in his desire for segregation by any means, the influence and prestige of his name helped give segregationists the ammunition to draw the color barrier.[14]

Spalding, meanwhile, continued up the corporate ladder as his playing career wound down. Having appeared in only four games in 1877 and just one in 1878, by 1883 he was club president of the White Stockings because Hulbert had died in April of 1882. In addition, his sporting goods company was thriving by supplying equipment to baseball teams across the nation. By the late 1870s,

---

[13] "On the Fly," *The Sporting Life*, June 24, 1883, 5. For Anson's career as an umpire baiter, or "kicker" in the parlance of the day, see Jaffe, *Evaluating Baseball's Managers*, 66-67, and Anson's SABR biography. For more about the rowdyism in 1880s and 1890s baseball, see chapters five and six of Rob Bauer, *Outside the Lines of Gilded Age Baseball: Alcohol, Fitness, and Cheating in 1880s Baseball*. This book also contains a glossary of terms popular in the 1880s but carrying different meanings today; look in the back if the meaning or usage of a word is unfamiliar.

[14] John Husman, "Toledo and Fleet Walker," Society for American Baseball Research, *Nineteenth Century Notes*, Spring 2010, 4-8.

The Cast: The Owners

Spalding had realized one of capitalism's eternal truths. Any worker, no matter how skilled at his or her craft, was still a worker, subject to the financial whims of the employer. The best route to wealth and power lay not with the most skilled performer on the field, but with the most skilled performer in the realm of ownership and management. Working from this realization, Spalding even developed his own marketing arm for his sporting goods business, *Spalding's Official Base Ball Guide*, published yearly. It contained statistical records and summaries of the recently completed season, to be sure, but also advertised Spalding's goods, bore his name, picture, and autograph on the cover, and disparaged the products of competitors.

Spalding also "won" the right to publish the official National League book in 1876 at the insistence of his club's owner, Hulbert. Although the contract merely stated Spalding had the right to publish the official league book (of rules of play and the league's constitution), and while the baseball guide was not an official National League publication, Spalding's obfuscation of this fact by using the word "official" on the cover went unchallenged until 1882. By then, the public mind already associated his name and products with being the official representative of major league baseball.[15]

The same was true regarding the Spalding baseball and, later, Spalding's uniforms. At the National League's yearly meetings, the league consistently voted (including Spalding, who voted as secretary and then, after Hulbert's death, as president of Chicago) to adopt Spalding's baseball as the official ball for all National League games. This allowed the guide to trumpet its ball as an official product and allowed Spalding to utilize one of the time-honored techniques of professional advertisers: allowing normal people to take part in greatness through association. By 1884, the guide listed other leagues using the Spalding baseball as a further testimonial (five of them in the 1886 guide, for instance, those five being the

---

[15] Levine, *AG Spalding and the Rise of Baseball*, 75-76.

National League, New York State League, Eastern League, New England League, and the College Association[16]), and by 1890, it touted the advanced technology used in their manufacture. The ball's patented plastic cement, the guide claimed, "makes it more elastic [and] . . . soft to the hands, and at the same time . . . retains its perfect shape." Spalding's catalog for his sporting goods also received free publicity when, for example, *The Sporting Life* mentioned it in its columns in the spring of 1886.[17] By that year, the catalog was even offering a newly invented baseball item, sliding pants.[18]

Like any good captain of industry, however, Spalding did not stop there. Instead, he continued pursuing both vertical and horizontal integration of his company. Horizontal integration, the practice of increasing market share through expanding production, buying out competitors, and so forth, came when more and more leagues began using his products. Spalding also engaged in vertical integration—controlling more than one link in a product's chain of production. Not only did Spalding sell balls, bats, and uniforms, but by 1879, his company manufactured all these products for itself, with *The Sporting News* estimating a production level of 1 million bats yearly by 1887. Soon, AG Spalding & Bros. also manufactured bicycles, skates, golf equipment, tennis rackets, dumbbells, caps, uniforms for multiple sports, and hunting equipment and clothing. Indeed, Spalding's company even designed the original basketball used by Dr. James Naismith in Springfield, Massachusetts. It also built the special bicycles used by the 25th Infantry (Colored) Bicycle Corps that operated out of Fort Missoula, Montana, starting in 1896, the first bicycle corps in the U.S. Army.

---

[16] "Something Extraordinary," *The Sporting Life*, March 3, 1886, 2.
[17] Levine, *AG Spalding and the Rise of Baseball*, 77-78; "Something Extraordinary," *The Sporting Life*, March 3, 1886, 2.
[18] Remlap, "From Chicago," *The Sporting Life*, March 3, 1886, 5. Remlap was the same person as Chicago sportswriter Harry Palmer, who spelled his last name backward in his 1886 letters to *The Sporting Life*.

The Cast: The Owners

Like many of his fellow tycoons, in 1892, Spalding reincorporated his company in New Jersey to take advantage of that state's lenient corporate laws, with the venture capitalized at $4 million. By then, his sporting goods empire included factories in Chicopee Falls, Massachusetts, manufacturing bicycles, skates, tennis racquets, dumbbells, and other sports equipment requiring steel, a baseball bat factory in Chicago, and a Philadelphia plant for leather goods. Spalding planned to open new factories in Ogdensburg, New York, for boat manufacture, and Brooklyn, where a new four-story plant of 40,000 square feet eventually employed over 1,000 workers creating bicycle shoes, stocking caps, football shoes and pants, jackets, hunting gear and clothing, and other general sportswear. All told, Spalding's sporting goods company employed about 3,500 workers and pulled in profits of several million dollars each year.[19] Spalding was the president of five corporations: A.G. Spalding Bros., the Spalding Manufacturing Co., the Casino Rink Co., the Chicago Ball Club, and the Western Arms and Cartridge Co.[20] He obtained a near-monopoly in the sporting goods industry after buying out his primary competitor, the A. J. Reach Company, in 1889.[21]

Spalding may not have been Andrew Carnegie, but for a $3,800 investment made just sixteen years earlier, it was impressive growth, demonstrating both Spalding's business acumen and the power of using an insider position to secure business contracts.[22] Even if he was not a self-made man, Spalding was a financially successful one, and he was also the National League owner most successful with his schemes and plots.

Al Spalding did not run the show single-handedly in the National League, however. Joining him among the NL's prime movers was the trio of men who controlled the Boston Beaneaters known as the

---

[19] Levine, *AG Spalding and the Rise of Baseball*, 79-80.
[20] Harry Palmer, "From Chicago," *The Sporting Life*, April 20, 1887, 6.
[21] "A Bold Stroke," *The Sporting Life*, September 4, 1889, 1.
[22] Levine, *AG Spalding and the Rise of Baseball*, 78-81.

Triumvirate. Its members were Arthur Soden, a roofing construction tycoon, J. B. Billings, who owned a shoe factory, and William Conant, who was involved in manufacturing hoop skirts and rubber goods. Although a three-way partnership, the man who usually spoke for Beaneaters' ownership in public was Soden. In a way, this was unfortunate, because it is hard to imagine a more greedy, self-serving, and generally disagreeable man than Soden, although according to contemporaries, his partners were little, if any, better. To give but a few examples of their approach to the business of baseball, collectively they owned about two-thirds of Boston's stock. After gaining the majority ownership of the franchise, they blocked smaller shareholders from sharing in the team's profits when they refused to issue dividends on the team's stock.

Not stopping with cheating their fellow investors, an official for a rival club, Chicago White Stockings team secretary John Brown, once described how, after one game in which he had requested four complimentary tickets for the family members of one player, the Boston treasurer demanded payment after the fact. Brown could not contain his amazement, stating, "Your people are the meanest set of skunks I ever saw engaged in the business. By God, sir, they are a disgrace to the game." Brown won his point, but the fact that Boston management was willing to alienate another club's executives over three dollars' worth of tickets speaks volumes. Speaking of Conant, Brown once said that he was "the closest fisted Judas I ever ran across. His mere connection with the Boston Club sours me against the whole business. I do not see how any player or business man can do business with him voluntarily and maintain his self-respect."[23] In a similar vein, consider the time in 1887 when Soden refused to split the gate from the team's Labor Day game against Philadelphia with the visitors. Holiday games usually drew large crowds, so league policy was that the teams split the gate fifty-fifty on holidays. Soden

---

[23] Harry Palmer, "Chicago Gossip," *The Sporting Life*, March 7, 1888, 3.

The Cast: The Owners

refused, however, simply because Congress declared Labor Day a holiday after the season began.[24]

The Triumvirs did not treat their players any better than the executives of other teams. In fact, they probably treated them worse. In 1880, Soden blacklisted one of his players, superstar outfielder Charley Jones, for his boldness when Jones asked for his June 1 paycheck on June 1. It took Jones *three years* to get back into the major leagues where he belonged.[25] A similar thing happened to ace pitcher Charlie Radbourn in 1887. Considered one of the best in the business, Radbourn struggled through a disappointing 1887, so in September, Soden suspended him for his "unsatisfactory work as a pitcher" and stated his belief that the Triumvirs "have been played for suckers long enough" and that they did not intend to take it anymore. In other words, he believed Radbourn was loafing and not giving the team his top effort. Because Radbourn was one of the rare players on the team who earned a salary commensurate with his talent and drawing power, the Triumvirate decided to suspend him, so they wouldn't have to pay him, thus saving a couple hundred dollars. Radbourn summed up the situation well when he said, "They are sore because they think I have not pitched as well as Madden, who gets a very small salary. As I get a big one they feel that I have somehow cheated them out of some money. Now, I signed a contract to pitch to the best of my ability. I have done that, and because they are disappointed in my work I am not to blame. I have lived up to my contract."[26]

---

[24] See Soden's SABR biography at http://sabr.org/bioproj/person/a1b2e0d0, accessed July 25, 2017; Mugwump, "From the Hub," *The Sporting Life*, September 14, 1887, 3. Mugwump was the pen name of Harvard graduate and assistant city editor of the *Boston Globe*, William D. Sullivan.

[25] David Nemec, *The Beer and Whiskey League: The Illustrated History of the American Association—Baseball's Renegade Major League* (New York: Lyons & Burford, 1994): 23.

[26] Mugwump, "From the Hub," *The Sporting Life*, September 14, 1887, 3. Madden was Kid Madden, a skinny, nineteen-year-old rookie who won 21 games in 1887.

There were big, dramatic incidents such as those with Jones and Radbourn, but the Triumvirs also antagonized their men on a day-to-day basis. When the team traveled, Boston players stayed at the cheapest hotels possible. The ballplayers also had to collect tickets before games, so Soden would not need to employ extra people for that duty. He also forced them to cut the grass at the ballpark, go into the stands to retrieve foul balls, buy their own uniforms, and pay the cleaning costs of those uniforms. The wives of married players had to buy a full-priced ticket to attend the game. The Triumvirs even eliminated the press section at their ballpark, the South End Grounds, so they could replace the press section with more seats for customers and eke out a few extra dollars that way.[27] As a result, Hall of Fame player Jim O'Rourke, who played in Boston before the Triumvirs took over management, once stated his belief that no player with a choice would ever willingly play for Boston.[28] Mike Kelly summed up the feelings of his Boston teammates with his 1888 statement, "I have no desire to play under this management any longer."[29]

The Triumvirs did not limit their parsimoniousness to their interactions with people, either. They also gained negative publicity for their refusal to spend much money on the upkeep of their field. Many observers considered it the worst in the National League, hands down, one writing, "The Boston ground has been so neglected that for the past three months it was the worst to play on in the League. The entire diamond needs re-sodding, else there will be great dissatisfaction among the players."[30] Another writer noted,

---

[27] See Soden's SABR biography at http://sabr.org/bioproj/person/a1b2e0d0, accessed July 25, 2017; Mugwump, "From the Hub," *The Sporting Life*, September 14, 1887, 3.
[28] Tim Murnane, "The Boston Boys," *The Sporting News*, January 22, 1887, 3.
[29] "Mike Kelly's Views," *The Sporting News*, July 21, 1888, 1.
[30] "Notes and Comments," *The Sporting Life*, September 28, 1887, 6.

The Cast: The Owners

"Boston has the roughest infield in the League, it being full of ruts, and there is evidently no attention paid to the grounds."[31]

Despite their lack of consideration shown to anyone who was not a paying customer, Soden and company were major players in the deliberations of the National League. Partly this was because of their outspokenness and partly because they played in Boston, a city noted for the great enthusiasm of its sporting public. Even though Boston won just one championship in the 1880s, the Triumvirs made a great deal of money, and their team was a major drawing card, so other owners had to take their views into account. Soden was also one of the architects of the reserve rule discussed in chapter one, giving him a bit of clout for helping create something his fellow owners found so useful.

One National League owner who kept a lower profile than either Spalding or Soden, but who usually shared their hard line, anti-player sentiments was John Rogers, owner of the Philadelphia franchise. A lawyer, Rogers generally stayed out of the spotlight unless player salaries were at issue, in which case he did not hesitate to state his views. To cite just one example, before the 1887 season, several of his players held out for better pay. Even though the club had a fine season in 1886 with a .623 winning percentage, Rogers had paid just two of the men $2,000 and none more than that, at a time when top players typically earned $3,000 to $4,000 in salary. One writer described Rogers: "It is a notorious fact that the Philadelphia club has had the cheapest salaried team in the League ever since it joined that organization."[32]

These three men, Spalding, Soden, and Rogers, led the hardliners in the National League. Not every owner shared their views, however. The most notable exception was New York Giants owner John Day, who made his fortune in the tobacco business but also had connections with New York's notorious political machine

---

[31] "Strange, But True," *The Sporting Life*, June 20, 1888, 4.
[32] "The Philadelphia Club," *The Sporting News*, March 26, 1887, 5.

in Tammany Hall. Day also owned the other New York baseball franchise for a time, the Metropolitans of the American Association, but sold it to Staten Island real estate developer Erastus Wiman in 1885. Unlike Soden and the Triumvirs, Day was popular with many of his ballplayers, partly because he usually paid them close to their market value and partly because he avoided the small, cheap, and petty things many of his contemporaries did. Granted, New York's market size and revenue stream meant his team earned plenty of money, but Day also traveled with his team to road games and made sure the players stayed in top-notch accommodations. As a result, when a rumor began that outfielder Jim O'Rourke was in a major contract dispute with Day, O'Rourke refuted the claim decisively. Regarding Day, O'Rourke stated he considered his owner "the very embodiment of honor. . . . His word is his bond."[33]

The one other National League owner who, at least in the 1880s, seemed more sporting and more interested in baseball simply for the enjoyment of running a team was Indianapolis owner John Brush. He was the owner of the first department store in Indianapolis, "The When Clothing Company," and he led the group that organized the Hoosier team and joined the National League in 1887. Brush did so partly so he could use the team and ballpark to advertise for his store, and when the club finished a distant eighth place with 37 wins and 89 losses, he took things in stride. In an 1890 interview, he stated, "I run a ball club . . . for the interest I take in the game and the recreation it gives me. I sell *pants* for money." He did very well in his business, too, and so did his partners in Indianapolis. A writer described Brush's company as "a mammoth concern which is a pride of the city." Considering that Brush and the rest of the Indianapolis ownership group had an aggregate worth over two

---

[33] See Day's SABR biography, available at http://sabr.org/bioproj/person/c281a493, accessed May 30, 2014; Jim O'Rourke, "Jim O'Rourke Objects," *The Sporting Life*, January 15, 1887, 1; Bryan DiSalvatore, *A Clever Base-Ballist: The Life and Times of John Montgomery Ward* (New York: Pantheon Books, 1999): 137-138.

million dollars, running a baseball team for interest and fun was unlikely to damage their collective bottom lines irreparably.[34] It is ironic, therefore, that in the 1890s Brush moved over to the hard-liner faction of owners, but in the 1880s, he remained one owner who might go either way, depending on the situation.

Finally, we must introduce two other men who were not National League owners in the 1880s but nonetheless had an enormous impact on the game and some impact on the formation of the Players League in 1890. Those two men are American Association owners Chris Von der Ahe of the St. Louis Browns and Charles Byrne of Brooklyn. Their personal rivalry, sometimes smoldering behind the scenes but at others blazing in the open, did much to influence the history of baseball in the late 1880s and 1890.

Part of the rivalry was personal and part professional. The Browns won four straight American Association pennants from 1885-1888 and seemed destined for a fifth in 1889. Byrne's Brooklyn club, however, had other plans. Partly driven by his intense dislike of Von der Ahe, Byrne wanted badly to win a pennant, both for the revenue it would bring and to put the Browns' owner in his place. Byrne had also, on several occasions, considered ditching the American Association and transferring his allegiance to the National League because, first, he could charge more for tickets in the National League, and, second, he thought the NL had better leadership. Additionally, once in the NL he would not have to deal with Von der Ahe anymore. Complicating his plan, however, was that on just as many occasions, Byrne stated he would not change leagues until Brooklyn won a pennant.[35]

---

[34] Charles Alexander, *Turbulent Seasons: Baseball in 1890-1891* (Dallas: SMU Press, 2011): 13; also see Brush's SABR biography, available at http://sabr.org/bioproj/person/a46ef165, accessed May 30, 2014; G. W. B., "In Earnest," *The Sporting Life*, January 5, 1887, 1.

[35] When it came to ticket prices, teams did not have the authority to set their own prices in the 1880s like they do today. Instead, National League teams charged seventy-five cents for grandstand tickets and fifty for seats in the bleachers. In

Outside the Lines of Gilded Age Baseball

What Byrne did, then, was in 1888 and 1889, he began stockpiling talent. His club lacked the superstars that some clubs had but compensated with excellent depth. Having made ample money in various business pursuits, cost was no obstacle. Byrne demonstrated this when he made his first move following the 1887 season, buying the entire franchise of the New York Metropolitans and transferring the Metropolitan players he wanted onto his own team. This gained him slugging first baseman Dave Orr, outfielder Darby O'Brien, outfielder/shortstop Paul Radford, and pitcher Al Mays, along with a few other spare parts like catcher Bill Holbert. Then he convinced Von der Ahe to sell him two of St. Louis's useful players, catcher Doc Bushong and pitcher/outfielder Dave Foutz. Next, Byrne cut a deal with Baltimore for one of its better men, outfielder/shortstop Tom "Oyster" Burns. Toward the end of the 1888 campaign, he bought second baseman Hub Collins from Louisville when Louisville's foolish owner Mordecai Davidson started running the Colonels into the ground. Before 1889 began, Byrne bought another player from St. Louis, pitcher Bob Caruthers, and found pitcher Tom Lovett to be the fourth arm on his pitching staff, finally giving him the talent needed to beat the Browns by a nose.

Looking back, it seems likely most men would have acted just as Byrne did regarding Chris Von der Ahe, had they been in his shoes. Indeed, it is a bit of a wonder that anyone could work with Von der Ahe for long. Often, he behaved as though he had a permanent chip on his shoulder. Perhaps this was because he was a relatively recent immigrant to the United States, a "new money" man who rose through owning first a grocery store, then a saloon, a butcher shop, and a food retail store. Von der Ahe was also the one owner who sports newspapers often made fun of in print, some

---

the American Association, it was fifty cents to sit in the grandstand and twenty-five for the bleachers.

referring to him as "the Boss President."[36] Sometimes, the sporting press printed his statements with the broken grammar and syntax of someone new to the country who spoke with a heavy accent, a dishonorable treatment usually reserved for African Americans. This treatment might have evoked some sympathy, except that Von der Ahe behaved so erratically that no one outside of St. Louis could put up with him. While he was not a grand schemer like Spalding, or a miser in the Soden mold, his tendency toward irrational anger and poorly considered actions made him a pain in the neck to all other owners in the American Association. He saw a conspiracy against his beloved Browns behind every move of his fellow owners, it seems, and at times attempted to bully those who disagreed with him.

Even a short list of some of his actions leaves one shaking one's head. Von der Ahe encouraged his men to argue every call that umpires made, engage in rough tactics with opponents, and employ stalling tactics whenever the situation seemed promising. If the umpire fined his players for their shenanigans, which umpires often did, he usually paid the fines and encouraged his men to keep at it, thereby contributing greatly to the on-field violence of the 1880s. Then, he sometimes used his power to get the offending umpire fired for not favoring his team often enough. Likewise, in 1887 Von der Ahe persuaded other American Association owners to amend the AA's constitution, allowing teams to blacklist players who refused to sign a contract at the price first offered by their team. He once claimed that he could not make any improvements to his home field, Sportsman's Park, because he did not own the property, even though he did own the property and merely sought to avoid the expense of upkeep. Von der Ahe once accused one of his best players, outfielder Tip O'Neill, of sulking and trying to lose games on purpose just because O'Neill was in a slump. Worst of all was his behavior

---

[36] "Base Ball," *The Sporting News*, February 5, 1887, 5.

during the last month of the 1889 pennant race with Brooklyn, described in chapter 13, which bordered on psychotic.[37]

Other than that, Von der Ahe was quite normal. The reason he could get away with such consistently inconsistent behavior was that he had the best team in the American Association, a team that drew lots of fans to games, on the road especially, and he knew it. If the growls of his fellow Association owners got a little too vocal, Von der Ahe simply floated some rumors that his club might jump to the National League, and usually that was enough to keep everyone in line.

While the drama with the Brotherhood of Professional Baseball Players unfolded, especially from 1887 onward, the group of baseball owners usually behaved true to their personalities outlined here. Spalding was the grand planner. Although not exactly a puppeteer who pulled the strings of the other owners, or a Godfather-like figure offering the others a deal they could not refuse, few things of importance happened without Spalding's approval and support. Arthur Soden played the role of tough guy and seemed happy to do it, unconcerned about having a reputation as the most disliked person in baseball. Other owners fell in line—John Day playing the role of mediator and occasional ally of the players in juxtaposition to Soden, John Brush the struggling little brother squealing for a fair chance to compete with the older kids, and so on, with Chris Von der Ahe such a wildcard that no one ever knew what he might do or say next. The other National League owners not mentioned here played the role of characters in a play with bit parts—appearing here and there, necessary to keep the story moving, but replaceable.

On the players' side, there were a host of personalities as well. Most important, of course, were the officers of the BPBP, led by the

---

[37] "A Blow at the Dead-Heads," *The Sporting News*, March 12, 1887, 1; Nemec, *The Beer and Whiskey League*, 97.

The Cast: The Owners

organization's president, John Montgomery Ward. It is now time to meet them and study the founding of their organization.

Chapter 3

The Cast: The Players

THE BROTHERHOOD OF PROFESSIONAL BASEBALL PLAYERS, quietly formed on October 22, 1885, was the first significant and lasting attempt of baseball players at unionization. While the organization did not go public right away, the Brotherhood's charter, primarily authored by New York Giants shortstop John Ward, pledged the organization to "protect and benefit its members, promote a high standard of professional conduct, and advance the interests of the national game."[1] In addition, members pledged to:

- Strive to promote the objects and aims of this Brotherhood, in accordance with the Constitution and By-Laws;
- Never to take advantage of a brother in good standing;
- Never to permit an unjust injury to be done to, or continued against, a brother in good standing, while it is in my power to prevent the same;

---

[1] David Stevens, *Baseball's Radical for All Seasons: A Biography of John Montgomery Ward* (The Scarecrow Press: Lanham, MD, 1998): 42.

The Cast: The Players

- Assist a brother in distress;
- Render faithful obedience to the will of the Brotherhood, as expressed by the decree of the council, or vote of my chapter.[2]

Based on these statements, the BPBP appeared little different from any number of the benevolent associations and societies common in the late nineteenth century. Many trades and professions had organizations with similar codes of conduct for their members. However, if the Brotherhood merely served these purposes, why keep it a secret in 1885? Partly, it was a matter of organization. Baseball teams had schedules that took them all over the country, and thus, it was not always possible to carry on business very quickly in the days before long-distance telephones. It was even tougher in the off-season when all the players dispersed to their homes throughout the nation. It is understandable that Ward and his fellow Brothers would take their time until they had perfected their plans and enrolled as many players in the organization as they could.

Clearly, Ward and company intended the BPBP to be much more than a mutual aid society, although it certainly could fill that role as well. In fact, Ward was one of the first players to donate to the February 1886 benefit for Curry Foley. Foley had a modest career as a pitcher and outfielder for the Buffalo Bisons and Boston Red Stockings between 1879 and 1883. He is also the first recorded major league player to hit for the cycle.[3] Sadly, in 1883, he developed rheumatism, which eventually left him physically incapacitated and broke. His team at the time, Buffalo, refused to release him, however, claiming he was faking to get his release. To rub salt in the wound, Buffalo's management did not pay him for the days he missed trying to fight his illness. Due to the reserve

---

[2] Di Salvatore, *A Clever Base-Ballist*, 176.

[3] A "cycle" is when a player hits a single, double, triple, and home run all in one game. It has happened about 300 times in major league baseball as of 2017, making it about as rare as a pitcher throwing a no-hit game.

clause, he could not escape from his contract with the Bisons. These circumstances of having to remain with a Buffalo team that would not pay him drained Foley's finances to the point where he had to reside in an asylum. Things were so bad that other ballplayers organized a relief benefit for Foley in the winter of 1885-1886 out of sympathy for his plight.[4]

In addition to such special cases, Ward and his Brothers envisioned the organization as a vehicle to redress their accumulating grievances over such issues as abuses of the reserve clause, player sales, and the 1886 salary limit described fully in chapter five. To do so, however, the players wanted to present a broad, united front to management. Before the Brotherhood could expand its influence, therefore, it needed members.

Ward and Jim O'Rourke, along with New York Giants teammates Tim Keefe, Roger Connor, Buck Ewing, Mickey Welch, Daniel Richardson, Mike Dorgan, and Joe Gerhardt, formed the organization's original core. This group contained men who were not only tremendous players on the field (Ward, O'Rourke, Keefe, Connor, Ewing, and Welch would all gain election to the Baseball Hall of Fame) but also, in accordance with the Brotherhood's charter, possessed sterling reputations for their comportment off the field. The organization sought to build its reputation through recruiting morally upright players who met certain standards of behavior and sobriety and who would encourage prospective members to reform if necessary before joining. Such was the goal, at least, even if the reality sometimes fell short of such lofty standards.

Everyone in baseball knew of Ward's learned stature. He was as close as a baseball player could get to the All-American boy who had it all. He was both the shortstop and field captain for one of baseball's best teams in one of its largest markets. In addition, he

---

[4] For more on Foley, see his SABR biography at http://sabr.org/bioproj/person/d8a0584a, accessed September 11, 2017.

owned a degree in law from Columbia University, where he graduated *cum laude* in 1885.[5] Ward had, in the words of one impressed contemporary, a "singularly correct knowledge of the English language."[6] Prestigious literary magazines published essays he authored, and Ward also wrote his own book, *Base-Ball: How to Become a Player* over the winter of 1887-1888. Finally, after the 1887 season, Ward married Helen Dauvray, one of the noted actresses of the age, on October 12.[7]

One of Ward's teammates and fellow organizers was "Orator" Jim O'Rourke, who had been in baseball so long that he participated with Al Spalding and Cap Anson in the 1874 tour of England to popularize baseball there. He was also a civic leader in his hometown of Bridgeport, Connecticut, and he refused both alcohol and tobacco. He graduated from Yale's law school in June 1887 and passed Connecticut's bar examination in November of that year. At one time, he declared his intent to run for office on the Democratic ticket. After the Brotherhood War and retiring from major league baseball, O'Rourke returned to his hometown and organized a team which included fellow Bridgeport native Harry Herbert. Herbert was black, and it was a rare occurrence to see an integrated team after professional baseball adopted its color line. O'Rourke also served on the Bridgeport Paving Commission, was a member of the Royal Arcanum, the Connecticut Bar Association, the Bridgeport Elks, and the Knights of Columbus. He died, appropriately enough, after

---

[5] Stevens, *Baseball's Radical for All Seasons*, 39.
[6] Thorn, *Baseball in the Garden of Eden*, 234-236.
[7] "The Ward-Dauvray Marriage," *Omaha Daily Bee*, October 30, 1887, 9. For more on Ward's courtship, marriage, and eventual divorce from Dauvray, see either of Ward's biographies, especially chapter four of Stevens, *Baseball's Radical for all Seasons*, and chapter eighteen of Di Salvatore, *A Clever Base-Ballist*. Helen Dauvray was a big fan of baseball, to the extent that she sponsored the Dauvray Cup, a trophy that went to the winner of the World Series each year in the 1880s. In 1887, for instance, the trophy traveled in its own railroad car when Detroit and St. Louis traveled across the country playing each other.

contracting pneumonia from braving a blizzard to consult with a legal client on New Year's Day, 1919.[8]

O'Rourke was also, as his nickname suggests, among the most loquacious and sesquipedalian players of the 1880s, so much so that the sporting press poked fun at his polysyllabic verbiage from time to time. In 1887, *The Sporting Life* printed a mock interview between Orator Jim and his team's owner, John Day:

Day: "How is everything down in Barnumville?"
O'Rourke: "You mean Bridgeport, do you not?"
Day: "Certainly; you don't suppose I mean any other place?"
O'Rourke: "I will tell you, Mr. Day, Barnum's 'Equescuriculum of Megatherian Monstrosities' have evacuated the town, and the grief of the demoralized and isolated population is inexorable."
Day: "What do you think of the umpiring for next season, Mr. O'Rourke?"
O'Rourke: "I will tell you, Mr. Day, we want unostentatiousness and the effervescence of imputrescibility conglomerated, and all umpires who are unsophisticated, incapacitated, or even men who get intoxicated, should be emasculated. My mottos are: Sesquipedalia Verba; Sic Semper Tyrannis Paregoric; Vive La Republique."[9]

Observers also considered O'Rourke among the most honest and reputable players in the game. The story of how he came to play for the Giants illustrates the point. In 1884, he was a member of the Buffalo Bisons, and when that team encountered financial

---

[8] Stevens, *Baseball's Radical for All Seasons*, 42-43; Di Salvatore, *A Clever Base-Ballist*, 175-177; also see O'Rourke's SABR biography at http://sabr.org/bioproj/person/b7e9aba2, accessed May 22, 2014; Looker On, "From New York," *The Sporting Life*, January 5, 1887, 4.

[9] Charles Foley, "Jim O'Rourke's Return from Yale College," *The Sporting Life*, March 30, 1887, 1. Bridgeport was also the home of circus entertainer P. T. Barnum, thus the reference to Barnumville.

difficulties at the end of its season and let him go, O'Rourke was in great demand. Giants Owner John Day met with O'Rourke and told O'Rourke that he would like to see him in a New York uniform the following season. They agreed the salary would be $4,500. Shortly thereafter, an agent from the Philadelphia Athletics contacted O'Rourke and offered him $5,500 to play in Philadelphia. O'Rourke only had a verbal agreement with Day, not a written contract, and could have easily gone back on his word but did not. Another writer attested to his honesty by stating, "O'Rourke, while a member of the Buffalo Club, was never reserved. He is one of those players that you don't have to reserve. You tell him at the end of the season that you want his services next year and if he says, 'all right,' that is sufficient."[10]

Another time, while playing for Boston, O'Rourke tried to score on a hit, but the defense threw him out in a close play at home plate. The Hub City crowd immediately called for the umpire's head and threatened to mob the field. O'Rourke calmed them down, shouting, "What is the matter, my friends? I was fairly out, and the umpire was clearly correct in his decision." The crowd then sat down, the game continued, and the umpire avoided an unpleasant confrontation that would have gone ill for him. Ironically, the umpire whom O'Rourke saved was none other than future National League president Nick Young.[11]

The other founders of the Brotherhood were like O'Rourke in attitude and comportment, even if lacking O'Rourke's refined and Latin-laced vocabulary. First baseman Roger Connor was the owner of baseball's record for career homeruns with 138 upon his retirement. He also hit 233 triples, most of any player who played exclusively in the nineteenth century. Connor was a quiet and dignified player who played in 1,998 major league games without a

---

[10] George Stackhouse, "New York News," *The Sporting Life*, September 19, 1888, 7.
[11] "Worthy of Emulation," *The Sporting Life*, August 28, 1889, 4.

single ejection and rarely sought the public spotlight. He "seldom, if ever, questions a decision of an umpire. He is beloved by his associates, and always has a kind word for everybody." However, despite his genial nature, Connor held firm views regarding the rights of labor and spoke strongly to encourage player solidarity in the new organization.[12]

The same was true of ace pitcher Tim Keefe. An early recruit to the cause of labor following an incident at age twenty when he had to sue simply to collect the wages due him for his work as a carpenter, Keefe's support for the concept of unionization solidified when his Troy, New York, team placed him on its reserve list in 1881. He tried to hold out for more money, but his gambit failed, and he played for the same contract, $1,500, as he had the previous season. He caught a break when the National League booted Troy out of its circuit before the 1883 season, and he was free to sign with the New York Metropolitans of the American Association, where both his pay, now $2,800, and his performance soared to new heights. However, he soon grew restive over the restraints imposed by the reserve clause and the way team owners manipulated it to the detriment of players.

The next chapter of his personal story illustrates his frustration, and the manipulations of ownership, perfectly. As the 1885 season neared, one man, John Day, owned both the New York Giants and the New York Metropolitans. Day favored the Giants and wanted to move Keefe from the Metropolitans to the Giants to strengthen that club. To do so, however, he would have to release Keefe from his contract with the Metropolitans, giving Keefe ten days to negotiate with other clubs. Knowing that a bidding war would result, Day instructed Giants manager Jim Mutrie to take Keefe and infielder Dude Esterbrook (who was not, of course, named Dude at birth but

---

[12] G. N. B., "League First Basemen," *The Sporting Life*, December 29, 1886, 4; also see Connor's SABR biography, at http://sabr.org/bioproj/person/4ef2cfff, accessed May 22, 2014.

all the sporting press called him Dude rather than Thomas because of his efforts to live a stylish, high-class lifestyle[13]) on a boat to Bermuda to visit an onion farm Mutrie owned. On the eleventh day of the trip, while returning from the Caribbean, Mutrie signed Keefe and Esterbrook to new contracts with the Giants. Keefe did get a three-year contract, along with some rest and recreation under the tropical sun, but he also wondered what he might have earned in a free market.[14] (Esterbrook, to finish the story, did not even enjoy the trip very much because he returned to Gotham with an acute case of seasickness that prevented him from manning his position at third base in some of the exhibition games the Giants played in mid-April.)[15]

The way that Jim Mutrie, the Giants manager, became the team's manager has similarities to Keefe's story. Mutrie managed the Metropolitans to the American Association title in 1884, the team posting a sterling record of 75-32. In the off-season, owner Day decided to transfer Mutrie to the Giants, and Mutrie agreed—sort of. In early March of 1885, he showed up at the American Association's yearly preseason meeting to represent the Mets. At this meeting, the Association passed a resolution to honor the National Agreement. This included provisions whereby the member teams of the League and Association would honor each other's player contracts. Mere weeks later, however, Mutrie transferred his allegiance officially, and on March 26 departed on his notorious cruise with Keefe and Esterbrook. Because of his treachery, the American Association banned Mutrie and nearly abandoned the National Agreement in

---

[13] One writer met him in 1887 and reported the Dude was wearing salmon-colored corduroy pants, a sky-blue vest embroidered "liberally" with yellow wreaths, a shirt of red and white bars with a flop-cornered white collar, a pea-green necktie, a black hat trimmed with ribbon, terra cotta-colored gloves, and sporting a cane. "Caylor's Comment" O. P. Caylor, *The Sporting Life*, October 5, 1887, 4.
[14] See Keefe's SABR biography at http://sabr.org/bioproj/person/6f1dd1b1, accessed May 22, 2014.
[15] "Baseball News," *New York Times*, April 20, 1885, 8.

anger over this breach of faith. They held a vote to expel the Metropolitans from the league in retaliation against John Day as well, although the vote garnered insufficient support and failed. The outrage was futile, however; Mutrie went on to manage the Giants through the 1891 season, by which time the American Association was on its last legs and set to dissolve.[16] Mutrie's actions, however, did earn him his derisory nickname of "Truthful Jim" from the angry pen of venerable baseball writer Henry Chadwick as well as a reputation from his enemies in baseball for questionable dealings that he never shook off.

Mutrie's reputation aside, when the opportunity to team with Ward and O'Rourke in forming the Brotherhood came around, Keefe wasted no time in joining. Like O'Rourke, Keefe neither smoked nor drank. Although not quite as well educated as Ward or O'Rourke, he studied shorthand at night, and when the Brotherhood held its first meeting in November 1885, the group selected Keefe as secretary-treasurer. He played an especially important role in Brotherhood affairs in 1889.[17]

The reasons that these individuals formed the core of the BPBP are not complex. When the moguls of baseball attempted a plan to limit salaries to a maximum of $2,000 per year (described in chapter five), many of the New York Giants players decided to hold out as a group. When they eventually came around and signed contracts for 1886 (it is unknown exactly what each player signed for, but contemporaries surmised that many of them received more than $2,000—the salary limit plan had numerous flaws and loopholes, as we will see), the players seemed content. Some, however, like Ward and O'Rourke, saw the writing on the wall and knew that some organization of players was desirable. Even if the salary limit plan of 1886 was not very effective, it was only a matter of time before

---

[16] See Mutrie's SABR biography at http://sabr.org/bioproj/person/430838fd, accessed May 24, 2014; Seymour, *Baseball*, 166.

[17] See Keefe's SABR biography at http://sabr.org/bioproj/person/6f1dd1b1, accessed May 22, 2014.

team owners hit on a plan that was. If the ballplayers wanted to maintain any freedom when that day came, they would have to work together.

The impetus to organize provided by the 1886 salary limit plan, along with the growing number of grievances individual players had over the restrictions of the reserve rule, plus the education and intelligence of these key New York players, led to the Brotherhood's formation in October of 1885. Within a year, the organization's existence was public knowledge. Predicting how people in the baseball world would look at this new entity was difficult, however. While plenty of unions and associations of working people existed in various industries around the country, baseball had never had one. A few people had floated similar ideas in the past, but this time, the Brotherhood was a reality.

Two groups' reactions mattered the most: the public, including the sportswriters, and the owners. How would spectators, the press, and the sporting public view the BPBP? Getting the press on the side of the BPBP was crucial because the press helped shape the attitudes and opinions of all the other groups in these years before radio, television, or the Internet. Most important, however, was how the owners reacted. Clearly, they were not going to be happy about this development because an organization of players working collectively was much more imposing than dealing with a handful of players speaking only for themselves. What would their approach to dealing with the BPBP be? Grudging toleration, or active opposition?

Chapter 4

Reaction to the Brotherhood of Professional Baseball Players

AFTER TAKING ABOUT NINE MONTHS to organize its affairs and prepare, the Brotherhood of Professional Baseball Players went public on July 27, 1886. Its president, John Ward, gave a special interview to *The Sporting Life*, describing the new organization and its goals. Ward chose his interviewer well, a lawyer friend named James Blackhurst who wrote under the pen name of "Layman."[1] In the interview, Ward was conciliatory and careful, even though the idea of unionism was not truly novel or radical in 1886. In fact, none other than Al Spalding had tried to form a union almost fifteen years earlier, although nothing permanent came of his attempt. Regarding Spalding's proposed union, in addition to the usual things with which unions concern themselves, former player Tim Murnane wrote, "As far back as 1872 Al Spalding, George Wright, Jim White and the other members of the old Boston Reds sat around the gymnasium on Eliot street and talked over the question, and finally

---

[1] Stevens, *Baseball's Radical for all Seasons*, 46.

Reaction to the Brotherhood of Professional Baseball Players

drew up a paper and presented it to members of the other clubs. . . . The object was to play with no club containing a player thought to be in the hands of the gamblers."[2]

Nonetheless, even if unionism was not radical, Ward wanted to highlight the respectability of the Brotherhood and downplay the threat it posed to the established order within baseball. The tragedy at Haymarket Square in Chicago on May 4, 1886, after which eight labor leaders were in prison awaiting trial for murders they did not commit while Chicago newspapers offered money to juries to convict them, might have been on Ward's mind as well. He disclaimed explicitly any desire to eliminate the reserve rule. When asked if the Brotherhood would attack the rule, Ward answered, "I should say that it will not be. I believe that the majority of ball players regard the reserve rule as a necessary institution, though they may consider that some abuses have arisen under it."[3] Instead, the BPBP would "meet the league officials, and in a spirit of fairness draw up a contract in which the equities of each might be reasonably protected."[4] Rather than emphasize how the new organization would challenge ownership, Ward focused on the commonalities of the team-player relationship:

> I believe this organization will be of positive benefit to them. Base ball, as a profession, has many features peculiar to itself. There is probably no other business in which the interests of employers and employees are so nearly identical. With the possible exception of the question of salary, they

---

[2] Tee Eye Emm, "From the Hub," *The Sporting Life*, October 5, 1887, 5. Tee Eye Emm was filling in for Boston's usual correspondent, "Mugwump" (W. D. Sullivan, of the *Boston Globe*) for this week because Sullivan had married during the preceding week, and this writer appears to be Tim Murnane. Not only was Murnane a Boston sportswriter for the *Boston Globe*, with the appropriate initials; he was also a player in the National Association in 1872 when this event took place, in fact the only player in the National Association that year with the proper initials.
[3] Layman, "A Big Surprise," *The Sporting Life*, August 4, 1886, 1.
[4] "The Brotherhood of Professional Ball-Players," *Chicago Daily Tribune*, August 4, 1886, 3.

seem to me to be entirely so, and even here there is not so much difference as would appear at first sight. . . . In all other respects I consider the interests of the players to be identical with those of the clubs.[5]

Ward then expanded on how the organization would help management, or at least not threaten it, saying, "There is one thing, however, which this organization does not propose to do. *It will not protect any man in wrong doing.* If any member of this organization misbehaves and subjects himself to discipline by his club, that is a matter with which the brotherhood should not and will not have anything to do." He did note that if a punishment was extreme or vastly different in magnitude from the seriousness of the offense, the Brotherhood might consider action, but he hoped these would be rare instances and that arbitration would suffice to remedy any gross injustices.[6]

In addition, both Ward and Blackhurst went out of their way to demonstrate that the men in the Brotherhood were of the highest caliber morally:

> The organization embraces *the entire intelligent and reputable element of the profession*. It includes among its members such men as Ned Hanlon, John Morrill, Jim O'Rourke, Arthur Irwin, Dave Rowe, Ed Williamson, Al McKinnon and Cliff Carroll. This is an array of names of which any organization may be proud. The mere publication of that list will insure the confidence and support of the public.

Ward also told Blackhurst that the Brotherhood claimed a membership of nearly 100 National League players recruited while

---

[5] Layman, "A Big Surprise," *The Sporting Life*, August 4, 1886, 1.
[6] Ibid.

the 1886 season was in progress.[7] Given that there were eight National League teams featuring thirteen or fourteen regular players, this signified that almost ninety percent of National League players had joined. The Brotherhood had even turned away a few players, unnamed in the interview, because of their moral failings. Only one Giant was not a member, catcher/outfielder Pat Deasley, who many observers believed had the undesirable moral failings in abundance.[8]

In addition to featuring men of good habits, the BPBP was democratic: "It is organized by chapters, each having its local officers; each chapter will choose one delegate or representative and all the representatives so chosen (eight in all) will constitute the council. This is the supreme executive and judicial body and its officers are the general officers of the brotherhood." Furthermore, and in marked contrast to the capricious discipline system of the owners that gave players no opportunity for arbitration, "The council shall have power to discipline any member by fine or suspension, but only after charges shall have been preferred in writing by his chapter or by any three members, and after the accused shall have been given an opportunity to be heard in defense."[9]

In early interviews, other members of the Brotherhood continued hammering at these themes concerning the organization's purpose and plans. In late October, *The Sporting Life* interviewed infielder Sam Crane on these very questions. When asked when the Brotherhood would call its first strike, Crane responded,

---

[7] Ibid. Writers often referred to Williamson as Ed Williamson at the time, probably because his given name was Edward, but most baseball references refer to him as Ned.
[8] "Notes and Comments," *The Sporting Life*, August 25, 1886, 5.
[9] "The Brotherhood of Professional Ball-Players," *Chicago Daily Tribune*, August 4, 1886, 3.

> I don't suppose such a thing will ever occur. That is not the purpose of the order. People think because it is a union, that like other unions, it must get up a strike, but there you make a mistake. The union was established mainly for the purpose of equalizing the rights and privileges of contracts between managers and players. . . . It is not the intention of the union to meddle with the salary question except that we believe there should not be a limit. . . . A man should be paid what he is worth.

Crane also emphasized that nearly all National League players were in the Brotherhood, and for that reason, believed that the League's barons would do the "square thing" and deal fairly with their concerns.

> With possibly two or three exceptions, every man on the League reserve lists is a member of the union . . . We will also probably have all professional players in the union by next season. If the joint committee [of NL and AA owners] . . . should formulate one set of rules for the League and Association, it will be but a short while until all Association players have combined with us, for then we will all be under the same contract.[10]

If enrolling close to ninety percent of National League players within one year seems impressive, the owners often contributed to the ease with which the Brotherhood bolstered its ranks. Consider the incident in Detroit, for instance, in which Wolverines ownership fined pitcher Charlie Getzien (also spelled Getzein) $100 for giving up an excessive number of runs in the eleventh inning of a game against the lowly Kansas City Cowboys. After the game, the owners also directed manager W. H. Watkins to chew out the rest of the

---

[10] "The Players' Brotherhood," *The Sporting Life*, October 27, 1886, 1.

team. Unsurprisingly, the Wolverines' entire roster proclaimed its willingness to join the Brotherhood shortly afterward. It is true that Getzien may have deserved some of the blame for this fiasco, according to news reports. Feeling let down by his teammates and the umpire, he lost his temper and his composure and began laying the ball in nicely for the Cowboys, who teed off and plated ten runs in the inning.[11] Still, the idea of fining a player such a hefty amount just for giving one poor performance did not sit well with the Wolverines.

Nor was this the only time that Watkins fined players just for making mistakes: "It was his custom to threaten to 'soak' a player $10 or $25 for a costly error." Wolverines players despised Watkins so greatly that following their 1887 championship season, they demanded his removal by refusing to play for him *en masse* from that point forward. Detroit management did not buckle under in the face of this threat, however, engaging Watkins for 1888 "at a handsome advance in salary."[12] Detroit's president, Fred Stearns, did not really believe the threat, anyway, and did not intend to allow his players to dictate to him how to run his ball club.[13] Stearns and Detroit management later tried to lay the blame for the whole episode on malingering second baseman Fred Dunlap, claiming he was behind the whole scheme in his efforts to extort more salary for 1888. Dunlap denied this, stating in an interview, "Some one has accused me of trying to work up the Detroit players not to sign unless Watkins ceased to be manager. That is also a lie. I never even thought of such a thing."[14] In the end, the two sides achieved something of a compromise when Watkins stayed on as team manager but did not sit on the players' bench during games.[15]

---

[11] "The Home of the Big Four," *The Sporting News*, August 2, 1886, 1.
[12] M. A. T., "Detroit Dotlets," *The Sporting Life*, December 14, 1887, 3.
[13] Mac, "Detroit's Great Loss," *The Sporting News*, December 24, 1887, 1.
[14] Hincker, "Fred Dunlap," *The Sporting News*, December 31, 1887, 4.
[15] "Chaff from Detroit," *The Sporting News*, February 4, 1888, 4.

Most players seemed satisfied, but veteran third baseman Jim "Deacon" White was not. White was forty years old by 1888 and had been in the game even before the National Association began play in 1871, so he had seen a thing or two. Displeased with Watkins, he maintained his refusal to take the field into March of 1888, to the distress of all Detroiters because the team had no other player to take his place at the hot corner.[16] White claimed his manager "backcapped" him repeatedly and adamantly refused to sign a contract. Opinions on the justness of White's decision seemed mixed. While some saw his move as an example of a player agitating to gain greater control over his fate, others backed the veteran, with the *Chicago Daily Tribune* writing, "There must be some strong grievance to make Jim White angry at anybody, for it is hard to find his equal as a man among ball-players."[17] When Watkins met White in March at the National League's meeting, he tried to talk White into signing a Wolverines contract for 1888, but White would not have it: "In this the manager utterly failed, and in addition received an extensive piece of the Deacon's mind, including the information that he would do no business whatever with Watkins."[18]

White felt so insulted, in fact, that by the next week he threatened retirement while the team tried to talk him out of such a drastic step.[19] This prompted Watkins to issue a public apology through the local newspapers, which appeared partly honest and partly intended to lure White back while the Wolverines scampered about to find another third baseman in case White remained unmoved. White accepted some of what Watkins said, writing, "I accept them as one gentleman is in duty bound to accept an apology from another," but he also replied, through the same local papers, that he did not consider the matter settled. Private issues did not

---

[16] Mac, "Jim White Wrathy," *The Sporting News*, March 3, 1888, 1.
[17] "Base-Ball Notes," *Chicago Daily Tribune*, March 13, 1888, 6.
[18] M. A. T., "Detroit Dotlets," *The Sporting Life*, March 14, 1888, 2.
[19] "Jim White's Position," *The Sporting News*, March 17, 1888, 1; "Hanlon, White, Baldwin," *The Sporting News*, March 17, 1888, 1.

prompt White's stance; instead, it was disparaging remarks about White's professional conduct and performance that impugned White's public reputation: "As you very well know, a ball player's stock in trade is his reputation as a man at all times and his skill on the field. Mr. Watkins, it is the using of your official position in giving out newspaper items intentionally reflecting on my professional reputation of which I accuse you and which I stand ready to prove."[20] White finally signed with Detroit for 1888, but this was not the last time he would enter the lists against the magnates of the National League.

Other teams, by imposing fines and other punishments in an arbitrary manner, also provided Ward and friends with ammunition to recruit new members. In August, Washington Nationals manager Mike Scanlon fined Cliff Carroll $100 and suspended him for the rest of the season. Simultaneously, he docked second baseman Jimmy Knowles and infielder Sam Crane $50 each just for poor fielding.[21] Writing about Knowles and Crane, a local sportswriter stated, "Of course it was a very bitter pill, but they had to swallow it. This was very harsh, especially so when these men were *trying* to do their work. . . . The effect of the above fines will work against the club, as the other players, not caring to share a similar fate, will not attempt to field difficult balls." This writer elaborated on Carroll's punishment as well, offering, "Another error of judgment was the suspension of Carroll, which was wholly unwarranted and very harsh treatment, simply because he had spunk enough to object to the continual experiments with amateur pitchers. The public is very tired also of these moss-agate failures and think it is about time that some of the profits be used in securing another pitcher." The players already felt aggrieved when Nationals management released Bob Barr, a mediocre pitcher having a down year because of an injured finger, and these episodes simply added fuel to the fire. At

---

[20] M. A. T., "Detroit Dotlets," *The Sporting Life*, March 28, 1888, 2.
[21] S. A. M., "Scared to Death," *The Sporting News*, August 9, 1886, 1.

least Barr looked on the bright side of things: "He is happy, however, and several of the players envy him, going even so far as to ask how he succeeded in getting the prize they want—his release."[22]

Carroll's punishment was so scandalous that Nationals manager Mike Scanlon wrote a piece for *The Sporting Life* trying to clear his name and the air surrounding the incident. He claimed that fining Carroll was necessary because "that player was not only meddlesome and very free with his unasked advice, but was unsteady in his habits and independent and insolent to such a degree that it could no longer be borne, and a lesson was needed. He got it, and the result is that since his reinstatement, after duly expressed penitence, he has played excellent ball." Rumors continued circulating, however, regarding the poisonous relationship of management and players in Washington. Things were so bad that manager Scanlon used the same piece to refute claims that he inflicted corporal punishment on some of his ballplayers.[23] Whatever the facts of his relationship with his team, it was soon irrelevant because Scanlon stepped down as manager the following week, with ex-umpire John Gaffney taking his place at the helm.

Had there been an American Association counterpart to the Brotherhood, its players would have voiced some of the same grievances. Always mercurial, Chris Von der Ahe in St. Louis was notorious for fining his men for poor play. Whenever the team went on a losing streak, even a short one, and his temper was up, St. Louis players risked fines for making mistakes. In 1888, for example, star left fielder Tip O'Neill was very sick and struggled to play his usual hard-hitting game. Choosing to disbelieve that O'Neill was ill, Von der Ahe instead concluded that O'Neill was purposefully dogging it to secure his release from the team. He then mulcted O'Neill $75 and laid him off without pay. At the same time, he fined pitcher

---

[22] W. U. D., "From the Capital," *The Sporting Life*, August 11, 1886, 1.
[23] "Notes and Comments," *The Sporting Life*, August 18, 1886, 5.

Reaction to the Brotherhood of Professional Baseball Players

Silver King $100 for not pitching at his usual level and accused rival Brooklyn of tampering with O'Neill and encouraging him to play poorly.[24]

The Brotherhood had not signed up any players from the American Association as of 1886, however. Possibly, this was due to the AA's reputation as the "Beer and Whiskey League," although this title referred more to how the owners of various franchises made their wealth outside of baseball and the fact that the Association allowed its teams to sell alcohol at the ballpark, rather than to any elevated level of dissolute living on the part of its players when compared to other leagues. The BPBP also thought it wise to take on just one league at a time.[25] Its decision also reflected the fact that Association players and League players did not have the same contract and so could not negotiate for the same things.

Ownership and management's reaction to the BPBP was not uniform. Although he would change his mind soon enough, National League president Nick Young appeared friendly at first, stating,

> It seems to be a move on the part of the most reputable men in the profession to secure for themselves and associates fair and equitable treatment at the hands of those in authority over them as well as to promote the general welfare of the sport. With such an object the organization is above criticism, and the fact that such men as John Ward, Jim O'Rourke, John Morrill, Ed Hanlon and Dave Rowe are the prime movers in the scheme, insures for it the respect and consideration of all who may be brought in contact with the workings of the institution.[26]

---

[24] "A Bad Break," *The Sporting Life*, July 18, 1888, 1.
[25] Stevens, *Baseball's Radical for All Seasons*, 45-46, 48-49.
[26] "Nick Young Friendly to the Players' Union," *The Sporting Life*, August 18, 1886, 1.

Ironically, considering his role in the drama to come, Al Spalding also gave the Brotherhood a cautious endorsement: "If they get the right men at the helm, such an organization can be made a power for the general good of the game, and for the benefit of ball players the country over in particular. I have great confidence in Johnny Ward's ability and energy, and if any man can make a success of such an organization he can." Spalding hoped, above all, that the organization would prove useful in curtailing drinking amongst the players. More than any other issue in baseball, Spalding obsessed about player drinking; his decision to hire private detectives to shadow his men and watch their after-hours behavior demonstrates this beyond doubt.[27] Management muted its overall response, however, perhaps because, while distrustful of any labor organization, the magnates wanted to wait and see what the new organization would do before they decided how great a threat to their arbitrary power it was.

What did baseball observers think about the Brotherhood? The *Chicago Daily Tribune* believed the Brotherhood offered the proper balance to the labor-management relationship in baseball. The *Daily Tribune* praised the organization for its intention to rectify the injustice of "the illegal and unjust contracts required in some clubs, where the parties of the one part sign away all right and the party of the other 'reserves' all." Furthermore, regarding the clause in the BPBP constitution stating that the organization could fine or discipline members only after a fair hearing, the paper regarded this as "a principle of justice which might fairly command the attention of the associations themselves." It closed its coverage of the Brotherhood's constitution by stating its belief that "this profession shows a most commendable appreciation of the rights of the individual members, and the section quoted is only a fair sample of

---

[27] Remlap, "From Chicago," *The Sporting Life*, November 17, 1886, 4.

Reaction to the Brotherhood of Professional Baseball Players

the discrimination and conservatism which pervades the entire document."[28]

Another Chicago baseball writer, Harry Palmer, saw the Brotherhood's emergence as the natural consequence of dictatorial and tyrannical moves by the magnates. Later events showed that Palmer did not always approve of the organization and its course of action, but clearly, he recognized why players joined. Throughout 1886 and 1887, some owners began applying the blacklist with greater frequency than hitherto, and enthusiasm for the practice was on the rise among some of baseball's capitalists. Thus, it did not surprise Palmer to see the players band together:

> When the blacklisting power began to be applied unjustly and innocent men were made to suffer by being deprived of the power to earn a livelihood at their profession, when fines began to be indiscriminately imposed upon players and other arbitrary measures exercised from which the player had no redress whatever . . . the spirit of self-protection which is strong in every man and only needs to be called forth began to show itself, and the result was the formation of the Brotherhood of Ball Players.[29]

Palmer then cut to the heart of the matter regarding salaries, with reasoning both logical and prescient:

> Club managers will acknowledge that if the same effect could be obtained through any other means it would be better to abolish the reserve rule and the odious black list, and yet it is a remarkable fact which no club manager can deny that the clubs themselves are directly responsible for the

---

[28] "The Brotherhood of Professional Ball-Players," *Chicago Daily Tribune*, August 4, 1886, 3.
[29] Harry Palmer, "From Chicago," *The Sporting Life*, March 30, 1887, 3.

necessity of the existence of such rules and the abuses that occur as the result of their existence. If a club did not feel that some other club would offer a crack player more money than the first club was paying him, there would be no reason for reserving that player, for the probabilities are that he would play with his old club so long as his salary and treatment were satisfactory. The manner in which the effort to check the exorbitant salary evil was prosecuted by the clubs of the National League is an evidence of their own weakness. The fact that an organization of professional ball clubs, organized for their own protection and benefit, should in meeting assembled have adopted a measure for their protection against exorbitant salary lists, and then each and severally have deliberately planned to defeat its object is a travesty upon base ball legislation, and such a policy, if continued, will create a feeling of distrust, perhaps open hostility, between players and managers which will eventually result in the death of base ball as a professional pursuit. Men will not be shipped about the country at the will of any base ball organization. Ball players are not nomads or Arabs.[30]

Henry Chadwick, witness to innumerable baseball campaigns, also gave the new organization his endorsement, stating, "Almost every line of labor in this country has its protective organization, and why not the ball players? The idea of the association is to uphold the players of the country, and prevent the enforcement of the unlawful rules which the managers have adopted. . . . These rules are distasteful to the players, as they allow managers to impose fines upon them for little or no cause." Chadwick also agreed with Ward regarding the mutuality of interest for players and teams, writing, "The interests of the players and of the leagues are of necessity

---

[30] Ibid.

Reaction to the Brotherhood of Professional Baseball Players

identical, for what damages the pecuniary interests of the clubs must injure the Brotherhood." Chadwick ended by encouraging the new organization to take some stand on the buying and selling of players against their will: "Its movement against the now prevalent custom of selling the release of players . . . is timely. I trust that the paying of $10,000 by one club to another for the virtual sale of the services of a player, held only under the reserve rule, and bound by no legal contract, is the culminating point of this new phase of the old slavery times of thirty years ago."[31]

Not everyone in the press greeted the Brotherhood enthusiastically, however. *The Sporting News* jabbed at the new organization, remarking, "There is nothing for Messrs. Young and Wikoff to do now but resign as John Much Gall Ward and the ball players' union have assumed the management of the base ball business."[32]

Obviously, National League President Nick Young and American Association President Wheeler Wikoff had no intention of resigning their posts. At least Wikoff did not have an Association brotherhood to worry about. In the middle of 1886, baseball's barons were still trying to sort out the repercussions of their decision to limit salaries at $2,000 for the 1886 season, and that seemed problem enough for the moment.

---

[31] Henry Chadwick, "Chadwick's Chat," *The Sporting Life*, March 30, 1887, 2.
[32] "Caught on the Fly," *The Sporting News*, August 9, 1886, 5.

Chapter 5

The Brotherhood and the 1886 Salary Limit Plan

AFTER THE 1885 SEASON, OWNERS IN BOTH MAJOR LEAGUES sought new ways to improve their bottom line. The reserve clause helped because reserved players could not negotiate with whoever wanted them, but that was not enough. In addition, with the Union War of 1884 receding into memory, there seemed no immediate threat from a new league that might cause more competition for players. That was not enough, either. Instead of standing pat, baseball owners made two decisions that they hoped would increase the profits already flowing from baseball.[1]

First, both leagues lengthened their schedules. In 1885, each had eight teams and each team played 16 games against all seven of their

---

[1] The Union War refers to the attempt to establish a third major league, the Union League, during the 1884 season. The Union League's owners managed to lure a handful of established players into their new organization, but it was a small handful. The Union League lasted but one year, and its overall caliber of play was demonstrably below what fans in the National League or American Association witnessed.

The Brotherhood and the 1886 Salary Limit Plan

opponents, making a 112-game season. For 1886, the National League added two games against each opponent for a 126-game slate, while the American Association was even braver, going to 20 games against each opponent and 140 games total. Not everyone agreed this was a good idea; it was an open question whether fans in northern cities like Chicago, Boston, Detroit, or New York would come to games in April or October when the weather threatened to make things miserable as often as not. Eventually, however, teams decided it was worth the risk to play more games under such conditions, and by 1888, a 140-game schedule was the standard throughout major league baseball.

The other major decision the owners made, and the one directly responsible for much of the early success of the Brotherhood of Professional Baseball Players in organizing and signing up members, was to implement a plan to limit player salaries at $2,000 maximum. The Salary Limit Plan, as observers called it, was about as simple as a plan can be. All teams vowed not to pay any man more than $2,000 for a season of play, and anyone making more than that in 1885 saw their salary dropped to that figure.

It is not hard to understand why players disliked this move, beyond the obvious fact that some would lose money. If baseball teams played longer schedules, they would realize more money from ticket sales. It stood to reason, then, that there would be more money available for player salaries, not less. Using this line of reasoning, most players viewed this plan as a grab for more money and control over players on the part of baseball owners, which, of course, it was.

The big question, then, was whether the owners would enforce their own rule and live up to it. True, the leagues wrote the new measure into the National Agreement, but this was hardly the ironclad guarantee it might seem. A team that decided to break the rule only faced punishment if two-thirds of the teams in a league voted to do so. Therefore, if all the teams broke the Salary Limit Rule, it was unlikely they would punish themselves.

Of course, all owners proclaimed their steadfast devotion to the new rule and vowed that none would ever violate it. To cite one of many examples, St. Louis Browns owner Chris Von der Ahe told the press that his players "will all sign for $2,000 and less, too. I see it stated in an Eastern newspaper that this rule can be easily evaded, and that it is charged that every manager in the country will violate it. Well, here is one that won't, and I know that no one else will." He continued, "No player is worth any more than that sum, and if there is anyone in my club who thinks he is he will find out his mistake when he suggests any plan for me to give him a greater sum."[2]

Many baseball observers were not so sanguine as Von der Ahe, however. Ted Sullivan, a man with long involvement in baseball and the manager of a minor league team in Milwaukee in 1886, stated, "No legislation of that kind can be made to work. If a club thinks it to its interest to pay a player more than $2,000, there is no way, so far as I can see, to prevent it being done. . . . There are a thousand ways such a rule can be broken. All the big players will receive more than the limit."[3] It was not long before rumors claiming exactly this started circulating. When Pittsburgh's management failed to sign a pair of players, Jim Manning and Arthur Irwin, it accused the teams successfully acquiring the players, the Detroit Wolverines and Philadelphia Quakers, respectively, of offering above the maximum to secure each man's services.[4]

It turned out that Ted Sullivan was much closer to the truth than Chris Von der Ahe. In fact, Von der Ahe violated the rule himself. True, he paid his catcher, Doc Bushong, the $2,000 maximum, but Bushong also got a $10 bonus for each game whenever he caught more than two games in a week.[5] Some teams simply gave their players money as a "gift," rather than as part of their salary.

---

[2] Olympus, "From the Mound City," *The Sporting Life*, November 4, 1885, 4.
[3] "Sullivan's Views," *The Sporting Life*, November 11, 1885, 1.
[4] "From the Smoky City," *The Sporting Life*, November 18, 1885, 1.
[5] "Von der Ahe's Plan," *The Sporting Life*, December 2, 1885, 1.

The Brotherhood and the 1886 Salary Limit Plan

Outfielder Harry Stovey of the Philadelphia Athletics, for instance, received an extra $100 gift that was "purely voluntary" on the part of his team and "unexpected" by the outstanding and defensively versatile player.[6]

The Louisville Colonels tried a different version of the same idea when they signed pitcher Guy Hecker to a contract for 1886. Rather than a gift of money, however, Hecker received $700 worth of stock in the new "Hecker Supply Company," conveniently founded just before the new salary limit went into effect. Hecker spent the off-season touring the South (where he suffered an arm injury throwing stones at a dog[7]) to hawk his new company's "billiards, pool, cigars, tobacco, stationery, and sporting goods."[8] It seems he scored some successes on his Southern tour, eventually securing the contract to provide uniforms for six of the eight teams in the Southern League.[9]

Another method teams used was to sign players at the $2,000 maximum but then sign them to separate personal services contracts to supplement the official pay. That way, the player got the salary agreed on but technically made just $2,000 for playing baseball. Typically, teams did not make these other contracts public knowledge, but sometimes word got out. Such was the case with Mike Kelly. Nicknamed the "King," most observers regarded Kelly with a mixture of awe and jealousy because he had great talent and enormous charisma at the same time. Fans loved him and flocked to see games whenever Kelly's team was in town. He was, therefore, almost worth his weight in gold as a drawing card. One of Kelly's teammates in Chicago, Ned Williamson, put it well when Chicago sold Kelly to Boston before the 1887 season. Williamson said, "Why, Mike was an attraction, viewed in a commercial sense, who

---

[6] "Notes and Comments," *The Sporting Life*, December 9, 1885, 3.
[7] O. P. Caylor, "Caylor's Screed," *The Sporting Life*, March 10, 1886, 1.
[8] J. I. M., "Affairs in the Falls City," *The Sporting Life*, November 11, 1885, 1.
[9] No title, *The Sporting Life*, February 24, 1886, 4; "Notes and Comments," *The Sporting Life*, February 24, 1886, 4; "From the Falls City," *The Sporting Life*, March 3, 1886, 1.

has brought thousands of dollars to the Chicago treasury, and Spalding will never again have a man in his team who will be to it what Mike Kelly has been. He is unquestionably the most popular player on the diamond today."[10] When Kelly arrived in Boston, his deal with the Beaneaters rewarded him with $2,000 a year for playing baseball and $3,000 per year for use of his photographic likeness.[11]

Another player with a lucrative personal services contract was star second baseman Fred Dunlap. When his 1886 team, the St. Louis Maroons, offered him only $2,000 to play that season, he "tendered his resignation" and announced his retirement.[12] Apparently, this convinced the Maroons to get creative and circumvent the salary limit because by December 29, Dunlap had signed on for another year in St. Louis. *The Sporting Life*'s St. Louis correspondent described the situation by writing, "Dunlap is very reticent regarding the matter. When the $2,000 salary limit is mentioned he smiles a significant smile. His salary last season was away over $3,000 and he says the sum he will receive next season will be quite satisfactory. So people can draw their own conclusions."[13] People did indeed draw their own conclusions: "In view of the fact that Dunlap took an oath, on his contract with Cleveland, to never again soil his dimpled hands with the mud which grows on the St. Louis diamond; that he would rather subsist on bread and water (fire-water) the rest of his days, there must have been some very substantial consideration to induce him to overcome his dislike of the Mound City."[14]

The Maroons disbanded after the 1886 season and sold Dunlap to Detroit in August of that year. Dunlap's new contract with Detroit

---

[10] Joe Pritchard, "From St. Louis," *The Sporting Life*, February 23, 1887, 4.
[11] "The Only Mike Kelly," *The Sporting News*, February 19, 1887, 1.
[12] Olympus, "From St. Louis," *The Sporting Life*, November 11, 1885, 1.
[13] "Dunlap Signs," *The Sporting Life*, January 6, 1886, 1.
[14] M. A. T., "Detroit Tips," *The Sporting Life*, January 6, 1886, 3. M. A. T. was Charles Matheson, sporting editor of the *Detroit Free Press*.

The Brotherhood and the 1886 Salary Limit Plan

remunerated him to the tune of $4,500 per year for two years. Detroit claimed it still observed the salary limit, however, stating that the extra pay above $2,000 consisted of a personal services contract with Dunlap and that they were only paying him the salary limit for his baseball activities. Thus, by signing Dunlap to two separate contracts, the Wolverines could observe the letter of the salary limit but still acquire the player whom they wanted and pay him a salary that kept him happy.[15]

Over in Chicago, team owner Al Spalding used special contracts of a different kind. Because he worried about drinking by players more than anything else, he offered Chicago's players extra money, in the form of "booze contracts," if they made it through a season and abstained completely. Spalding even provided the *Chicago Daily Tribune* with a copy of the contract after a dispute with several players on whether they had met their obligation.[16] In this dispute, Spalding also admitted to paying players above the salary limit when he said, regarding Mike Kelly, "I consider him the best ball-player in the country and will pay him more money than any other man in the nine."[17]

It is clear, then, that ballclubs found many ways to pay players a salary the player found agreeable while claiming they had not violated their rule. As a result, the rule became a dead letter, and everyone knew it before long. That is not the end of the story, however. The repercussions went much deeper than temporarily ruffling the feathers of a few well-known players who made above $2,000 in 1885. That is because, after the limit became public knowledge, several New York Giants, a majority of the team, in fact, decided to hold out as a group in protest. As one sporting paper put it,

---

[15] "More Sensations," *The Sporting Life*, August 11, 1886, 1; "A Prince of Ball Players," *The Sporting News*, August 16, 1886, 1.

[16] Remlap, "From Chicago," *The Sporting Life*, November 17, 1886, 4; "Only Temperance Men," *Chicago Daily Tribune*, December 2, 1886, 2.

[17] "Only Temperance Men," *Chicago Daily Tribune*, December 2, 1886, 2.

> They have held meetings and have thoroughly discussed the action of the joint conference committee in reference to the grading of salaries, or rather the $2,000 limit clause. A thorough understanding was arrived at, and the club, in a body, have agreed to stand by one another in regard to this question of such vital importance. The upshot of the whole thing is that the players will not hear of a reduction in their salaries from last season, and, in fact, some few of them even want an increase on the salary they have previously received.

Joe Gerhardt, the club's second baseman, remarked he might accept a minor reduction from his current salary of $3,500, but Jim O'Rourke, still one of the game's top players after fourteen major league seasons, "very emphatically stated that he is worth every cent of the money he received last season and that he will not sign for one cent less than he received last season."[18] The *New York Times* quoted an unnamed Giants player (although from the vocabulary employed, either team captain John Ward or O'Rourke appear the likely candidate) speaking about conditions:

> The time has arrived when the players must take some action in the matter. Since the organization of the League and American Association, the legislation has been solely in the interests of the clubs. The players have been ignored at every meeting, and restrictions one after another have been placed upon them until now they can stand it no longer. The first piece of injustice was the adopting of the reserve rule. A club can engage a player, reduce his salary to $1,000, and compel him to play for that sum, although he may have a standing offer five times that amount elsewhere. . . . At first, only five

---

[18] O. B. S., "New York on the Anxious Seat," *The Sporting Life*, December 9, 1885, 1.

The Brotherhood and the 1886 Salary Limit Plan

men could be reserved. We made an effort to have this broken. To show presumably their contempt for the players they changed the number from five to eleven. At Saturday's meeting they went still further and made it 12. Players have been treated unfairly long enough, and I assure you the stockholders of clubs will find before long that they have placed the last straw upon the camel's back. We make the money, and it is only just that we ought to get a fair share of the profits.[19]

By January and February, most of the key players for the Giants signed contracts to play in 1886, although a few men, notably pitchers Tim Keefe and Mickey Welch, did not. Buck Ewing, Joe Gerhardt, John Ward, Jim O'Rourke, and Danny Richardson all inked deals in those two months, although the sporting press remained curiously silent as to what caused their change of heart.[20] The players involved seemed to keep a low profile as well, leading to the usual speculation over whether the salary rule had stood up. One sportswriter offered that, "We would like to see the expression on President Young's face when he reads the contracts of these players preparatory to approval" because the writer believed "this salary limit rule, as we remarked some time ago, would be observed only in its breach."[21]

The story of these New York players is important because they formed the core of the BPBP. Like we saw in the previous chapter, Ward, O'Rourke, and Tim Keefe all had important roles in the founding of the organization, and Ward and Keefe both served as officers. For them, "the last straw upon the camel's back" came in 1885. It took them a little while to sign up other players, but not too long, if their claim of representing about 100 players by 1886 is

---

[19] "Return of the Giants," *New York Times*, October 19, 1885, 8.
[20] "Baseball News," *New York Times*, January 12, 1886, 8.
[21] Layman, "New York News," *The Sporting Life*, February 17, 1886, 2.

anywhere near the mark. Even if certain men, such as Dunlap, Kelly, or the New York holdouts, managed to keep their salary near its previous level for 1886, not all players had. With the schedule longer than ever and thus more shekels flowing into team coffers, this did not seem right, and these New York players led the effort to do something about it.

As a result, the BPBP centered its earliest efforts around the issue of eliminating the salary limit and trying to equalize the language in its contract with the National League. The Brotherhood, as Sam Crane of Detroit explained, wanted to do away with salary limits, however easily teams evaded them. They did not want the reduced salaries of the 1886 season to become a new baseline of what was normal. The owners, in contrast, publicly hoped that these lower figures did become a new basis for acceptable pay. In fact, they even wrote the salary limit into the second article of the National Agreement in the 1886-1887 off-season. That article read, in part, "no club shall pay to any of its players for one season's services a salary in excess of two thousand dollars, nor any advance payment for such services prior to the first day of April." This prompted the wry observation from prestigious baseball writer Henry Chadwick, "This rule of the National Agreement, which is now in force, seems to have been lost sight of by a majority of club managers, or else the salaries paid to players have been greatly overstated."[22]

In its effort to form policy regarding the salary issue, the Brotherhood held its first annual meeting in mid-November of 1886, just prior to major league baseball's winter meeting of the Joint Rules Committee. One chapter attended from each club in the National League, represented by John Ward (New York), Mert Hackett (Kansas City), Sam Crane (St. Louis Maroons, having joined the Maroons from Detroit in mid-season), Cliff Carroll

---

[22] Henry Chadwick, "Chadwick's Chat," *The Sporting Life*, February 16, 1887, 2.

(Washington), Charlie Bastian (Philadelphia Quakers), Arthur Irwin and Charlie Buffinton (Boston), Dan Brouthers (Detroit) and Ned Hanlon (also from Detroit but delegated to represent Chicago). They chose officers for the coming year, electing Ward as president, Brouthers as vice president, and Tim Keefe of New York as secretary and treasurer. With monthly dues for each player set at fifty cents, they reported $1,000 in the Brotherhood's treasury. The most important thing on the agenda, however, was to choose a representative to attend baseball's Joint Rules Committee meeting, and to no one's surprise, Ward received the nod from his Brothers, with instructions to recommend certain revisions to the rules of play on their behalf.[23]

The winter meeting of the National League and the American Association to discuss changes to the rules of play was an important moment for the Brotherhood. For the first time ever, the players had representation when baseball's moguls sat down to discuss business. Although only John Ward went on behalf of the Brotherhood, baseball's owners also extended invitations to fellow players Cap Anson of Chicago, John Morrill of Boston, Ed Swartwood of Brooklyn, Charles Comiskey of the St. Louis Browns, and Harry Stovey of the Philadelphia Athletics, although only Ward, Anson, and Comiskey managed to attend in Chicago. Officially, the magnates invited these men so that those who played could advise them on the merits and demerits of proposed rule changes. In any case, it was somewhat of a victory for the players because no player had ever gone to this conference before.[24]

Ward's mission on behalf of his Brothers, therefore, primarily included airing their views on various rule proposals. One was to simplify the responsibilities of the umpire to lessen the number of judgment calls he had to make. Another umpire-related suggestion

---

[23] J. F. B., "The Players," *The Sporting Life*, November 17, 1886, 1.
[24] "Better Baseball Rules," *New York Times*, November 15, 1886, 8; "The Maroons Victory," *The Sporting News*, November 20, 1886, 1.

was that only team captains could discuss calls with an umpire, and then only to question the interpretation of a rule, not the accuracy of the umpire's decision. The intention was promoting a more orderly and fast-moving game that more fans would appreciate, rather than one bogged down by constant complaining and challenges to the umpire's judgment because most spectators disapproved of this. Ward also declared a desire to prohibit coaching for the same reasons. (In the 1880s, "coaching" was the term used for what later observers called heckling or trash talking. It did not refer to the role of the team's manager or captain in instructing players.)

Ward also wanted to regularize the method by which the pitcher delivered the ball to home plate to eliminate the chaotic variety of motions and deliveries many pitchers used to deceive the batter. This would allow more batting, something fans liked. Finally, Ward and the other players wanted to have pitches hit into foul territory declared strikes, in part in reaction to abuse of this rule by players such as Arlie Latham who simply fouled away one pitch after another while waiting for four balls, so they could walk to first base. This rule would, in addition, make the games quicker, another bonus in the eyes of spectators.[25]

Interestingly, none of Ward's aims at the meeting had anything to do with player rights, the salary situation, the reserve clause, or any related issues. Besides the fact that, technically, the owners only wanted to consult Ward and his fellow players on the issue of potential rule changes, it appears he and the rest of his Brothers were still feeling their way as to how aggressive their organization should be. The list of proposals the players made did have a consistent theme, however, and one in line with the Brotherhood's avowed intent to promote the game. Each of Ward's suggestions attempted to make the game cleaner, more orderly, less confrontational, and more pleasing to fans by promoting action over delay and disputes.

---

[25] "Better Baseball Rules," *New York Times*, November 15, 1886, 8.

The Brotherhood and the 1886 Salary Limit Plan

Ward and the BPBP felt these changes would advance the interests of baseball among the patrons of the game.[26]

Although it confined its formal actions to suggestions on reforming the rules, this is not to say that the Brotherhood sat idle all winter. Far from it. Instead, the players sought legal advice regarding what contractual practices of baseball's magnates were legitimate and which were questionable. Although perhaps showing some premature bravado, one anonymous player told the *Chicago Daily Tribune* that the BPBP had "obtained the best legal advice in the country as to our rights and know that in a court of justice the league and association's contracts and rules which give them the right to discharge us, reserve us, or sell us, are not worth the paper they are printed on." Despite this, "We don't propose to make any trouble so long as members of the brotherhood are treated fairly.... There is one thing that base-ball managers must stop, and that is fining men because they happen to play badly.... Fines must not hereafter be imposed on members of the brotherhood without cause; whenever they are there will be lawsuits."[27]

In all, the organization kept a low profile for most of the year following its formation and statements of intent in the summer of 1886. Participating in drawing up new rules for the game was a step toward greater involvement, but only a small step. Building its membership effectively was rather more significant, with 107 players in the fold representing every National League team by the

---

[26] Besides the incidental fact that the owners did adopt most of the rules proposed by the players, one of the most interesting changes made by the Joint Rules Committee was to substitute a square of white rubber instead of a stone for home plate. Prior to this, home plate itself was a frequent source of injury to players. "The Maroons Victory," *The Sporting News*, November 20, 1886, 1. For a thorough discussion regarding how and why baseball owners and players alike wanted to improve their sport through promoting more consistent action, see Rob Bauer, *Outside the Lines of Gilded Age Baseball: Gambling, Umpires, and Racism in 1880s Baseball* or Rob Bauer, *Outside the Lines of Gilded Age Baseball: Alcohol, Fitness, and Cheating in 1880s Baseball*.
[27] "Base-Ball," *Chicago Daily Tribune*, March 13, 1887, 22.

end of the 1886 season.[28] Baseball's owners, at least in their public statements, seemed not to take much notice of, or interest in, the BPBP during the winter of 1886-1887, and because the organization did not issue any major public challenges on behalf of its membership during those months, perhaps the magnates hoped they could ignore the new organization. In 1887, however, the situation changed. As the '87 campaign wound down, Ward and his brethren began, in the eyes of ownership, taking an unhealthy interest in the salary and player contract questions.

---

[28] Stevens, *Baseball's Radical for all Seasons*, 46.

Chapter 6

The Winter of 1886-1887

IN THE ESTIMATION OF MOST OBSERVERS, the Salary Limit Plan of 1886 failed. When baseball's owners looked around at the end of the season and evaluated its effectiveness, they seemed to agree because over the next two seasons they made little effort to continue it. A few owners paid the salary limit lip service; many did not even bother to do that much. On the positive side of ownership's ledger, the salary limit probably did result in a few players receiving less money. On the negative side, the decision generated a great deal of new resentment, and many of the noteworthy players continued making about the same figure as they had before. In addition, it caused contention and distrust between the owners themselves. Those who wanted to hold the line and enforce the limit felt backstabbed by their fellows when other owners got creative and signed players with gifts and personal services contracts.

As a result, the winter of 1886-1887 featured a bit less drama than the previous one had. It was not so much that the quarrels over players and salary fell off; instead, they shifted to a new phase. The major issue of the winter of 1885-1886 had been the salary limit. In

1886-1887, by contrast, baseball saw an increase in the number of players holding out, demanding to play for another club, or both as their method of protesting their current situation.

When club managers and executives had to deal with more of these demands, rumors naturally started circulating that one club had offered another a large sum for the release of an important player who seemed discontented. Like most sports rumors, the stories usually featured more fiction than fact, but that did not stop the press from believing that there might be some truth somewhere and that their local team might be involved. Rumors, as we know, often take on a life of their own.

This also shows that the Brotherhood was not yet ready for a major move, or alternately, was uncertain about what move it should make. The two issues uppermost in its calculations were the language of contracts and ending the sale of players without their consent. The Brotherhood's leaders went to work on the first of these issues but did not have much success with the second.

That meant that many ballplayers had to find their own means of bargaining for more pay and gaining negotiating leverage. Although the reserve clause limited their options considerably, by this time a handful of potential methods existed for doing this. Which one a player chose depended on his individual circumstances. The threat of retirement was one strategy available to players disgruntled over their compensation. Players such as Jim McCormick, Fred Dunlap, and Bob Caruthers used this ploy in their disputes with team management prior to the 1886 season, and McCormick trotted it out again after the season concluded. It was a very popular approach, although not always a successful one.

Of course, the better the player, the more leverage he gained. If a backup catcher tried it, team executives were unlikely to lose any sleep, but if an important player used this threat, it carried more weight. For instance, Charles Baldwin, a pitcher with the Detroit Wolverines who had just won 42 games and pitched 487 innings in 1886, tried out the "retirement racket" while trying to secure a fatter paycheck for 1887. Most teams could not simply ignore a threat from a player of this magnitude.[1] His teammate, outfielder "Big Sam" Thompson, considered doing the same, once remarking he might sit out 1887 and spend the year "resting." Thompson eventually compromised with the club, however, and by late January, both he and Baldwin were on board for the upcoming campaign.[2] A good thing, too, because Thompson lived up to his nickname, putting up a punishing batting line of .372/.416/.565, for an OPS+ of 166. He led the National League in both batting average and slugging percentage, not to mention at bats, hits, triples, runs batted in, and total bases.

For other players, owning a business, or threatening to open one, was a popular technique to gain leverage, especially when combined with the retirement gambit. Players often stated that their business, real or envisioned, offered enough profit that they could do without the game and retire if their club did not see things their way. Washington's Cliff Carroll, still angry over the heavy fine leveled on him by manager Mike Scanlon in 1886, asked the club's owners for $2,500 in 1887, saying he would sign for that figure or else devote his attention to the billiards parlor he recently opened in Bloomington, Illinois.[3] He also made plans to open a restaurant across the street from Washington's ballpark, the Swampdoodle Grounds, and the establishment, known as "The Bouquet," opened in March.[4] Carroll's defiant stance stemmed from this spat with Washington's management, and the conclusion of his situation nearly produced the first grievance between baseball's magnates and the BPBP.

After the 1886 season concluded, Carroll went to Washington's president, Walter Hewitt, to discuss a new contract for 1887. Carroll

---

[1] "Notes and Comments," *The Sporting Life*, November 17, 1886, 3.
[2] "The Detroit Club," *The Sporting News*, January 29, 1887, 1.
[3] W. U. D., "From the Capital," *The Sporting Life*, December 15, 1886, 4.
[4] "Caught on the Fly," *The Sporting News*, February 19, 1887, 5; Sam, "The Washington Club," *The Sporting News*, March 19, 1887, 1.

protested his fines from 1886, believing them unjustified, and to Carroll's face, Hewitt expressed his sympathy and agreement. Furthermore, Hewitt attempted to smooth things over with the disgruntled player by telling Carroll he would pay back the $100 in fines if Carroll signed a contract. His dignity satisfied, Carroll signed, but when he went to the bank to present his check and receive the $100, the bank refused to pay because Hewitt had ordered the bank to stop payment on the check. Carroll immediately concluded, correctly, that Hewitt had hoodwinked him just to get his signature on a new deal, and he informed the Brotherhood of this rank injustice. The BPBP formed a committee to confront Washington's president. Hewitt finally paid, but only after his fellow National League owners urged him to settle quietly. Apparently, Hewitt's shenanigans were so petty and unfair that they were out of bounds even for baseball's capitalists.[5]

While most of these threats were hot air, every now and then a player followed up on the threat of going into business rather than playing ball, or already was in business and doing well, thus endowing the claim with a veneer of plausibility. For example, when it tried to put its team together for 1887, the Cleveland Blues lost out on a pitcher the team coveted, Charley Klump. Klump's family objected to his playing sports for a living, and he had a comfortable position in the Eberleard Manufacturing Company.[6] Even when so notable a baseball personage as Cap Anson attempted to persuade the young man to try out for the Chicago nine, Klump would not budge.[7] The same held true for a player the Philadelphia Athletics were after in 1888, an amateur pitcher named W. H. Whitaker. Other professional teams had attempted to sign him previously, but because his parents objected, and he already had a solid position with the Pottstown Iron Works, none succeeded.[8]

---

[5] "The Washington Club," *The Sporting News*, December 31, 1886, 1.
[6] F. H. Brunell, "From Cleveland," *The Sporting Life*, January 12, 1887, 4.
[7] F. H. Brunell, "Brunell's Budget," *The Sporting Life*, August 1, 1888, 3.
[8] "Philadelphia Pointers," *The Sporting Life*, January 18, 1888, 2.

The Winter of 1886-1887

Another example was shortstop Frank Fennelly of Cincinnati. The club's president, Aaron Stern, paid Fennelly a personal visit when attempting to ink Fennelly to a contract for 1888. To his considerable surprise, Stern discovered Fennelly was the owner of a Falls City, Massachusetts, grocery with "four wagons and as many clerks constantly employed." Realizing that Fennelly's business had the potential to bring in about twice the money he planned to offer, Stern said, "I saw at once that he was independent of base ball as a means of a livelihood, and, though pleased to find him so prosperous, was fearful after all that he might remain firm in his purpose and refuse to come to Cincinnati." As a result, the owner had to offer Fennelly $2,000 plus "a handsome bonus besides." Stern did, however, safeguard his interests a bit by including a clause stating that Fennelly would have to remit $500 in salary should he touch liquor during the playing season. This was probably a wise move considering that once an umpire fined Fennelly nine times in one game for arguing because Fennelly was drunk.[9]

Better off still was Otto Schomberg of Indianapolis. Following a fine season with the Hoosiers in 1887, he looked toward his life off the field (unusual for a player just twenty-two years old) and employment in a family business, Henry Schomberg & Co., manufacturing hardwood lumber and coopers' stock in Good Harbor, Michigan. He spent the off-season scaling logs at the head of a platoon of 150 men. While his father and brother opposed his returning to the diamond for 1888, Schomberg decided to play one more year despite health problems: "His physician ordered him to quit using tobacco and assures him that he will never again experience any trouble with his heart, if he leaves tobacco alone. He proposes to follow his physician's advice and feels confident that he will lead the League in batting next season." Schomberg did not make good on his boast concerning his batting prowess, stumbling

---

[9] "One of Cincinnati's Two Grocerymen," *The Sporting Life*, January 11, 1888, 1.

to a mere .214 batting average in 1888, and did not appear in the major leagues again. His heart condition was serious, as it turned out, rendering him physically incapacitated at times in 1888.[10] He tried to play with various minor league teams for a few more years before giving up playing ball in 1890 and attending to the family's lumber business. He eventually incorporated the operation, putting up $15,000 in capital, and the mill cut about 8 million board-feet of timber at its peak while the company, by now named Schomberg Hardwood Lumber Company, also operated a hotel, two stores, and a saloon in Good Harbor.[11]

Veteran pitcher Jim "Pud" Galvin used one final variant of this approach before the 1888 season when he became upset over the Pittsburgh Club's treatment of him. Galvin was one of the true stalwart pitchers of baseball's early years. He had pitched at least 370 innings every season going back to his first full campaign in 1879, going as high as 656 for Buffalo in 1883, and given his durability and dependability, Galvin felt sore at Pittsburgh's management for its treatment of him the previous two seasons. He said to team secretary Al Scandrett, "I ain't going to say what I want until I am ready to sign, and I may not be ready to talk business until April 1. You had me in a hole for two years and want to get me again, and I have not decided whether I will play ball or not." Galvin's reference to being in the hole referred to an incident where the team denied him pay in 1885 for one of his rare arm injuries, causing Galvin to say, "I will see them in hell before I sign for their price.... They signed me in Buffalo for $3,500, and when my arm gave out cut me down to $2,000 in 1886. Last year they gave me $100 of an increase."[12]

---

[10] "Notes and Comments," *The Sporting Life*, January 18, 1888, 5.
[11] See Schomberg's SABR biography at http://sabr.org/bioproj/person/d6ce5342, accessed November 10, 2014.
[12] Circle, "Pittsburg Pencilings," *The Sporting Life*, January 4, 1888, 3; "Affairs at Pittsburgh," *The Sporting News*, January 7, 1888, 1.

The Winter of 1886-1887

Galvin signed before his self-imposed April 1 deadline. Near the end of February, he worked things out with Pittsburgh and signed for $3,000, somewhat closer to his Buffalo salary than what he had made the last two years in the Smoky City.[13] He offered the Alleghenys a choice of paying him $3,500 with no advance money up front, or $3,000 with $1,000 advanced before the season began, and the club agreed to his second proposition.[14] His negotiating success stemmed from playing a neat trick on the team to get the management to up its offer. Galvin pretended to take over the primary ownership of a saloon in which he had an interest, even putting his name on the sign out in front of "his" grog shop. This convinced Allegheny management that he probably could hold out until April 1, just like he said he would, and believing that this reduced its leverage over the veteran pitcher, the team decided to accept one of Galvin's offers.[15]

Another approach to getting a team to increase its salary offer, besides the "retirement" and "going into business" ploys, was to form a group and bargain collectively. Hoping that this would work better than acting individually, players on the Philadelphia Quakers, grumbling that only two team members had made the salary maximum in 1886, decided to form a "combination" to see that the same fate did not befall them in 1887. Only outfielder Ed Andrews and shortstop Charlie Irwin got the maximum in 1886, and this seemed a tad miserly to the other Quakers. Although the team finished in fourth place, its record of 71 wins against 43 losses gave

---

[13] Carter, "Jimmy Galvin Signs," *The Sporting News*, February 18, 1888, 1.
[14] "The Exact Figures," *The Sporting News*, February 25, 1888, 1. Paying players advance money was a common practice in the Gilded Age, even though teams hated it. Often, players who were unscrupulous with their finances needed some extra money to get them through the winter until the next season began and so would demand advances from their clubs when signing their contracts. In other cases, players did not truly need the extra money right away, but because teams were in the practice of agreeing to advances would ask for one anyway to get their hands on their pay sooner.
[15] Circle, "Pittsburg Pencilings," *The Sporting Life*, February 29, 1888, 2.

it a winning percentage of .623, one of history's greatest performances by a fourth-place team. Hoping for more reward for their winning ways, various players pressed for better pay, and some pulled out creative reasons for their demands. They needed all the creativity they could muster because "it is a notorious fact that the Philadelphia club has had the cheapest salaried team in the League ever since it joined that organization."[16]

Outstanding pitcher Charlie Ferguson (1886 ERA+ of 161) and fellow hurler Dan Casey (also coming off an excellent season with an ERA+ of 132) justifiably looked to get their hands on a bit more currency, Ferguson hoping for a raise from his $1,800 compensation for the season just completed. Outfielder Jim Fogarty wanted more than $1,600, $900 more, in fact, claiming he had an offer to play in his native San Francisco for $1,500 plus no traveling across the country. Charlie Bastian put in a claim for a raise from $1,600 and said that if he did not get it, he would retire to his liquor business. Catcher Jack Clements, best known for being the last regular catcher in major league baseball to throw left-handed, wanted his recompense doubled, from $1,400 to $2,800, on the theory that his work in 1886 greatly exceeded his reward, and so doubling his salary for the current season would even things out for the two seasons put together. Clements also used another familiar threat, that his well-to-do mother objected to him playing ball for a living, to prove he had sufficient fallback if the Quakers thought he was bluffing.[17] Clements did not hold out that long, however, signing by mid-December for an undisclosed amount that was "not the extravagant figure he at first demanded, and yet is a deserved increase on this season's stipend."[18]

The "combination" was not the iron-wrought brotherhood the players originally hoped it would be. Shortly after Clements inked

---

[16] "The Philadelphia Club," *The Sporting News*, March 26, 1887, 5.
[17] "The Local Clubs," *The Sporting Life*, November 17, 1886, 4.
[18] "Philadelphia Chat," *The Sporting Life*, December 15, 1886, 4.

his pact, Fogarty and third baseman Joe Mulvey also agreed to new deals. Fogarty may have lost money in the saloon business, requiring him to take a sure thing rather than hold out for more but risk getting less.[19] Outside of this trio, however, some Quakers continued agitating for more pay. Despite these three defections, Quakers management could not persuade Ferguson, Casey, Bastian, outfielder George Wood, reserves Ed Daily and Andy Cusick, or first baseman Sid Farrar to sign so easily. Ferguson sought $3,000, but because his team was "opposed in principle to excessive salaries, and believes in graded increases year by year to such as are deserving," the holdout lingered into March.[20]

When the Quakers departed for their southern exhibition tour in late March, Ferguson was not on the train. Casey and Bastian were not, either. Farrar did sign "for a substantial increase over last season," but Ferguson, even after lowering his demands to $2,800, would not budge further when manager Harry Wright countered with $2,500 for 1887. Ferguson coached the Princeton college team on the side and claimed he was content to continue doing so should the Quakers continue lowballing him. Bastian also had a fallback option, his liquor business, stating, "I am not compelled to play ball, and I do not propose to play for the Philadelphia club for a thousand dollars less than I can command with some other club." Ferguson finally signed in early April, in time to enter the pitcher's box for the exhibition series with the Quakers' city rivals, the Athletics.[21]

Tragically, the 1887 season was Ferguson's last. He died, of typhoid pneumonia, on April 29, 1888. He was only twenty-five years old, and his early death ended what promised to be a remarkable career. Between his pitching and hitting skills, he had already accumulated 32.1 WAR in a mere four years. Ferguson had married in 1885 and had one child, but the child, too, died shortly

---

[19] "Local News," *The Sporting Life*, January 5, 1887, 1.
[20] "The Local Clubs," *The Sporting Life*, February 23, 1887, 5.
[21] "The Philadelphia Club," *The Sporting News*, March 26, 1887, 5.

after birth. He certainly ranks amongst the best players that baseball history has forgotten, possibly the best combination of hitter and pitcher other than Babe Ruth.[22]

Later, one Philadelphia writer revealed that the salaries for some of these holdout players were as follows: Farrar and Casey, $1,750 each, Ferguson $2,500, Ed Andrews and Fogarty, $1,800, Wood $2,200, and Joe Mulvey, who had not held out, $1,600.[23]

One final strategy that might work, given proper conditions, was that good players on bad teams might put their club in a tough position if they threatened to use any of the tactics mentioned above. Washington was another team that struggled to fill its roster for 1887 because the Nationals had a quartet of quality men hold out for more pay, and considering how poorly the team played in 1886, it could not afford to go without the few decent players it did possess. The four Nationals, outfielder Paul Hines, pitcher Frederick Shaw, outfielder Cliff Carroll, and catcher Barney Gilligan, realizing this, wanted to leverage their situation into a larger paycheck.

Things took an interesting twist over in the American Association, and it is no surprise that St. Louis and Chris Von der Ahe were involved. Although he had worked the system successfully and received $3,500 for his pitching in 1886, Bob Caruthers wanted more dough in 1887. In fact, he declared he would travel to Jerusalem and sit out the season if the team did not raise his pay to an even $4,000 for that year. In classic form, Von der Ahe's response to Caruthers' bravado was, "When I want Mr. Caruthers I'll send for him." Von der Ahe explained his penny-pinching by describing his players as ungrateful for his liberality and by asking anyone who would listen, "Who were they when I took them in

---

[22] "Pitcher Ferguson Buried," *New York Times*, May 2, 1888, 5; "A Great Player Gone," *The Sporting Life*, May 9, 1888, 3. For more on Ferguson's remarkable but short life, see his SABR biography at http://sabr.org/bioproj/person/727aabbe, accessed December 20, 2014.

[23] "In the Quaker City," *The Sporting News*, January 7, 1888, 3.

hand? I made them what they are, or at least gave them the first opportunity to make themselves."[24]

Parisian Bob did not back down. Tossing out some reliable bargaining chips, along with a few new ones, he told his hometown paper, the *Chicago Daily Tribune*, "I will not play for $3,000, as Von der Ahe wants me to. I am not obliged to play ball; my folks want me to quit it, my health is not as good as I would like, and it's a pretty sure thing I won't play any more. . . . I am losing weight and am not satisfied with my condition."[25] The claims of sickness were real enough. Von der Ahe verified them in a personal visit to see Caruthers at his home in the Windy City, and Caruthers said he would see how he felt in March and consider a contract at that time.[26] The condition afflicted both his heart and lungs, according to the family physician, and as January melted into February, Caruthers limited himself to a combination of bed rest and daily "electric baths" in his efforts to pull out of his malaise.[27]

When March arrived with Parisian Bob still unsigned, Von der Ahe escalated the situation. Relying on a new provision in the American Association's constitution that allowed for blacklisting players who would not sign the contracts first offered them—a provision Von der Ahe personally pushed through at the most recent American Association meeting—Von der Ahe threatened his pitcher with that punishment should he not sign and report for the season by March 21. Because he had wealth, however, Caruthers had the option of consulting legal counsel. His lawyer told him to disregard the notice and initiate a suit in U.S. District Court if Von der Ahe chose such extreme measures.[28] It was not long before others decided to join the suit, should the situation go that far. Teammates

---

[24] "The St. Louis Browns," *The Sporting Life*, December 15, 1886, 3.
[25] "Is it Another Bluff?" *The Sporting Life*, January 5, 1887, 1.
[26] Pritchard, "From St. Louis," *The Sporting Life*, January 26, 1887, 5.
[27] Eli, "The Browns' Pitcher," *The Sporting News*, January 29, 1887, 1.
[28] "Von der Ahe's Threat Against Caruthers," *Chicago Daily Tribune*, March 15, 1887, 3.

Dave Foutz and Arlie Latham, as well as outfielder Hub Collins, shortstop Bill White, and first baseman Paul Cook, all three of Louisville, announced their intent to challenge the same rule just one day after Caruthers.[29]

Perhaps this brought Von der Ahe to his senses. Probably both sides were just using negotiating tactics. In any case, he soon had Caruthers under contract, just in time for a preseason exhibition rematch of the 1886 World Series with the Chicago White Stockings. That series would be very interesting indeed, and not just for the action on the field. Over in Chicago, Al Spalding had had some problems of his own, and the team he brought to the field to meet the Browns was nowhere near the one that had lost to St. Louis the previous October.

It should not surprise us that Chicago played a major role in escalating the situation with the BPBP. Usually, when big events happened in baseball, Chicago owner Al Spalding was involved. His White Stockings teams of 1885 and 1886 were historically great teams. Both won league championships, and both won over 70% of their games. It would be more than twenty years before another team did the same. Spalding, however, was not happy with the state of the White Stockings even while the team won game after game. It is no exaggeration to say Spalding was fanatical about the issue of drinking by baseball players. He hated it. He employed Pinkerton detectives to shadow his players during the season and made them take temperance oaths and sign special contracts pledging abstinence from alcohol. Even his decision to send the White Stockings to spring training in Hot Springs, Arkansas, in 1886 stemmed partly from his desire to have all his men train in one spot where he could control their behavior more effectively.

Unfortunately for Spalding, the great team he had assembled featured its share of heavy drinkers. More than its share. Ned Williamson, Silver Flint, Mike Kelly, Jim McCormick, and George

---

[29] "Base-Ball Brevities," *Chicago Daily Tribune*, March 16, 1887, 9.

The Winter of 1886-1887

Gore all loved C_2H_5OH more than most, and even such a staunch disciplinarian as team captain Cap Anson could not keep everyone in line all the time. As a result, before the 1887 season, Spalding decided to start selling off players who did not share their owner's passion for clean living and public respectability. McCormick and outfielder Abner Dalrymple went to Pittsburgh, and George Gore ended up in New York with the Giants. The sale that occasioned the greatest comment, however, and brought up the issue of player sales for the Brotherhood, was Spalding's decision to sell Mike Kelly to Boston for $10,000.

The trouble between Spalding and Kelly stemmed from the special contracts Spalding had each player sign regarding player drinking. Spalding had fined Kelly and McCormick $375 each in 1886, mostly for excess drinking, and both were sore about that. In addition, McCormick stated that his deal with the White Stockings promised him bonuses (to evade the official salary limit of $2,000) that would raise his pay from $2,000 to $3,000 (Spalding claimed $2,500) if his team won the National League championship but that the team did not follow through and pay the bonuses. Consequently, both men threatened retirement over the winter of 1886-1887.

Joining Kelly and McCormick in their outrage, although not in their threats of retirement, was veteran catcher Frank "Silver" Flint. A major leaguer going back to the National Association days of 1875 when he caught for the St. Louis Red Stockings as a nineteen-year-old, Flint was not much of a hitter by 1886, just finishing his third consecutive campaign with an OPS+ below 70. However, he had been with the club since 1879, and anyone who survived the wear and tear of catching in the major leagues for that long had some professional credibility. In an interview, Flint described how players such as himself, McCormick, Kelly, and others knew that, technically, they had violated the section of their contract promising bonus money if they both won the National League championship and abstained from intoxicating liquors while doing so. Flint reasoned that, since the point of a clause about not drinking was to help the team win the championship, and the team had indeed won the championship, whether players had imbibed along the way was unimportant: "We had no idea Spalding would hold it out until he did so, and what makes us kick is that the club won the championship and the stockholders made a lot of money." When his interviewer asked Flint why the players had not insisted on having their contracts worded with this scenario in mind, he replied, "Oh we didn't ask for it, and had been in the habit of taking Spalding's word for everything. All I want now is my release and he can keep the money."[30]

Spalding did not see things the same way. Speaking about alcohol use in general, he said in December, "Now, that sort of thing has got to stop. We owe it to the patrons of base-ball in this city that we have trained athletes on the field and we are going to have them. Our detective's report shows that before one game one of our men drank thirteen glasses of beer. . . . Next year we will have a temperance club." Regarding the recalcitrant Mike Kelly, Spalding stated, "So far as Kelly is concerned the Chicago club will go on even if he does not come here; it will go on if he does; but I am free to say I hope he will be here. I consider him the best ball-player in the country and will pay him more money than any other man in the nine. He is a great ball-player and is popular and I like him; still it would be all nonsense to say he can come here and do as he pleases."[31]

Spalding held fast to this line throughout the winter. Although Kelly still had not signed as January wore away, Spalding continued to profess his admiration for Kelly's skills, personality, drawing power, ability to work with younger players, and ingenuity in devising creative ways to bend the rules.[32] Kelly played right along. He continued to maintain that he would not don the Chicago uniform

---

[30] "Only Temperance Men," *Chicago Daily Tribune*, December 2, 1886, 2.
[31] "Only Temperance Men," *Chicago Daily Tribune*, December 2, 1886, 2.; "Pitcher Jim McCormick," *The Sporting News*, January 22, 1887, 1.
[32] "Spalding and Kelly," *The Sporting News*, January 15, 1887, 1.

in 1887: "I was perfectly satisfied with the amount of salary that I received, but my objection to becoming a member of the Chicago Club for 1887 was solely because I would have to play under Spalding, Anson & Co. If Mr. Spalding refuses to let me go I will retire on my laurels."[33]

In another interview, Kelly tried to stand up for the players fined by Spalding, himself included, with whom the White Stockings wanted to part ways. He said that, "President Spalding and Capt. Anson have not treated me properly.... The officials of the Chicago Club never fail to take advantage of any opportunity to impose a fine upon a player. McCormick, Gore, Flint, myself, and several other members of the team were fined for no cause whatsoever." When queried about the Pinkertons and the proof that players were drinking, Kelly replied, "As for McCormick and myself, I will say that there is no truth in this charge.... McCormick pitched splendid ball at the beginning of last season, as every follower of the game is aware, and only fell off when the officials of the club treated him badly." Kelly finished by stating his belief that all the drama over alcohol, "was simply drummed up in order to lessen the salary list of the club. If the team lost money and a scheme of this kind were resorted to in order to simply lessen expenses it could be overlooked, but they made plenty of money and have no such excuse to offer."[34]

Besides the fines that he believed unjustified, McCormick also offered an additional reason for his desire to leave the Pale Hose: his wounded pride. It seems that for much of 1886, the team only allowed him to pitch against the National League's weaker opponents. He did not have the chance to face the stronger clubs of the NL, those being the New York Giants, Detroit Wolverines, and Philadelphia Quakers. McCormick interpreted this to mean that his team lacked confidence in his work and did not trust him. It did do

---

[33] "Kelly Will Not Play with the Chicago Nine," *Chicago Daily Tribune*, February 10, 1887, 3.
[34] "Tired of Chicago," *New York Times*, January 3, 1887, 8.

wonders for his won-lost record as a pitcher, however. He won his first eighteen decisions of the season and finished with 31 wins against just 11 losses. This perceived lack of trust, however, in addition to the fines, left him with no desire to pitch in Chicago in 1887.[35]

Some in the press supported the players in their accusations against the team. The *Chicago Evening News* agreed with those observers who felt the buying and selling of players without their permission was wrong and singled out Kelly and McCormick for praise because

> They are the only members of the Chicago nine who have had the pluck to stand out against the petty tyranny of the managers of the organization . . . so that they were able to resist the Russian methods of the Chicago club directors and earn a living in the face of the apparently determined efforts of their former employers to reduce them to the level of serfs.

The paper wondered why their teammates did not join them, writing, "Kelly and McCormick are, however, exceptions. They have been able to throw off the yoke, but it is time that the other players vindicated their privileges as American citizens. The courts are open to them, and they should appeal to the law to protect them from the rapacity of the stockholders who interfere with their right to earn their living wherever they choose." The *Evening News* claimed that the people of the city backed the two men, as well, writing, "The purchase and sale of human beings inaugurated by the directors of the Chicago club is disgusting, and it is time that the system that permits it should be wiped out. This traffic has been unpleasantly commented upon by the people of Chicago, and they

---

[35] "Kelly and McCormick," *The Sporting News*, February 12, 1887, 1.

are prepared to applaud the action of the only two men who have dared to defy these dealers in white slaves."[36]

By February, however, Spalding became more confrontational when asked about the King. As Kelly continued holding out, Spalding said, "If he keeps on in that spirit I'll make him eat hay with his horses before he is much older. He has been mad long enough now, and it is pretty near time somebody was getting mad at this end of the line. . . . If Mr. Mike Kelly does not sign a contract with Chicago pretty damned quick, he will have cause to regret it. That is all."[37]

It was a bluff. The next week, Spalding cut his losses and sold the incomparable Kelly to the Boston Beaneaters for $10,000. Kelly did well out of the deal, in some respects at least. Although he saw none of the sale price personally, he did negotiate a new contract with Boston's ownership that rewarded him with $2,000 a year for playing baseball and $3,000 per year for use of his photographic likeness. The combined value, $5,000, was a nice jump over the $2,000 and potential no-drinking bonuses the White Stockings rewarded him with in 1886. The sale stunned his teammates, however. Shortstop Ned Williamson, when informed of what had happened, lamented, "We were like brothers on the Chicago nine. We traveled together in fair weather and foul. When Kel went broke I went with him. When he was flush I too had money." When asked about Chicago's chances at a pennant without the King, Williamson was honest, or depressed, enough to admit, "No, it will hardly be able to do that."[38]

---

[36] "Kelly and McCormick Defy the Chicago Slave-Dealers," reprinted in the *Chicago Daily Tribune*, April 22, 1887, 3. The "Russian methods" refer to the autocratic government of the Russian Empire under the rule of the tsars, which still had a reputation, in many ways deserved, for oppression even though Tsar Alexander II had ended serfdom in 1861.
[37] Harry Palmer, "From Chicago," *The Sporting Life*, February 16, 1887, 2. The reference to eating hay with his horses was a response to the rumor that Kelly's brother wanted him to retire and join him in his horse breeding enterprises.
[38] "The Only Mike Kelly," *The Sporting News*, February 19, 1887, 1.

Williamson also understood the drawing power Kelly wielded: "Why, Mike was an attraction, viewed in a commercial sense, who has brought thousands of dollars to the Chicago treasury, and Spalding will never again have a man in his team who will be to it what Mike Kelly has been. He is unquestionably the most popular player on the diamond today."[39] Chicago sportswriter Harry Palmer agreed: "The enormous figure paid for Kel's release is more than double that ever paid in the history of the game to the best of my knowledge. Yet I believe that Kelly will prove himself worth several times the amount to Boston, for he is just the man to imbue it with confidence and incite it to increased effort.[40] Williamson also demonstrated how demoralizing Kelly's loss might be to holdover players, regretting his decision to sign with a team that seemed determined to clear out his friends and battle-tested teammates: "When I signed I supposed we would have the old nine; if I had thought that Kelly and Gore were going to be released my signature would never have gone on that contract."[41]

Boston's Triumvirs offered Spalding $5,000 for Kelly at first. Spalding cabled back, "We couldn't think of letting Kelly go at the figure you offer, but perhaps for double that amount we might consider it." The Triumvirs soon raised their figure to the stratospheric sum of $9,000. When Spalding stood firm and again asked for ten grand, they decided a mere $1,000 would not stand in the way of acquiring the defending National League batting champion and most popular player in the game and decided to meet Spalding's asking price. Jubilation reigned in Boston at the electric news, and forecasts of increased patronage abounded: "People here have been in the habit of going to see the Chicagos play here who never see any other games. . . . Many who have never seen a game of professional baseball are talking about going to see the $10,000

---

[39] Joe Pritchard, "From St. Louis," *The Sporting Life*, February 23, 1887, 4.
[40] Harry Palmer, "From Chicago," *The Sporting Life*, February 23, 1887, 5.
[41] "Diamond Dust," *Chicago Daily Tribune*, March 6, 1887, 16.

man. The interest in the game which has seemed in danger of waning has taken a boom." Furthermore, when Kelly's old team, the White Stockings, came to town, "those Chicago games alone will about pay for Kelly's release."[42]

The team also promised Kelly he would be the team captain, which did raise a little bit of a question mark because John Morrill had held that title, along with that of team manager, for several years. A man described as having a "quiet, retiring temperament"[43] and respected by the team because "he does not address his companions with vituperative language after a game, because he is quiet, yet firm, and because his head is not inflated,"[44] but ever the professional, Morrill pledged to work with captain Kelly (Morrill retained his position as manager) to make the Boston nine a winner in 1887.[45]

Prodding Spalding in this surprising direction was Cap Anson. When Spalding first broached to Anson the possibility of selling Kelly, the grizzled first baseman replied, "Let him go." When the owner, surprised, asked Anson how the club could get along without the King, Anson replied the team could "get along without anybody who don't want to stay with us. If there is anyone else dissatisfied, let him go, too." To reporters, Anson kept up the bravado: "The Chicago Club without Mike Kelly, is stronger than it ever was before. . . . Oh, well, you may howl, but I tell you we'll be around next fall, as usual, when the pennant is given out." He later remarked, "It would be necessary for Soden to purchase the entire Chicago team before he could have the slightest hope of capturing the much coveted rag."[46]

---

[42] Mugwump, "The Kelly Deal," *The Sporting Life*, February 23, 1887, 1.
[43] Ibid.
[44] "Notes and Comments," *The Sporting Life*, January 11, 1888, 5.
[45] Mugwump, "The Kelly Deal," *The Sporting Life*, February 23, 1887, 1.
[46] "Evidently Not Stuck on Kelly," *The Sporting Life*, February 23, 1887, 1; "Chats with the Ball Men," *The Sporting News*, April 23, 1887, 5.

Joining Anson, also surprisingly, was Harry Palmer. Even though he extolled Kelly's virtues at the turnstiles and on the field, Palmer thought the White Stockings well-stocked with talent and depth: "I have said that Kel's release will not materially weaken the Whites this year, and my reasons for thinking so may be found in the personnel of the team as it now exists. We are far better off today in playing strength and resources than we have been for two years past."[47] Perhaps Palmer, usually friendly to Spalding in his columns, was trying to spin a bad situation into something less dire for the Chicago faithful, or perhaps he shared Spalding's delusion that any player was replaceable. In any case, it appears that Palmer, Anson, and Spalding confused quantity with quality. The idea that the White Stockings could continue to win 70% of the time while removing star players and replacing them with younger, unproven ones seems wishful thinking in retrospect, but that is what the team did. And Spalding chose this course mainly because of alcohol.

Spalding took his anti-liquor crusade to new heights for the 1887 campaign. The godfather of the box score, Henry Chadwick, described Spalding's plan to enforce temperance as follows: "Every spree will cost League players this season $200, and the fine will be enforced every time." Spalding himself said, "The Chicago Ball Club is bound to have its games played by sober men or not at all. . . . We are bound to weed out the whiskey drinkers from the ranks of the White Stockings, and we are impelled to this course both for the good of the men and the good of the game." Spalding continued trying to strike a high moral tone: "I may have peculiar and somewhat advanced ideas on this subject, but I am only anxious to elevate this great game of base ball and put it on a plane of respectability where we shall be proud to acknowledge it as our National sport."[48]

---

[47] Harry Palmer, "From Chicago," *The Sporting Life*, February 23, 1887, 5.
[48] Henry Chadwick, "Chadwick's Chat," *The Sporting Life*, March 9, 1887, 3.

The Winter of 1886-1887

It is tough to conclude that Chicago benefitted in any way from Kelly's sale. Over in Boston, Kelly's purchase made the turnstiles spin like windmills on a blustery spring day. Attendance in Chicago remained at a high level for a couple more years, but then, after Spalding sold off a few more veterans and the team slid to the middle of the pack in the National League, fewer and fewer fans came to watch Chicago's sober and gentlemanly athletes play.

From the players' point of view, however, most of these considerations did not matter very much. What the players saw was that Boston could afford to pay $10,000 for Kelly, without Kelly receiving any of the sale price, even though it was Kelly, not Spalding or the White Stockings, who produced the value on the field to justify such a price in the first place. The same was true of all players, of course. It was just that Kelly's sale price was so high that the injustice of the situation was even more glaring.

This gave the BPBP one of the issues it needed to work on when the 1887 season ended. Buying and selling players without their consent, in addition to the restrictions of the reserve rule, gave the clubs too much power, it thought. Another outgrowth of the practice of selling players was for teams to increase the number of offers that they made to each other, hoping perhaps to secure a premium performer who might be on the market before a rival did. This created its own problem, however. When news about potential deals of this kind made the rounds, even players who had never complained about their situation started to worry that they would be involved in the next transfer. This increased fear, in turn, gave the Brotherhood another issue in its program for reform. The BPBP could urge resistance to this practice as a recruiting tool to build its membership, even if it already had plenty of useful tools, and portray teams buying and selling their players without consulting the men involved as tyrants building their fortunes on the backs of the aggrieved ballplayer. The average crank, of course, just wanted to see his nine on the field compete and win some games, but when the Brotherhood's calls for reform went unheeded, the drama surrounding player sales would only build, not decline, in the years to come.

Chapter 7

The Winter of 1887-1888

TYPICALLY, THE BROTHERHOOD of Professional Baseball Players did little publicly while a season was in progress. After all, the players had games to play. They had to travel around the country, making it nearly impossible to get all the key members of the BPBP together at the same time to coordinate effective group action. Absent such twentieth-century contrivances as the telephone, the players simply had no way to conduct private business unless they met in person.

That is why most of the BPBP's major decisions came during the off-season. Although the Brotherhood undertook no major moves between 1886 and 1887, the issue of player sales, most notably of Mike Kelly for $10,000, gave it another recruiting tool and issue to mull over. Rather than seek reform on a single issue, however, what the Brotherhood eventually did was attempt to reform player contracts, hoping fairer contract language would remedy several ills simultaneously.

The first sign that the organization was ready for a more active off-season came in August of 1887, when *Lippincott's*, a literary magazine, published an essay by BPBP President John Ward discussing the reserve rule and its abuses. Ward posed the question, "Is the Base-Ball Player a Chattel?" when trying to make his case for reform. The essay described the three main reasons baseball's owners put the reserve rule in place: ensuring greater stability, limiting salaries, and achieving a monopoly to reduce the independence of the players.

Ward had some sympathy for the owners' desire for more stability. Without it, investors would be reluctant to finance baseball teams because it was very difficult to gauge the value or potential return on an investment if a team gained or lost many valuable players on a yearly basis. If, however, a club could hold over most of its players from one year to the next, or at least the best ones that the team depended on, investors could put money into teams with greater confidence, improving franchise stability. Another consideration was the connection between spectators and their favorite players. Ward recognized that if each club fielded a brand new nine each season, these bonds would not develop, and attendance might suffer if fans saw their favorite players going somewhere else after every season.

Greater stability aligned with Ward's second reason for the existence of the reserve rule, limiting salaries. Before the reserve rule appeared in 1879, each player was, in today's terminology, a free agent after each season. With all clubs competing for the best talent each year, players demanded, and often received, healthy salaries because they could negotiate in a free market. If most of these players were not available, however, there would be fewer bidding wars for top talent, depressing the total amount of money spent on salaries. Therefore, the reserve rule was the most important single consideration in the finances of baseball. Allowing teams to reserve their men and denying most players the chance to negotiate on the open market prevented bidding wars because less competition existed for the services of each player.

The Winter of 1887-1888

The third goal of baseball's magnates, in Ward's view, was monopoly. If the National League could reserve all the top talent to itself and gain a reputation for superiority in the eyes of spectators and the sporting press, the League could dictate terms to both players and competing leagues alike. No monopolist of industry could have put it better.[1]

In the rest of Ward's essay, he described how management manipulated the reserve rule to reduce players to near-slavery, professionally speaking. When more leagues in organized baseball entered into the National Agreement, which forced them to observe the reserve rule and not try to sign players whom other teams reserved, the players' choices narrowed to playing in a fringe league for miniscule pay or taking what their major league team offered in exchange for a potential career of service with one team. This led Ward to state that however bad a player's situation might be, or how he might try to escape the reserving team, he was always

> at the disposition of his former club. Like a fugitive-slave law, the reserve rule denies him a harbor or a livelihood, and carries him back, bound and shackled, to the club from which he attempted to escape. We have, then, the curious result of a contract which on its face is for seven months being binding for life, and when the player's name is once attached thereto his professional liberty is gone forever.[2]

Clubs, in contrast, could release players at their option by giving the player ten days' notice, with no further liabilities. Ward commented, "That is to say, the club may hold the player so long as it pleases, and may release him at any time, with or without cause, by a simple ten days' notice; while the player is bound for life, and,

---

[1] "Is the Ball-Player a Chattel?" John Montgomery Ward, *Lippincott's*, August 1887. Copy of the article obtained from Michigan State University, http://history.msu.edu/hst324/files/2013/05/ward.pdf, accessed May 23, 2014.
[2] Ibid.

no matter what his interests or wishes may be, cannot terminate the contract even by ten years' notice."³

Following this, Ward provided readers with several examples of how clubs had abused the reserve rule, rendering it a detriment. Besides describing the *ex post facto* nature of the rule (in 1879, teams decided to implement the rule after the players had already signed their contracts, meaning the players had not known that their teams might reserve them when they signed), Ward referenced the case of Curry Foley described in chapter three as an extreme example of how abuses of the reserve rule harmed players.

The reserve rule also inflated the sum a team obtained for selling a player. Ward noted that when Chicago sold the legendary Mike Kelly for $10,000 prior to the 1887 season, the reserve clause made that price tenable from Boston's perspective. The Beaneaters were not just buying Kelly's services for 1887, but potentially for the rest of his career. Additionally, Chicago sold Kelly without his input and Kelly did not see a single penny from the sale. When some defenders of the reserve rule pointed out that players sometimes did well financially after their sale to a new team, noting that Kelly made about $5,000 per year playing in Boston, Ward answered, "The assertion that the player is always benefited by an increase of salary, though not necessarily true, would only prove the injustice of his former reservation by showing that the selling club had paid him a less salary than he was really worth. The reserve rule was made that a club might retain its players, not that it might sell them."⁴

Finally, Ward pointed out the St. Louis Maroons-Kansas City Cowboys debacle. Following the 1886 season, the National League expelled these two teams from its ranks. While one might assume this freed their players from the reserve clause because their former teams no longer existed to reserve them, such was not the case. Prior

---

³ Ibid.
⁴ Henry Chadwick, "Chadwick's Chat," *The Sporting Life*, December 26, 1888, 4.

to the 1886 season, the National League modified the reserve rule so that the league itself reserved all the players, rather than their individual teams. This meant that all the Kansas City and St. Louis players were still under contract to the National League, despite having no team to play for, and therefore they could not seek to sign on with another team, either in the NL or in some other league, that might want them. Instead, the players had to wait while the league office shopped them to other NL teams. In April, the National League finally released those players for whom it found no takers, but now they were at a significant disadvantage in finding teams for 1887 because the rosters of most teams were full already.[5]

What made this incident even more galling and hypocritical was the fact that this came after the 1886 incident in which National League president Nick Young complained about a Southern League team, Nashville, doing the same thing. After a writer spoke with Young, he wrote, "The club of that place has disbanded entirely . . . yet they retain control of a lot of their best players and are trying to sell them to the highest bidders. Now this is entirely wrong in letter and spirit, and President Young said that his mail was loaded down with protestations against such proceedings."[6] After observing these shenanigans, Ward commented, "It is all well enough to keep the reserve list in force. This is a good thing and I believe in it, but I fear that this way of saying to a man, you shall go here or you shan't go there, is too much."[7]

One reason this essay proved timely was that after the 1887 season, the players-for-sale rumor mill cranked into high gear immediately. Rules allowed teams to sign new players for the next season starting October 20. Rumors, however, did not have to wait until October 20. Late in the 1887 campaign, talk circulated that the

---

[5] Ward, "Is the Ball-Player a Chattel?" copy of the article obtained from Michigan State University, http://history.msu.edu/hst324/files/2013/05/ward.pdf, accessed May 23, 2014.
[6] "Important, if True," *The Sporting Life*, August 25, 1886, 3.
[7] "General Sporting," *Chicago Daily Tribune*, March 12, 1887, 11.

Pittsburgh Alleghenys offered the Chicago White Stockings $10,000 (after the Kelly deal the previous year, it seems that anything sensational enough to compare had to have a rumored value of $10,000[8]), and later raised their figure to $15,000, for Chicago's captain and first baseman, Cap Anson. Given that the big Iowan was Al Spalding's right-hand man, as well as a minor stockholder in the Chicago Club, this seemed more fanciful than hopeful on Pittsburgh's part. Perhaps Pittsburgh figured that after Chicago shocked everyone by selling Kelly, it never hurt to ask.

Anson's unavailability did not mean, however, that other key White Stocking players were untouchable. Boston, hoping to repeat what the purchase of Mike Kelly did for its bottom line in 1887, was in the market for a new pitcher to team with the still-formidable Charles Radbourn and up-and-coming young left-hander Kid Madden in the pitcher's box for 1888. Baseball had no finer pitcher than Chicago's John Clarkson, and the Triumvirs cast their covetous gaze westward once again as the 1887 season reached its final days.[9] They hoped to move quickly, perhaps because word reached them that the Cincinnati Red Stockings were also after the great pitcher. Rumor had it Cincinnati was willing to pay the White Stockings $7,000 for Clarkson's release.[10]

Sadly for the Red Stockings, Clarkson poured cold water on their hopes when he declared his intent to play for an Eastern team in 1888. He was born in Cambridge, Massachusetts, and said he wanted to make his home near relations in the East and help his father in business, although, seeing that players had trotted out the "going into business" line so frequently that it was cliché, no one much believed that part by now.[11] Clarkson left no doubt, however, that he would play somewhere else in the coming year, saying, "Yes,

---

[8] "Pittsburgh Club News," *The Sporting Life*, October 26, 1887, 1.
[9] "Clarkson and Chicago," *The Sporting News*, October 1, 1887, 4.
[10] "A Hunt for Players," *The Sporting News*, October 22, 1887, 4.
[11] "The Latest from Clarkson," *The Sporting Life*, October 26, 1887, 1; "Diamond Dust," *St. Louis Daily Globe-Democrat*, October 28, 1887, 8.

The Winter of 1887-1888

I am on the market, but don't know where I shall bring up. I am anxious to get away from Chicago."[12]

Meanwhile, Clarkson's employer, Al Spalding, started signing every promising minor league player in sight, perhaps preparing for a major move by the Brotherhood or for the sale of more of his old standbys, or both. The story of how he signed pitcher Gus Krock, from Oshkosh of the Northwestern League, illustrates how competitive the winter hunt for new blood could be. One day in early November, Spalding was in his office talking with the Detroit Wolverines' manager, W. H. Watkins, about signing players. Word was out that Watkins was also after Krock and that he had dispatched an agent to Milwaukee to search the town "with a fine-tooth comb" to find Krock and sign him to an agreement. While the two men sat talking, Krock just happened to poke his head into Spalding's office in the hope of negotiating a White Stockings contract for 1888. Luckily for Spalding, Watkins was facing away from the door, so Spalding excused himself and immediately hustled the young pitcher down the hall and away from his office. Threatening Krock with death (figuratively, we hope) if he were to say anything, Spalding led him through the mail room, hid him in a corner, piled shipping boxes and a bicycle on top of the bewildered player, and warned him not to move a muscle until Spalding returned. A short time later Spalding did, and inked Krock to a pact on the spot. This goes to show the level of exertion to which some clubs went to acquire a prospect of Krock's magnitude. Baseball observers described Krock as "a giant in size, with fearful speed in delivery and really excellent command of the ball. Although big, he is said to be even more active than Anson and to be a steady and reliable batsman."[13]

Regarding Clarkson, for the rest of 1887, rumors circulated that he would go elsewhere for 1888, and while Spalding did his best to

---

[12] M. A. T., "Delighted Detroit," *The Sporting Life*, October 26, 1887, 5.
[13] Harry Palmer, "Chicago News," *The Sporting Life*, November 16, 1887, 4.

squelch them, they never quite died. In January of 1888, Detroit's ex-president Fred Stearns cranked the rumor mill back into motion, stating, "Clarkson may go to Boston this year. I know that Spalding will release him.... Clarkson is not the valuable man he used to be, and Spalding will sell him if any club will offer what he is worth, or rather what Spalding thinks he is worth."[14] Later, Clarkson himself became more particular, stating it was Boston or the business world for 1888. He claimed to have no beef with Chicago and no ill will toward Al Spalding or Cap Anson, merely that he disliked moving from his home to Chicago for half of every year, away from family and friends.[15]

Clarkson also added some complexity to the situation by making one of the Brotherhood's main points, stating, "He is the sole owner of his skills as a ball player, and if any pecuniary consideration is necessary to obtain Chicago's consent to the release, he should come in for his share of the money so paid. He believes that the full sum given should come to him, but is willing to allow the club from which he is released 50 per cent of the 'purchase' money."[16] Another rumor concerning Clarkson making the rounds, too, claimed he had secured the services of fellow Massachusetts resident, former Civil War general, Congressman, supporter of the ex-slaves, and current lawyer Benjamin F. Butler, to aid him in his attempt to escape from Spalding's clutches, but later this proved unfounded.[17]

When they sensed the possibilities of a deal once again in February, the Triumvirs poured on the charm in their efforts to woo Clarkson. After a meeting with Boston management, Clarkson said, "My dealings with the Boston management have been anything but unpleasant. I am prepared to defend them from the aspersions which are constantly being hurled at them by newspaper writers who never

---

[14] "Stearns on Clarkson," *The Sporting News*, January 7, 1887, 1.
[15] Mugwump, "Hub Happenings," *The Sporting Life*, January 18, 1888, 2.
[16] T. I. M., "The Great Pitchers," *The Sporting News*, February 4, 1888, 1. T. I. M. was Boston sportswriter Tim Murnane.
[17] Bob Larner, "Washington Whispers," *The Sporting Life*, February 8, 1888, 3.

saw either one of the gentlemen."[18] Interestingly, Spalding continued to downplay the entire situation to such an extent that one wonders if he really believed any of it. He said, in answer to a letter from Clarkson, "Of course the inference was that he wanted to play in Boston, but he has never said the Boston people wanted him, nor have they ever said to me that they would engage him if his release could be obtained."[19] As late as March, Spalding appeared unconvinced that Clarkson was in earnest, or at least he let the public believe he was unconvinced. As Clarkson put it, "Mr. Spalding seemed to think it was a huge joke when I asked him to name a price for my release, as I was ready to pay a good sum for it. He thought I was joking, but I wasn't, and I shall not weaken, either."[20]

The intermittent three-way negotiations between Clarkson, Spalding, and Boston's management reached their final stages at the National League's spring meeting in New York City. Clarkson attended the meeting and, in a talk with Spalding, refused to budge, telling him, "It's no use talking, Mr. Spalding, I won't play in Chicago next season under any conditions." The Chicago magnate countered by stating, "John, I can't let you go. You know how the Chicago people felt when I let so many strong players go last summer. They won't stand another transaction of that sort, especially when it comes to parting with you, who are a great favorite in the city." Unmoved, Clarkson answered, "Mr. Spalding, it's not a matter of salary with me at all, and you can not name any price that would be an inducement for me to play in Chicago next season, not even if it were largely in excess of the one I now receive."[21] This may have finally gotten Spalding's attention. When Boston writer William Sullivan asked him what he planned to do with Clarkson, the purveyor of sporting goods told Sullivan, "I hate to let John go. I shall have to go back to Chicago and think it over.

---

[18] T. I. M., "The Boston Players," *The Sporting News*, February 4, 1888, 1.
[19] "President Spalding," *The Sporting News*, February 4, 1888, 4.
[20] Mugwump, "Hub Happenings," *The Sporting Life*, March 14, 1888, 2.
[21] "A Stormy Meeting," *The Sporting News*, March 10, 1888, 5.

I think John is perfectly honest in all he says. But I don't see how I can let him go. Yes; I know they need him in Boston, but so do I need him in Chicago. John is a great pitcher and I know it as well as anybody. If I let him go there will be a howl in Chicago."[22]

Spalding eventually re-opened negotiations with Soden all the same, hoping to salvage something and avoid total defeat. "Soden came to me and asked me if I would release John, but the amount of release money he offered was so far below anything I would consider that I closed the interview in short order."[23] Spalding then made another move for Clarkson. "I told him I would pay him a salary which would satisfy him. He replied that it was not a question of salary. I then said I would much prefer to have him return at a higher salary than to receive $10,000 for his release." With Clarkson refusing to budge and Boston trying to lowball him, Spalding let out that he was also entertaining offers from other clubs for the ace right-hander.[24] One report had it that, instead of a straight sale to Boston, that Chicago would receive Charlie Radbourn and some cash in exchange. Another had Clarkson going to Philadelphia in return for the best pitcher the Quakers had to offer, Charlie Ferguson.[25]

The agony of both the cranks and team officials in Boston over Clarkson continued into the very last days of March, but finally, the Triumvirs got their prize. Usually the master of spin, the best that Spalding could say was, "We had the championship before Clarkson pitched for us, and we can win it again without him. I don't know anything about what he intends to do, and I don't care. We have five good pitchers in Van Haltren, Krock, Sprague, Brynan, Clark, and Baldwin, and that's enough." Spalding's anger was sufficient that the reporter taking his statement did not bother mentioning that Spalding had just listed six pitchers rather than five.

---

[22] Mugwump, "Hub Happenings," *The Sporting Life*, March 14, 1888, 2.
[23] Harry Palmer, "Chicago Chat," *The Sporting Life*, March 14, 1888, 4.
[24] "Is Clarkson Going to Sign?" *The Sporting News*, March 17, 1888, 1.
[25] Eli, "The White Stockings," *The Sporting News*, March 17, 1888, 1.

The Winter of 1887-1888

Thus, the peerless Clarkson pitched for the Beaneaters in 1888. Soden and his fellow Triumvirs certainly worked Clarkson enough to get their money's worth on the field, even if he did cost them $10,000 in purchase money and another $4,000 in salary for 1888. Clarkson went on to start 54 games that year and 72 in 1889, more than half of Boston's contests the second year.[26] When Clarkson finally inscribed his name on a Boston contract for 1888, fans in the Hub were ecstatic: "At the hotels, theatres, and clubs the topic of conversation among admirers of the National game was the lucky stroke of the Boston management. . . . Nothing since the signing of Mike Kelly has created such a sensation in base-ball circles in this city."[27] Soden, Billings, and Conant must have been ecstatic as well, envisioning both more wins on the field and more coins ringing in the cash box.

It would not be an off-season in major league baseball without some drama emanating from Bob Caruthers. As usual, he entered November regretting that the recently concluded season was his last. This time, the plan was to join his brother James selling hardware at James' store on 186 Kinzie Street in Chicago: "Positively I will quit. I guess I have pitched my last ball. I know people will think me to be working for a bigger salary but they will find out that they are in the wrong." He did leave the door open for a return, just barely, saying, "If I should ever play ball again which is almost out of the question, I want it understood that it will not be in St. Louis. Mr. Von der Ahe has not treated me as he should and for that reason I will shun him forever. . . . I will without a doubt settle down in business and once settled down will remain there." Chris Von der Ahe, savvy to the right-hander's bluffs by now, appeared unimpressed: "I suppose he expects me to run after or to call on him

---

[26] "Clarkson and Chicago," *The Sporting Life*, April 4, 1888, 1; Mugwump, "Settled at Last," *The Sporting Life*, April 11, 1888, 1.

[27] "Base-Ball Notes," *Chicago Daily Tribune*, April 8, 1888, 2.

but I don't propose to do any thing of the kind. If he wants to see me he can call at my office."[28]

It did not take long for the ruse to become transparent to all. Within a week, Caruthers was negotiating with Brooklyn to play in the City of Churches in 1888. The team offered $4,500 while Parisian Bob sought an even $5,000. While he still claimed to have communications from his family telling him to make no deals for any reason, he already had let people know that "$5,000 for six months' work is a good deal of money and he would like to sign a contract with any one for that salary."[29] Cincinnati also was in the hunt for Caruthers, however, especially when Caruthers' mother sent him another letter stating that she would "sever the bonds of filial affection and love existing between them if he persisted in going to Brooklyn to play ball." Apparently, she believed that her twenty-three-year-old son might succumb to the vices and temptations of the big city. Mrs. Caruthers' dislike of baseball does seem sincere, at least. In an interview at her home, 530 La Salle Avenue in Chicago, she said, "I have never seen a game of baseball, and will not go to see one as long as he is connected with the game.... During the last two weeks I have received telegrams from base-ball Presidents and their agents, but paid no attention to any of them. I didn't even answer them."[30] His father James, a former state attorney and judge in Tennessee, did approve of baseball, but had died the prior year.[31] Caruthers' new tune was to claim, "I can't go to Brooklyn; that's settled. I'll play in Cincinnati next year, or I'll be behind a counter in Chicago selling hardware." Rumor had it that,

---

[28] "The Case of Caruthers," *The Sporting News*, November 19, 1887, 5.
[29] "Caruthers Thinks He Will Go to Brooklyn," *Chicago Daily Tribune*, November 27, 1887, 15.
[30] "Bob Caruthers is Here," *Chicago Daily Tribune*, December 2, 1887, 3.
[31] "The Great Caruthers," *Chicago Daily Tribune*, December 4, 1887, 11.

The Winter of 1887-1888

in response, Cincinnati offered St. Louis $9,000 for Parisian Bob's release, along with a $5,000 yearly salary.[32]

By then, baseball observers knew that they should take nothing Caruthers said regarding money or contracts at face value. The denouement came when he agreed to go to Brooklyn in mid-December. His mother took a great deal of convincing but relented eventually. For Brooklyn, the price was steep. The Bridegrooms paid $8,250 to St. Louis to secure Caruthers' release and then signed Caruthers at a salary north of what Mike Kelly received from Boston the previous year. The parties did not reveal the precise terms to the press but did confirm the sum was nearer to $6,000 than to $5,000. Brooklyn owner Charles Byrne summed up the enormity of the transaction by stating, "We had started in to get Caruthers, and were forced to follow him up until we got him at an enormous cost. Still, in my opinion, he is the best ball-player in the country and is worth more than any other. We expect to get the benefit of the deal out of the increased price of admission, and the large crowds that a good team will attract, not only in Brooklyn, but everywhere we go."[33]

Byrne realized what Mike Kelly's deal with Boston the year before had proven—the seemingly astronomical sums of money paid to acquire premier talent could end up a bargain because they increased fan support dramatically. With his signing of Caruthers, Byrne was hoping to achieve the same coup that Soden and company had in Boston. Indeed, to increase the hype, Byrne constantly mentioned that the Caruthers deal exceeded the value of the Kelly deal from 1887, in the hope of stirring interest and enticing cranks to Washington Park to see baseball's highest salaried player in 1888. It was a great winter all around for Parisian Bob—he also married

---

[32] "Cincinnati Likely to Get Caruthers," *Chicago Daily Tribune*, November 28, 1887, 3.
[33] "Caruthers Goes to Brooklyn," *Chicago Daily Tribune*, December 14, 1887, 1.

that March in Chicago, pledging his eternal devotion to "a prominent north side belle."[34]

Perhaps the study of Caruthers and his salary-seeking antics deserves some analysis. This chapter shows that even with the reserve rule, dissatisfied players could still, on occasion, get away from teams they disliked. Sometimes, their attempts were simply a scheme to inveigle more money, while, at others, genuine grievances existed. It would be easy, and to some extent justified, to cast a player like Caruthers into the first of these two groups without thinking twice. Yet, given the presence of something like the reserve rule, it is difficult to see what other option a player had in his effort to get the salary he was worth in an open market. Because owners showed hostility toward the idea of multi-year contracts, perhaps fearing the effect that such job security would have on player motivation, a player could do little else besides whine, complain, or, like the kid on the playground whom we all hated growing up, threaten to take his ball and go home. Therefore, while in retrospect it is easy to lambaste a person like Caruthers for his apparent lack of honor, we should keep in mind that he and other players had few other options. Or, perhaps, we can lament his lack of honor while admiring his creativity at the same time. The situation is more complex than it seems.

Things were not always straightforward for the teams, either. It is true that because of the reserve clause, they had no obligation to move a petulant player. They could simply reserve the man, work out a salary, and that was it. There were risks in such a way of doing business, however. For one, an unhappy player might not give premium effort. Anyone who has played baseball knows many ways exist to give less than full effort without obviously dogging it. Pitchers might experience unusual bouts of wildness. Infielders could accidentally make bad throws, while outfielders could get a late jump on a fly ball or lose the ball in the sun, and it was next to

---

[34] Eli, "Our Bobby Married," *The Sporting News*, March 10, 1888, 1.

impossible to determine if these mistakes were genuine or planned. Replacing sulking players was not always an option, either, because clubs only carried fourteen or fifteen players (oftentimes, even fewer than this on road trips, to save on travel expenses), of which most were extra pitchers and catchers. Most teams had one or maybe two substitute fielders because carrying more would cost money the team was unwilling to spend. In addition to this, if a club acquired a reputation for stinginess, it risked that new players would be unwilling to sign with it, and thus might struggle to keep up its talent level as the years passed. All these factors meant that it was a delicate task, for both players and their teams, to negotiate salary from one year to the next.

Fred Dunlap's story shows one method teams had to fight back against players who tried to work the market, and that was by casting doubt on the character of the player. When Detroit finally sold Fred Dunlap to Pittsburgh for $5,500, the Wolverines portrayed Dunlap as a malcontent, stating that he was "a disturbing element . . . a born agitator, and very keen" who also "showed too grasping a spirit," leading one Detroit sportswriter to claim that while "I regard Dunny as a marvelous ball player and found him an agreeable fellow," in the eyes of Detroit management "he is not accused of any specific serious offense, but was simply not regarded as a desirable man for any club."[35]

Part of Dunlap's dissatisfaction stemmed from the possibility of moving from a championship-level team, Detroit, to a mediocre one, Pittsburgh. Therefore, when he realized negotiations were heating up, he told the press he wanted part of whatever money Detroit received for selling him. He claimed that if he were to go to Pittsburgh, he wanted half of the sale price, or else he would not go willingly.[36] Detroit owner Fred Stearns' response was a canny one.

---

[35] M. A. T., "Another Big Deal," *The Sporting Life*, November 9, 1887, 1; M. A. T., "Detroit Dotlets," *The Sporting Life*, February 8, 1888, 4.
[36] "Dunlap and Stearns," *The Sporting News*, November 26, 1887, 1.

He decided to release Dunlap outright, after getting agreement from all other teams in the National League not to negotiate with him, so that only Pittsburgh could sign the second baseman. It seems Stearns determined that if Dunlap wanted half the price paid for his release, Stearns must find a way to deny his request, obviously fearing that future players would emulate the Sure Shot and demand a share of the boodle for themselves: "I believe in treating players generously, but when they attempt to gouge us, why they won't make much by it. Dunlap won't get half of the release money, because none will be paid."[37]

Despite this setback, Dunlap had not exhausted his maneuvers. He went to Pittsburgh and met with the team's president, Nimick, to inform Nimick of his decision to play ball in the Smoky City in 1888. Nimick, delighted at the news, asked what salary Dunlap requested. The Allegheny executive surely knew the second baseman would not come cheap, given that he had garnered $4,500 with Detroit the previous year. At least according to some accounts, Dunlap floored Nimick, literally, when he said, "I have decided to play with Pittsburg next season, provided I get $7,000 for doing so."[38]

Dunlap also had an ace-in-the-hole to evade Stearns' simple release strategy. One of his contracts with the Wolverines was a personal services contract, so should Pittsburgh not accommodate his desires, he planned to insist that Detroit honor the second year of his two-year personal contract with the club.[39] The second baseman also continued his propaganda offensive in the press. When asked about his reputation as a troublemaker, he stated, "Some people say I am a disorganizer. That is a lie. I will leave it to any player in the Detroit team if I ever had an angry word with any of

---

[37] "Dunlap to Be Released," *Chicago Daily Tribune*, December 20, 1887, 3.
[38] "Dunlap and Nimick," *The Sporting News*, December 17, 1887, 4.
[39] M. A. T., "Detroit Drift," *The Sporting Life*, December 28, 1887, 2; "Fred Dunlap," *The Sporting News*, January 7, 1888, 1.

them."[40] In the end, Dunlap got a nice deal for himself. He went to Pittsburgh for the 1888 season, with a contract said to cover two years and pay $5,000 annually, and got $2,000 of the money paid for his release as well.[41] Nimick, however, disputed these figures, saying the salary was "less than a great many think." Pittsburgh's correspondent for *The Sporting Life*, while given the opportunity to see the contract personally, declined to reveal the exact figures.[42]

What is also interesting is that players such as Dunlap and Caruthers received frequent condemnation from the sporting press. One writer, for instance, referred to Dunlap as a "bloated capitalist" after his maneuvers to go from Detroit to Pittsburgh.[43] When a player worked the market for all it was worth and succeeded, this was somehow a bad thing, or reflected negatively on their character by implying greed, yet team owners who did the same to fatten their bottom lines only rarely received such censure. Writers tended to refer to them as capitalists (without the bloat), conservative men of sound principles, sensible businessmen who wanted to put the game on a permanent basis, and the like. A smart manager who succeeded at signing new players was a "hustler," a term with largely positive connotations at the time, but players rarely were.

Furthermore, condemning players for their role in pushing up salaries ignores the role that club managers played in the process. Frequently, players agitated for their release and justified their desire to leave by claiming another club was willing to offer them more. This was sometimes a bluff, but sometimes not. It was not against baseball's rules for a manager to make an offer to a player under contract to another club per se, but the practice did risk unduly aggravating their fellow team executives. In their enthusiasm to

---

[40] Hincker, "Fred Dunlap," *The Sporting News*, December 31, 1887, 4.
[41] "Base Ball Notes," *Chicago Daily Tribune*, January 8, 1887, 15; "Nimick's Big Capture," *The Sporting News*, January 7, 1888, 1; "Number Two," *The Sporting Life*, January 11, 1888, 2.
[42] Circle, "Pittsburg Pencilings," *The Sporting Life*, January 11, 1888, 2.
[43] M. A. T., "Detroit Dotlets," *The Sporting Life*, January 11, 1888, 2.

procure top players, then, managers often tried to lure players away from their current team but did so indirectly, employing a journalist, a friend who also played ball, or another well-placed individual as a go-between with talented players. It is difficult to blame a player for wanting to go somewhere else if promised more money, especially considering that their baseball career had a finite length and they could only earn money through playing ball for a relatively brief span of years.

This was the situation that the Brotherhood stepped into during the winter of 1887-1888. With rumors flying everywhere about selling this or that player (one even had John Ward going to Washington or some team in the American Association, although New York Giants owner John Day quickly squashed it) for ever-rising sums of money, Ward and the BPBP decided they should take a stand on this practice. Not only did it show them how much they might be worth without the reserve clause in their contracts, but also, the players resented not getting any of their purchase price because they were the ones who created the value in that sale price.

However, the players could not do much without collective action. The question was, could they get the owners to even listen to their grievances? Late in 1887, they decided to try.

Chapter 8

The Brotherhood Grows in Stature

WE HAVE SEEN THAT, for the first year of its career, the Brotherhood of Professional Baseball Players kept a low profile. Between July 1886, when it announced its existence to the public, and July 1887, it played a marginal role in major league baseball. It would be going a bit far to say that people forgot about it entirely during the first months of the 1887 season, but for most observers, it was a minor blip on their radar. This began to change in August. In that month, the BPBP involved itself in the intertwined questions of player salaries and the language in player contracts. Although this was almost inevitable, by taking these questions up and addressing them publicly, the Brotherhood raised its profile considerably. The players in major league baseball began looking at it in a new light, and the moguls who ran the game did as well, although the light appeared either brighter or dimmer, depending on the observer.

In August, *The Sporting Life* printed excerpts of a lengthy interview with Ward about the intentions of the Brotherhood, and Ward stated that he, on behalf of his Brothers, had asked for a conference with National League owners to work out a new form of contract. Ward stated his belief that "the old form has outlived its usefulness. The absolute power which it gives to the club may have been necessary at the time it was first made, but times have changed, base ball is a different game, ball players are not the same men and it is no longer necessary that the clubs should possess such an arbitrary power." He also repeated one of the key themes of his *Lippincott's* essay: "Ball players are at present forced to subscribe to contracts giving the clubs the most absolute control over them, and many of the grievances of the players, with which the public have become familiar through the press, are authorized and, to a certain extent, legalized by these contracts."[1]

Ward then described the revisions he sought. One problem was that the current contract contained phrases binding the player to uphold all articles of the National League's constitution and the National Agreement between the National League and the American Association. Ward and other players disliked these references to outside documents and wanted all responsibilities stated in the contract because "it is simply impossible for a player to know what those documents are. They are changed from time to time and one cannot keep track of them at all." He also pointed out that "if the player is willing to concede the right of reservation to the club, let that be stated in the contract, and if there are any limitations on the right, let them also be stated. Let the words of the contract itself contain the entire agreement between club and player, then any player may at any time know what to expect and what is expected of him."[2]

Speaking further about the reserve rule, Ward reiterated that it was necessary in some form but also proposed modifications to it that, incidentally, bear some similarity to the current system whereby a player becomes a free agent after six years of major league service time. Ward said, "I do not think the time has yet come

---

[1] "League Players," *The Sporting Life*, August 24, 1887, 1.
[2] Ibid.

when base ball can do away with the reserve rule. The great majority of players still favor it, though they think it needs modification. The time during which a club may reserve a player should be limited to, say three or five years and the number of reserved should possibly be reduced." Furthermore, instead of the current practice by which every contract was a one-year agreement with a team option for the following year, Ward offered, "Contracts should be signed for one, two, or five years if agreeable to both parties. A player could then take his family with him and feel secure of his stay for a definite time."[3]

Ward concluded the interview with a statement calling for the end of his personal nemesis, the buying and selling of players: "A club has a right to sell its claim on a player under contract to it when the player also agrees to the transaction. But let it be distinctly stated that in such a case the buying club buys only the unexpired term of the contract and not the right of reservation or sale, and at the termination of the contract the player goes free upon the market." Ward pointed out this simple change would end players sales almost entirely because there would be little value for the acquiring team without the right of reservation: "As for the selling of a player not under contract, let no such right be recognized at all. A player released from reservation to be free upon the market to all clubs, and no such thing tolerated as a release of a player from one club to another."[4]

In a separate interview, Ward used the celebrated case of Mike Kelly to reinforce this last point: "What did the Chicago club ever give Kelly in return for the right to control his future services? Absolutely nothing; and yet that club sells that right so cheaply acquired for $10,000. But I repeat it never gave such a right, and any such claim by one set of men of the right of property in another is as unnatural to-day as it was a quarter of a century ago." Ward

---

[3] Ibid.
[4] Ibid.

concluded by stating, "Kelly received his salary from the Chicago Club . . . and returned every dollar of it several times over, and yet the Chicago Club makes $10,000 for releasing Kelly from a claim for which it never paid him a dollar, but which it acquired by seizure some years ago."[5]

The magnates of the National League received the Brotherhood's request at their mid-August meeting. They did not comment to the sporting press immediately, however, and "it was not divulged what action was taken upon it."[6] Ominously, they did not even send Ward any immediate answer, although because they stonewalled the media, no one could say whether this was an act of disrespect toward the BPBP or an act to buy time to coordinate a response.[7]

Undeterred, the Brotherhood forged ahead. Brother Fred Pfeffer, representative of the White Stockings, described its plans, saying, "I don't know what we will do, but there will undoubtedly be some action in reference to the one-sided character of the contracts with players as they now exist. We don't want to make any row in the league, but there is a degree of justice that should be recognized in dealing with players, and we propose to find a remedy that will effect this." He believed that "the brotherhood is strong enough to make any demands it might choose to do, but no extreme measures will be proposed or tolerated. . . . We believe that the club officials can be induced to deal fairly with us. So far as I am personally concerned I have no complaints to make, but there are men I know who don't get a fair show." He finished by stating, "I don't believe we shall be able to do anything the effect of which will be felt

---

[5] "Base Ball Slavery," Chicago, *The Daily Inter Ocean*, July 16, 1887. The event of twenty-five years previous was, of course, the end of slavery in the United States via the Emancipation Proclamation and thirteenth amendment to the U.S. Constitution.
[6] "Current Topics," *The Sporting Life*, August 24, 1887, 1.
[7] "The Brotherhood Will Meet," *The Sporting News*, August 27, 1887, 1.

The Brotherhood Grows in Stature

immediately, but that our organization will be able to bring about needed reforms I am certain."[8]

The BPBP held its meeting on August 28. The delegates in attendance were Fred Pfeffer of Chicago, Arthur Irwin from Philadelphia, Cliff Carroll from Washington, Mert Hackett representing Indianapolis, Ned Hanlon on behalf of Detroit, Ward and Tim Keefe from New York, Abner Dalrymple of Pittsburgh, and Jack Burdock from Boston. They drew up a new contract "which is not so slavish" as the existing one and decided to present it to the National League's owners at the League's next meeting, hoping that body would acknowledge the fair-mindedness of their reforms. Just as Ward and others had said all along, they made no move against the reserve rule: "Many people thought that the players would attack the reserve rule and tear it to pieces, but they did not. It was the sentiment of all the players that the reserve rule should stand. They say that it might be improved with a few minor changes, but that the rule, in the main, is in the interest of base-ball and the players." In addition to asking concessions on the language of contracts, the Brotherhood also condemned the sale of players. Finally, it stated that if a club released a player, the release should free the player from all obligations, and the player should be able to go wherever he wanted to. The same should be true in cases where a player's team disbanded.[9]

They offered the League something in return, stating, "The brotherhood will give the league all the help it can in fighting drunkenness among players, and resolutions will be submitted to the league suggesting that a player who drinks shall be fined $25 for the first offense, $50 for the second, and $100 for the third. Then if the player has no intelligence left the fourth offense shall be punished with suspension and the blacklist."[10] This pronouncement probably

---

[8] "Notes of the Game," *Chicago Daily Tribune*, August 28, 1887, 11.
[9] "Reforms Proposed by the Brotherhood," *Chicago Daily Tribune*, August 29, 1887, 2.
[10] Ibid.

had a few goals. First, by repudiating the drunken element, the BPBP could earn respect and support from the general sporting public. This could be quite valuable. The sporting public could hurt teams where it counted most, in the pocketbook, by withholding its patronage and not going to games. Having the public's support was no small matter, and earning its trust meant counteracting stories like what had just happened on August 24, when a minor league player's companion in Eau Claire, Wisconsin, broke into a brothel, intimidated the owner with his firearm, trashed the furniture, jumped out a window, pistol-whipped another man, and then fled from the authorities who tried to arrest him.[11]

The same goal, improving the organization's public image, held for relations with the sporting press. Because the press was the only means for disseminating information in the Gilded Age, having the newspapers on your side, or at least neutral, was very important. In addition, the players knew perfectly well that Al Spalding was the most influential owner in the National League, and they also knew how much he abhorred drinking, both for the damage it did to his own team and to the game's image. Getting his support for, or at least toleration and acknowledgment of, their brotherhood might go far toward getting other owners to fall in line. The players still had no idea how the League might respond, however, so they finished by stating that should the League refuse to treat with them, they would work out the necessary reforms on their own. The meeting concluded after appointing a committee consisting of Ward, Irwin, and Hanlon to carry forward the Brotherhood's resolutions and meet with ownership on the BPBP's behalf.[12]

It appears this course met with approval from League players. While the Brotherhood held its meeting, most of the Pittsburgh club voted to join. The Brotherhood had not had the chance to organize

---

[11] "Another Player on a Rampage," *The Sporting Life*, August 31, 1887, 1.
[12] "Reforms Proposed by the Brotherhood," *Chicago Daily Tribune*, August 29, 1887, 2; "Base Ball," *Galveston Daily News*, August 30, 1887, 6; "The Players Up in Arms," *The Sporting News*, September 3, 1887, 1.

The Brotherhood Grows in Stature

the Pittsburgh players, other than Abner Dalrymple, who had come to Pittsburgh from Chicago, because the team had been a member of the American Association until 1887, but now its players joined the fold. Thus, the Brotherhood now had members from all eight National League franchises, with most players from every franchise as members.[13]

The Brotherhood's decision to offer its help with combating drinking was a timely one. National League owners continued to debate the temperance question and how best to discipline recalcitrant drinkers. Part of the League's problem was its lack of cooperation. All too often, when one club grew tired of the shenanigans of a lushing player, another club would step in and offer money for the release of the wayward man, hoping to have better luck with him. This did not exactly encourage drinking or reward the player directly, but it did not encourage them to shape up, either. The only real penalty, as things stood, came when a player had let down so many teams time and again, like Sadie Houck, Charlie Sweeney, or Billy Taylor, that no one was willing to take a chance on them any longer.

This lack of procedure also offered no solution of what to do with the likes of Jim McCormick or Mike Kelly—players who imbibed too frequently but had enough talent that someone would always want them, regardless. As things stood in 1887, teams could only fine them or deal with them however the club's manager thought best. As a result, the League's magnates considered unilaterally putting a temperance clause into the language of player contracts for 1888. The plan the owners discussed included fining the player through the league office, rather than through the individual teams, so the response would have greater uniformity. They also considered coming down on repeat offenders with suspensions, with the other owners barred from asking to purchase any player under suspension: "This it is thought will effectually

---

[13] "Joined the Order," *The Sporting Life*, August 31, 1887, 1.

weed out the drinking element or make them abandon the habit entirely for six months in the year."[14]

This indicates that, under the right circumstances, ground for cooperation between the players and owners existed. The players offered help in weeding out alcoholism, which all owners favored. The moguls could reciprocate by giving a little on the issue of player releases, player sales, and the language used in contracts. The question was, of course, would the owners meet with the players? Doing so would advance them toward one of their most cherished goals. The risk, however, from ownership's point of view, was that if the players negotiated concessions here, they might want more in the future, and the Brotherhood might grow bolder. This idea, of giving any voice to labor, was anathema to many capitalists in Gilded Age America, so no one could say for sure how the owners might respond.

The potential for compromise existed alongside the potential for conflict, and the sporting press realized it. One writer, with either inside knowledge or a fair amount of prescience, offered that, concerning contracts, "Suppose the directors of the League refused to grant it? Suppose, further, that the players thereupon should form a co-operative league of their own, apportion their own players and their territory, and begin next season on their own hook?" While conceding, "very likely nothing of the sort will be attempted so soon," the author also believed "such a thing is by no means impossible, and in case no change is made in the present constitution of the League and the Association it is hardly improbable. Base ball is a new business, comparatively—less than twenty years old—and its principles are not yet thoroughly determined." In the end, the writer sided with the players, writing regarding the state of baseball, "Pecuniarily, it is a tremendous success, but the relations between

---

[14] "Temperance in Base Ball," *The Sporting Life*, August 31, 1887, 1.

The Brotherhood Grows in Stature

employers and employees are not yet settled, and are not likely to be until they are put upon a fairer basis than the present one."[15]

Similarly, New York sportswriter George Stackhouse wrote regarding the Brotherhood, "If the members continue in their present manly course, the organization will be a benefit to base ball as well as the players. The meeting was a quiet and orderly one, and if some of the League moguls had heard some of the speeches made they would have at once become convinced that the brains of base ball are not all incased in the skulls of the directors." After speaking with Ward, Stackhouse agreed that the organization was gaining strength and warned that its suggestions of today might become its demands of tomorrow, should baseball's capitalists fail to take heed.[16]

When asked about his thoughts on the Brotherhood's request, Al Spalding said he would approve of meeting their representatives because "it would enable club officials and directors to explain many points in connection with the question which Ward brings up which I think they do not fully understand. I shall always be ready and willing to discuss any questions bearing on the relations between the clubs and their players, if such discussion will make our relations any more satisfactory."[17] When questioned on specifics, however, such as when to meet, his personal views on the organization and its objectives, and the like, Spalding returned to the noncommittal stance of his capitalist brethren, telling Chicago sportswriter Harry Palmer, "Why discuss Christmas presents during the ice cream season?"[18]

Speaking of Harry Palmer, he was a good example of how the print media could help or hurt the cause of the Brotherhood. He took a cautious view of the BPBP and its motives, although because of his close association with Al Spalding, looking back it is sometimes

---

[15] "It's in the Air," *The Sporting Life*, August 31, 1887, 1.
[16] George Stackhouse, "New York Mention," *The Sporting Life*, September 7, 1887, 4.
[17] Harry Palmer, "From Chicago," *The Sporting Life*, August 31, 1887, 2.
[18] Harry Palmer, "From Chicago," *The Sporting Life*, September 7, 1887, 3.

hard to tell where Spalding's views ended and where Palmer's began. He was not quite Spalding's mouthpiece in the press, but at times his personal views made it appear that way. In 1887, some of Palmer's columns set forth various points that critics of the Brotherhood often raised. While Palmer sympathized with some of the organization's complaints, he also worried it might become an exclusive organization that would work to the benefit of its members rather than the general benefit of the game. He saw danger in the possibility that the Brotherhood might request multi-year contracts for some or all its players, believing this might become a tool for existing members to preserve their own positions in baseball and keep out younger talent.

Palmer also worried what these contracts might do to player motivation. Would they continue to work and strive for improvement if their contract guaranteed employment several years into the future? He therefore cautioned younger players to think twice before joining the organization. Palmer also repeated several complete or partial fallacies regarding the players, writing such nonsense as that ballplayers dressed their wives in silks and diamonds and that they worked just seven months of the year.[19]

One thing that Palmer did not bring up, but should have to help make his point, was what would happen should a player take a major injury and lose his effectiveness before the contract was up? Given the injury history of players, especially pitchers, in Gilded Age baseball, this was no small matter. He also neglected to mention, considering the other side of the issue, that a long-term contract had benefits. Foremost among these was that it achieved the same purpose as the reserve rule—that is, keeping the player on the team and the core of the team intact over an extended period—but without the negativity produced by the restrictiveness of the reserve rule. It would also avoid the yearly disputes over salary that had done so much to complicate the lives of owners such as Spalding and Chris

---

[19] Harry Palmer, "From Chicago," *The Sporting Life*, September 14, 1887, 2.

Von der Ahe in recent years. Finally, a long-term contract gave each club more predictability. If a team were to sign a player to a three-year deal, for instance, the team could better predict what its costs would be three years into the future and plan accordingly, instead of having to worry about what would happen should an important player become dissatisfied and demand more cash before signing their next contract.

In a way, however, this point was moot because the Brotherhood spent the fall of 1887 discussing the language of contracts rather than their length. Ward also responded to Palmer's critique, writing a letter to *The Sporting Life* describing Palmer's position as misinformed. Ward tried to clarify that the Brotherhood did not desire to make multi-year contracts obligatory. Rather, "I expressed the opinion, individually, that there was no good reason why contracts, instead of for one year, might not be made for two, three or even five years, and I meant, of course, *if agreeable to ball club and player*. But as for making this condition obligatory, I never entertained any such absurd idea." Seeking to avoid burning bridges unnecessarily, Ward also said of Palmer, "Several of the ablest articles on the subject of the players' wrongs have been contributed by your Chicago correspondent. . . . We confidently expect his continued co-operation."[20]

Ward's words did not mollify Palmer, however. He believed the Brotherhood in the wrong to focus on the issue of player sales and tried to turn around Ward's story of the Kelly sale to make his own point. In his eyes, "When Kelly's release was sold to Boston it was sold because Kelly had positively refused to play another season in Chicago. *Before* it was sold, however, Kelly was consulted by the purchasing club. He stated that the transfer was agreeable to him and named the salary he would play for. Was there any '*slavery*' in this transaction?"[21] At the same time, Palmer conjured up fanciful new

---

[20] John Ward, "What They Want," *The Sporting Life*, September 21, 1887, 1.
[21] Harry Palmer, "From Chicago," *The Sporting Life*, September 28, 1887, 4.

fears regarding the Brotherhood's intentions. He warned that if the BPBP succeeded on the contract issue, other leagues would, in short order, have their own brotherhoods and that eventually these separate brotherhoods would consolidate. Taking new players into their ranks as fast as the clubs discovered them, the consolidated brotherhood would then destroy baseball within one season.[22]

While Harry Palmer wavered in his support of Ward and the BPBP, many other writers were taking Ward's side, at least some extent. One Baltimore writer observed that listening to the Brotherhood cost the League nothing and required no concessions but would convince both the players and the public that it had the game's best interests in mind. He reminded his readers that calling the BPBP a secret organization, which various owners had done, was "thoroughly inconsistent, for both the League and Association hold secret meetings and the latter body is red-handed from the outrage of expelling a member merely for publishing the standing of a vote on one of the most senseless and damning pieces of legislation that ever disgraced the record of a sane assembly." He also pointed out that, when it came to the League or the Association, "if there are any good reasons why these meetings of the employers should be star chamber affairs, the argument would apply equally well to the employed." While admitting that there were some players so ignorant that they could not tell their own name "from the sign of a Chinese wash house," not all owners were the intellectual heirs of Voltaire, either; they often did the kind of petty, tyrannical, and borderline dishonest things that the players wanted to eliminate.[23]

---

[22] Harry Palmer, "From Chicago," *The Sporting Life*, October 5, 1887, 4.
[23] T. T. T., "League Vs. Brotherhood," *The Sporting Life*, October 5, 1887, 1. Regarding the quote about the red-handed behavior of the American Association, T. T. T. (Albert Mott) refers to its treatment of O. P. Caylor, whom the Association barred from a previous meeting even though Caylor was the manager of the New York Metropolitans because he had the nerve to publish the record of the Association's vote on the matter of blacklisting players who would not sign the contracts offered them by their clubs. The decision to adopt the

The Brotherhood Grows in Stature

Interestingly, this writer, Albert Mott, also expounded what we might call the Modified Labor Theory of Baseball Value to support the Brotherhood's cause. In its simplest form, Karl Marx's Labor Theory of Value holds that since workers take raw materials and turn them into finished products, their labor creates the value of the product beyond its original value as a raw material. When a capitalist then sells the finished product, keeping most of the profit for himself while giving only a fraction of it back to the workers, the capitalist steals from the workers because their work is what gave the item its increased value. Because the workers increased the value of the item, they deserve most of the profit from its sale. Applying this concept to baseball, Mott stated some obvious truths, such as "the public do not visit the Polo Ground on account of Mr. Day or Mr. Mutrie, and certainly, in Baltimore, if Barnie was the card offered it would not draw like an army mule. People go to see well-known players play a game . . . and they would go see them whether offered as a show by Mr. Day or Mr. Ward, Mr. Barnie or Purcell, or even an unknown employer." Similarly, "how many people would the Jersey City or the Newark Club draw in New York even if named the New York Club?"[24]

The word "modified" is appropriate here because, like Mott also realized, clearly the clubs provided things of value as well. They furnished a place to play the games, advertising to draw fans, administrative time to create the schedule and make travel arrangements, and so forth. Still, it is probably fair to say that sports like baseball come closer to the Labor Theory of Value than most businesses. The workers at a fast food chain are expendable because almost anyone can perform their tasks satisfactorily. Few people, however, can hit a baseball traveling at ninety miles per hour or throw a baseball accurately at that speed, so those who command

---

blacklisting measure was the "senseless and damning" measure mentioned in the quote.
[24] Ibid.

those skills create a great deal of value through the rareness of their talents. That is why major league baseball games draw tens of thousands of fans while most high school baseball games draw one hundred or so. Or, as the *Baltimore Herald* put it,

> It is high time that the idea that crack ball-players get more than they are worth was exploded. Men like Latham and Comiskey are scarce. Ten thousand men might be examined before one could be found combining all the qualifications of a first-rate ball player, mental and physical, as they do. They are very different from the average man, and are worth a great deal more. They are experts in their business, and experts in nearly every other calling in life are higher paid than these men. They may have been cart-drivers before they became professional ball-players, but they are as different from ordinary cart-drivers as Daniel Webster and Rufus Choate were from the ordinary 'shyster' lawyer who carries his office in his hat. It is no argument to say that players like Robinson of the Browns, Hanlon, and Dunlap could not earn more than $15 a week at any other occupation. Neither could the Rev. Dr. Talmage as a book-keeper.[25]

This discussion frames most of the arguments made by both sides. The players, knowing their skill was what made baseball popular and convinced that baseball had many needed reforms, had a plan of how to proceed. It is not clear if National League owners were of the same mind because they did not make their discussions regarding the Brotherhood public knowledge, although later events demonstrated they had not been idle during the summer months.

That meant that by the end of the 1887 championship season, the issues were no closer to resolution than they were when the season began. The leaders of the Brotherhood made their intentions and

---

[25] "Base-Ball Notes," *Chicago Daily Tribune*, October 30, 1887, 13.

The Brotherhood Grows in Stature

desired reforms known to the sporting public. The owners of the National League did not respond. As long as the players had games to play, they had few options regarding the issue because it was difficult to get the necessary people together for a meeting. After the season ended, however, that major obstacle no longer existed. As a result, October and November of 1887 witnessed the first major showdown between the Brotherhood and the National League.

Chapter 9

The Brotherhood and Player Contracts, 1887-1888

ALTHOUGH, WITH A FEW EXCEPTIONS, the views of the baseball public supported many of the Brotherhood's goals, to make headway on contract language, the Brotherhood of Professional Baseball Players needed official recognition from the National League. As of mid-September 1887, that recognition was not forthcoming from anyone in baseball's senior organization, and the Brotherhood's leadership became restless. Perhaps seeking to divide and conquer, or to test the BPBP's cohesiveness and resolve, National League president Nick Young and associates told Ward they were happy to meet a delegation of players but that the delegation could not represent the Brotherhood.

When informed of this, in an interview in Pittsburgh, John Ward said, "If this resolve is persisted in there will be trouble. The brotherhood has come to stay, and not one of us will sign a contract until a delegation from our organization confers with the representatives of the National League. . . . President Young and others look upon us as something weak, but they will find out their mistake if a conflict takes place."[1] The owners were unmoved, however. When a sportswriter queried Pittsburgh's president about his views on the organization, he simply stated, "I know nothing about it."[2]

When asked what the Brotherhood would do if the League continued its course and the players refused to sign, Ward said, "I am not at liberty to say what we will do. Let me say, however, that there is plenty of money at our disposal to organize any association or league. We know of any amount of capitalists who want to invest their money in base-ball. I will go further and say that we will be recognized as an organization, and we will all play next year whether the league people like it or not."[3] We might interpret this hint at forming a rival organization in several ways. Perhaps it was premature confidence on the part of the Brotherhood. Ward might have been bluffing, hoping to startle the National League into showing its cards. Finally, these statements might have been Ward's attempt to throw the owners off balance when they were already arguing amongst themselves through the press about the merits of returning to a percentage system for distributing ticket revenues for 1888.

In this Pittsburgh interview, Ward also drew attention to the benefits the Brotherhood already provided its members to cast the organization in a fair and reasonable light. He mentioned the case of Boston Beaneaters pitcher Charles "Old Hoss" Radbourn. The ownership in Boston, the Triumvirs, suspended Radbourn without pay in September 1887 for what they deemed ineffective pitching,

---

[1] "The Brotherhood of Base-Ball Players Demand Recognition," *Chicago Daily Tribune*, September 19, 1887, 3; Stevens, *Baseball's Radical for all Seasons*, 50; Di Salvatore, *A Clever Base-Ballist*, 194; "Sporting Notes," *Morning Oregonian* (Portland), September 19, 1887.
[2] Circle, "From the Smoky City," *The Sporting Life*, October 19, 1887, 1.
[3] "The Brotherhood of Base-Ball Players Demand Recognition," *Chicago Daily Tribune*, September 19, 1887, 3.

with insinuations that Radbourn was not giving his best effort each day, thus defrauding them of money. The fact that the Triumvirs reversed course within a few days, Ward felt, was a testament to Boston's fear that the Brotherhood might take up Radbourn's cause. He told his interviewer, "The union meant to respect the reserve rule, but would not tolerate a system by which honest players can be cast aside for weeks without pay simply because he is not playing as well as the club directors would like to see him."[4] As another member of the Brotherhood put it a short time later: "The point I made in his case was that *indefinite* suspensions are illegal under the contract or otherwise. It is not proposed to uphold wrong-doers, but in all cases the player must, and *will*, have a hearing, and the punishment must not be *unreasonable*, etc."[5]

Nor was Radbourn's case the only time observers suspected a team of suspending a man just to save money in 1887. A Washington sportswriter believed the same fate had befallen one of the Nationals' players as well. In a general critique of the club's management offered to explain the team's weak performance, in September Robert Wood wrote of the team's president, "Only this week he suspended a player for an offence committed prior to June 16, and after the man has been upon the field and played several good games. I do not think it was so much his desire to correct abuses as it was to curtail the expenses of the club."[6]

The day after Ward's interview, the *Chicago Daily Tribune* printed a lengthy piece that, while not attributed to Ward, glowed in its references to the Brotherhood while demonizing National League ownership. Discussing the "one-sided" contracts, it stated that they gave the clubs, "absolute control over every player that could be induced to sign a contract—have held their players in a state of bondage, and have in numerous instances sold and assigned them

---

[4] Ibid.
[5] "What the Brotherhood Did for 'Rad'," *The Sporting Life*, September 28, 1887, 1.
[6] W. U. D., "From the Capital," *The Sporting Life*, September 28, 1887, 6.

like so many slaves." These contracts were "clearly illegal, and have been so pronounced by the courts, and the practices of the league in dealing with players have been repugnant to every idea of freedom, if not hostile to American institutions." As if that was not enough, the article also reported, "it is only a short time since the President of a league club, in speaking of the players in his team, said, 'Those men belong to me body and soul, and I'll make them play ball,' emphasizing his remarks with appropriate profanity. An organization whose methods can justify such assertions does not deserve well of the American people." Not stopping there, "The league, however, appears to be considerable of a foreign element. It claims to have done much to promote the game, and possibly it has, but all its work has been of a mercenary character." After casting all these aspersions of un-Americanism at the League's owners, the article went on to applaud the BPBP's manly course and called on its readers to support the players should the situation develop into a showdown. It closed by pointing out the great financial rewards realized by ownership as justification of why the owners could afford to share a bit more with their players.[7]

As September neared its end and storm clouds continued gathering, both sides took their argument to the sporting press. Nick Young published an exchange of letters between himself and Ward in *The Sporting Life*. He acknowledged receiving Ward's letter describing how the Brotherhood had appointed a committee at their August 28 meeting at Earle's Hotel in New York City. Young's evasive reply on September 1 was to write, "In the absence of a League meeting, which could not conveniently be held at a very early day, I had no authority to recognize any communication from the Brotherhood, and at the same time suggested that he adhere to or renew his original request that the League officials meet a

---

[7] "The Ball-Players League," *Chicago Daily Tribune*, September 20, 1887, 3.

committee of its players, etc."⁸ This, according to Harry Palmer at least, was a lie. Young had no reason to call a League meeting to discuss the Brotherhood because the League's magnates already had discussed it by that time and decided to deny the Brotherhood recognition even before Ward and the Brotherhood decided to ask for it.⁹ Given Palmer's access to Al Spalding, his version of events is probably the correct one.

Ward did not buy Young's reply any more than his unexpected ally Palmer did. Ward's response on September 3 called out Young for his obfuscation. Ward pointed out that Young and the National League already had authority to meet a delegation of the Brotherhood. The National League had already given him such authority, at its joint committee meeting on rules, which the minutes of that meeting demonstrated. Ward stated, "A refusal to recognize the Brotherhood now will look very much like hostility toward it, simply on the ground that it is an *organization* of the players. . . . Will the League go on record as opposed to any organization of the players on that ground alone?" He also warned Young, "Delays are always dangerous and an unsettled condition at the close of the season might prove a serious misfortune."¹⁰

While, clearly, Young's delaying tactics perturbed Ward, he offered some conciliation as well in his September 3 letter. Ward repeated a theme he had brought up often: that the interests of the players and the owners were much the same.

> Presidents Stearns, Reach and Day are successful businessmen outside of their base ball interests, while, on the other hand, Hanlon, Irwin and myself are entirely dependent on base ball for a livelihood. Are we not, therefore, relatively

---

[8] Nick Young, "The League's Position Defined," *The Sporting Life*, September 28, 1887, 1.
[9] Harry Palmer, "From Chicago," *The Sporting Life*, October 5, 1887, 4.
[10] Nick Young, "The League's Position Defined," *The Sporting Life*, September 28, 1887, 1.

The Brotherhood and Player Contracts, 1887-1888

as much interested in the game's welfare as they? If then the game has nothing to fear, but the officials themselves have, we must conclude the interests of the game and that of the officials are two different things. I am sure you will not agree to see any such distinction drawn.[11]

Young again split hairs in his response. In his answer, written September 10, he pointed out that at the rules committee meeting Ward referenced, the minutes merely named Ward, along with three other players, as prominent players interested in the proposed rule changes. He further claimed that his financial records showed Ward attending at the National League's expense, rather than the Brotherhood's, another attempt to deny that the BPBP ever enjoyed official status or sanction.

Ward refuted this claim also. He pointed out that, first, the League had invited him. Ward was its guest, and the League paid for his trip, just as it did the other players. He also possessed a telegraph from Al Spalding and John Day specifically stating his presence as a member of the Brotherhood, and that, furthermore, John Day officially referred to him as such in front of the entire rules committee.[12]

Despite this, Young again denied having authority to recognize the Brotherhood's delegation and insisted "no emergency demands that I take a vote of League clubs by mail or telegraph, as suggested." He then closed with a statement intended to achieve a combination of discrediting the need for the Brotherhood, casting doubt on its motives and loyalty to American values, and threatening what might happen if the BPBP persisted: "I cannot understand what difference it makes to the players whether their proposed amendments to the contracts are to be considered as emanating from

---

[11] Ibid.
[12] John Ward, "Ball Players' Brotherhood," *New York Times*, October 2, 1887, 3.

individual players, or from a secret society whose membership is mainly composed of League players. If you accomplish equitable results, why quarrel with the form or method of their consummation?" Furthermore, "The very marrow or essence of the good you are seeking can as well be reached by the old and usual means as by the new, without compromising the existing status of anyone."[13]

Following Young's epistle, the paper gave the Brotherhood a final chance to air its side of the story, and Ward gave another interview upon alighting from his train at Pittsburgh: "Yes, it is true that the League refuses to recognize the Brotherhood. The League evidently regards us as of no importance, yet there are not nine players of any note whatever in the League that are not members of the Brotherhood." When reporters asked Ward what he and his Brothers proposed to do should the impasse remain, he restated their intent not to sign contracts for 1888 and again pontificated on the evils the Brotherhood justly sought remedy for. He said, "Men can be suspended without pay or fined at the whim of any set of directors, and still be held by an iron grip. Take for instance the case of Radbourn. . . . He was suspended without pay because the officials of the team allege that his work was not satisfactory. Mark you, no charges were made against him, and he was refused his release." Referring to the reporters present, Ward reminded them, "Now, if you fail to satisfy your employers they can either discharge you or you can quit. In Radbourn's case they simply held him by an iron-bound contract without pay, and had he quit the club he would have been debarred from playing in any club recognizing the National Agreement in the United States." Going on concerning the arbitrariness of the present system, Ward said, "Under the present contract system a player can be fined for walking around the corner and buying a cigar if the officials of a club in their wisdom see fit to

---

[13] Nick Young, "The League's Position Defined," *The Sporting Life*, September 28, 1887, 1.

The Brotherhood and Player Contracts, 1887-1888

construe the act into an offense." Finally getting to the Brotherhood's main point, Ward told the reporters, "But what we most object to is being sold like cattle. This evil must be checked, or it is going to injure the National game. It is on this point that the League refuses to recognize us, for it has been a great source of revenue to its clubs in having the privilege of selling its best players wherever and whenever it liked."[14]

Ward's teammate and fellow Brother, "Orator" Jim O'Rourke, also spoke to the assemblage. He reiterated Ward's theme that the National League had recognized the Brotherhood at its rules committee meeting and promised that should the magnates decide on a showdown the players were ready. Describing the organization's membership, he said, "Well, we have our club, Boston, Philadelphia and Washington entire; about eight men in Indianapolis; all of the Pittsburg nine, except Smith, Whitney and Beecher, and they are willing to go in; nearly all of Detroit, and three men in Chicago, Pfeffer, Williamson and Flint." O'Rourke also sounded a note of hope, however, when he finished by saying, "I don't think there will be any occasion" when asked about a possible strike by the entire Brotherhood.[15]

When asked for his views, Brother Jack Burdock of Boston said that while the players were not yet in position to challenge the League directly,

> the day is near at hand when they will be in that position. We are satisfied with the reserve rule and the salaries paid, but we are not at all satisfied with the form of contract now in use by the managers. No player who is a member of the Brotherhood of Base-Ball Players will ever again sign that contract. We must and will have a new form. The present

---

[14] John Ward, "The Brotherhood's Side," *The Sporting Life*, September 28, 1887, 1.
[15] Ibid.

contract won't stand law. It is too one-sided and gives the player no show. As soon as a man signs it he binds himself for life to a club and becomes a mere chattel so long as he depends upon base-ball as a means of livelihood. The managers can do with him as they please. If they don't want him to play ball he can't, and must remain idle forever. The manifest injustice of this appears when it is understood that in such an event he does not receive a salary. The managers of a club can lay a player off without pay, and even, under the present ironclad contracts, prevent him from signing with another club that might be glad to avail itself of his services. That means that they have it in their power to take the bread and butter out of our families' mouths.[16]

The Sporting Life then canvassed "leading base ball men," in other words, team owners, on their reaction to the developing drama. It seems clear they had been in conversation with Young since his September 10 letter to Ward and that the owners had decided to play up the angle that the BPBP was a secret organization with questionable loyalty to America. They also chose to obfuscate the questions surrounding the contract by trying to shift the terms of the debate and portray the players as out to injure the game with a hopeless scheme to get up a new organization. President Young wrote, regarding his reasons for his refusal to recognize the Brotherhood, "In the first place, if the Brotherhood was organized solely for mutual benefit, as many other societies are, there might be no reasonable objection to its recognition by the League, though there would be no special reason and certainly no necessity for such action." Then, seeking to cast doubt on the motives of the Brothers, he continued, "If, on the other hand, it is organized for the purpose of guaranteeing to its members immunity from the consequences of violating the laws and contracts of the League, its attitude is

---

[16] "Base-Ball Notes," *Chicago Daily Tribune*, October 30, 1887, 13.

distinctly antagonistic, and its promoters have no right to expect recognition at our hands." He closed his statement by implying which of those two scenarios he found more likely: "The disposition of all the officers of the League clubs is most friendly to the players, but they do not see that any good purpose can be served by recognizing a secret organization among them."[17]

New York Giants owner John Day did not offer personal comment when *The Sporting Life* tried to obtain his views but sent an unnamed "right hand man" instead. This individual tried to uproot the basic grievance of the players by portraying the present contract as entirely correct and appropriate: "The Brotherhood object to our contract and insist upon one that would take the control of the players out of the League, both on and off the field. There are certain terms of our contract which may appear rather grinding, but they are never enforced. For instance, the stipulation that the player shall assume all risk of personal injury on the field or otherwise is not enforced. . . . It is merely a provision to guard against unreasonable litigation on the part of any cranky players."[18]

This statement was very far from the truth. In fact, the reader can almost hear Bobby Mathews choking. Mathews was a stalwart pitcher with the Philadelphia Athletics, and in 1886 the team laid him off without pay when he suffered a sore arm. He started just two games after July 21, and Philadelphia denied him $541 in salary due to inactivity.[19] After the season ended, Mathews tried to retaliate, refusing to sign a contract for 1887 until the club paid him back the money it had withheld. While the team held out, he coached a college team to bring in some cash while waiting for Philadelphia to

---

[17] Nick Young, "Various Opinions," *The Sporting Life*, September 28, 1887, 1.
[18] Ibid.
[19] For more on Bobby Mathews, see his SABR biography at http://sabr.org/bioproj/person/e7ad641f, accessed July 4, 2014; "Local News," *The Sporting Life*, February 9, 1887, 5. This man is surely the least known pitcher in baseball history with 297 or more wins.

see the light.[20] Management refused to budge, with team official Billy Sharsig making the case that not only did Mathews provide no value while hurt but that after returning he appeared just three times while receiving $600 compensation for those three appearances.[21] Mathews finally signed a contract for 1887 in late March, although sadly the sporting press did not specify whether he got his money back, stating only that Mathews reached an "amicable adjustment" with the club. Later reports suggest, however, that he got the money due him.[22] Sharsig did not hold a grudge, apparently, stating that Mathews' velocity was as good as ever, and so was his arm, and that he could probably pitch three times per week if needed.[23]

The 1887 situation in New York concerning Dave Orr was like that of Mathews. The Metropolitans fined their beefy first baseman in September when he sat out some games. Orr claimed illness and a lame arm but as team executive O. P. Caylor explained, "He was not too ill, however, to get into a row at home and whip an officer, whereupon I telegraphed for him to report at Cleveland, which he failed to do on account of a lame arm. I found that the lame arm was due to a fall down stairs during the fight mentioned." Caylor concluded, "As he was not injured in the discharge of his duty there was no reason why he should be paid for his loss of time and I justly mulcted him. Thereupon he became abusive and his suspension followed."[24]

Both Orr, and the New York Court of Special Sessions, had a different view of things. Orr claimed he sustained his injury at his boarding house at 241 East 112th Street on August 16 while defending his landlady against drunken assault by the lawyer

---

[20] "The Quaker City," *The Sporting News*, February 19, 1887, 1; "The Philadelphia Players," *The Sporting News*, March 5, 1887, 1.
[21] "Philadelphia News," *The Sporting Life*, March 16, 1887, 5.
[22] "Spalding and His Surplus Players," *Chicago Daily Tribune*, November 3, 1887, 6.
[23] "Philadelphia News," *The Sporting Life*, March 30, 1887, 5.
[24] "The New York Clubs," *The Sporting Life*, September 14, 1887, 1.

The Brotherhood and Player Contracts, 1887-1888

serving her with divorce papers. In Orr's effort to remove the intoxicated lawyer from the premises, both men fell down the stairs, and Orr sustained injuries to his arm, thumb, and ankle. After the landlady, Mrs. Heinzel, corroborated his story, the courts immediately discharged Orr, clearing his name. The fine stood, however.[25] Despite this, Orr may still have gotten the best of things in the end. Early in 1888, New York sportswriter George Stackhouse spotted the hefty first baseman near City Hall Park, with none other than recent divorcee Emily Heinzel on his arm.[26]

The 1888 case featuring Detroit Wolverine right fielder Sam Thompson was probably the worst example of the practice of refusing pay to injured players. The big outfielder hurt himself early in the season and played in only fifty-six games for the year. In late July, tired of seeing their great player sitting out, Detroit decided to lay him off without pay until he was ready to perform once more. Thompson threatened to sue them to recover his pay. He later tried to go back into the outfield, but his arm injury was so severe that he could barely throw the ball to an infielder, thus providing indisputable evidence that his ailment was quite real.[27]

The hypocrisy on this issue aside, *The Sporting Life* spoke to Al Spalding about the Brotherhood, of course, but the Chicago owner was far too sly to say anything too dramatic or inflammatory. As usual, he took the opportunity to portray the present contract system as necessary, a reasonable act on the part of respectable businessmen that avoided placing control in the hands of an unruly mob of undisciplined players. When queried on whether the current contract was one-sided, he replied, "Necessarily so. The power must be placed in the hands of the club, which is a responsible organization. It is much safer when in such keeping than if it were in the hands of

---

[25] "David Orr as a Bouncer," *Chicago Daily Inter Ocean*, October 28, 1887, 2.
[26] George Stackhouse, "New York Mention," *The Sporting Life*, January 11, 1888, 4.
[27] M. A. T., "Detroit Dotlets," *The Sporting Life*, August 1, 1888, 5. M. A. T. was Charles Matheson, sporting editor of the *Detroit Free Press*.

roving players with no special responsibility. It is much safer in the hands of a club by whom it will be judiciously used. I claim it is for the interest of the players themselves."[28] Judicious, responsible men, doing what was best for the roving, childish players who did not know what was in their own best interest. Nothing more, nothing less.

Not so reserved in his remarks, John Rogers, owner of the Philadelphia Quakers, joined Nick Young in tossing accusations of disloyalty and un-American principles at the players: "The League really could not afford to officially recognize a secret organization within its ranks of whose intentions and methods nothing is known, and whose work is done in the dark." Rogers made this claim even though the Brotherhood was not secret, publishing its goals and organizational structure back in 1886. Nonetheless, Rogers continued spouting nonsense, stating the fallacy that a new contract preventing owners from buying and selling players at will was part of a grand plot to take over the League: "To make such a precedent now would be only the commencement of an interminable series of demands and concessions, the possibility of which would outstrip all conception, and would ultimately leave the League utterly powerless in the hands of its subordinates." He meant to emphasize, of course, that he feared any concessions to the players would embolden them and give them some control over their fate. Like many Gilded Age capitalists, Rogers had difficulty conceptualizing a situation in which this could work; he assumed, or wanted the sporting public to assume, that given any power, the players would act just as tyrannically as he would.[29] He was already sour because the Columbian Bank in Philadelphia, of which he was a director, was collapsing, and the $7,500 the Quakers had with the bank was

---

[28] Ibid.
[29] Ibid.

in danger of disappearing into thin air, so perhaps this seemed a good opportunity to take out some personal frustrations.[30]

When interviewed later, Boston Triumvir Arthur Soden expressed similar ideas. In his conversation with Boston writer "Mugwump," he offered, "I am in favor of hearing our players whenever they wish to meet us in conference, but I don't quite believe in recognizing them as a Brotherhood. . . . It is establishing a bad precedent. A manufacturer will receive his own employees, but don't fancy entertaining a committee of the Knights of Labor. That is the way I feel in this case." When Mugwump pointed out that receiving the Brotherhood as an organization was the same thing as receiving his employees, since the organization consisted solely of players, including his own, Soden weakly changed the subject. Unlikely as it may seem, Soden was more favorable toward the BPBP than his fellow Triumvir, Billings: "He don't like anything secret, and is death on the Brotherhood. He don't want anything to do with the organization, and if he had the casting of Boston's vote, I am afraid it would be thrown against hearing John Ward's communication."[31]

Regarding the impending crisis with the National League, Ward continued to stand his ground in interviews. He pointed out that the League could not reject the proposals of the Brotherhood as unreasonable because it had not accepted any proposals. Therefore, the League's objection must be to the organization itself. He reiterated the Brotherhood's intent to discuss its proposals and withdraw any demands that the owners could demonstrate were unreasonable, but clearly, that could not happen until the two sides met on an equal footing.[32] He also reversed Young's statement that it made no difference whether changes for the players emanated

---

[30] "Philadelphia's Loss by a Bank Failure," *Chicago Daily Tribune*, October 2, 1887, 13.
[31] Mugwump, "Hub Happenings," *The Sporting Life*, November 16, 1887, 5.
[32] "Ball Players' Brotherhood," *The Daily Inter Ocean* (Chicago), October 2, 1887, 2.

from individual players or the Brotherhood, stating, "What possible difference can it make to you whether you confer with a committee of individual players or a committee from the brotherhood, since the brotherhood practically is the players?" He also smashed the fallacy propagated by Young and Rogers that the Brotherhood was in any way secret, stating, "Its business meetings, like those of many other bodies—the League, for example—are not open to the general public, but there is no obligation of secrecy imposed upon any member, and its constitution and bylaws are free at any time for your inspection."[33]

The verbal sparring continued into October. While the Brotherhood's committee of Ward, Irwin, and Hanlon worked on their own version of a new contract, Nick Young continued in the fantasy that "the League is in no way responsible for the present condition of things," and proclaimed that "contracts will be prepared as usual and submitted to the players for signature. This test of the sincerity of the men will be a crucial one, and will serve in a measure to indicate how much in earnest they are in this movement."[34]

The Brotherhood's committee, with the help of James Blackhurst, finished its work at the Bingham House in Philadelphia in mid-October. They planned to submit their work to the eight Brotherhood chapters for ratification, which was all but assured. They also, through Blackhurst, reached out to the barons of the League by contacting Philadelphia owner and lawyer John Rogers in another effort to calm the seas. Despite his inflammatory comments earlier, Rogers appears to have cooled down along with the October weather. He and Blackhurst held "amicable" discussions that "led to the clearing away of some doubts and misconstructions" on the contract and Brotherhood recognition questions. A glimmer of hope, at least, returned.[35]

---

[33] John Ward, "Ball Players' Brotherhood," *New York Times*, October 2, 1887, 3.
[34] Nick Young, "The Next Move," *The Sporting Life*, October 19, 1887, 1.
[35] "As to Contracts," *The Sporting Life*, October 26, 1887, 1.

The Brotherhood and Player Contracts, 1887-1888

Philadelphia Quakers co-owner Al Reach, a man who rarely discussed baseball affairs in print, also offered fans the possibility that the two sides might work out some of their differences, remarking in a Pittsburgh interview, "I am confident that when the league meets next week the brotherhood will be frankly recognized. We have nothing to fear. If the brotherhood proposes anything that will elevate the national game of course we will agree to it, as our desire is to make the game as pure and honest as possible." Reach later denied saying that the League would recognize the BPBP, however, claiming his interviewer quoted him incorrectly, and claimed he had merely said the NL would listen to suggestions.[36]

Either way, Reach did not mention how the League would react on the contract question. Regarding the Radbourn situation and the Brotherhood's request to end the practice of suspending players without pay, he said, "I don't think that that request will be granted. If that rule is abolished it will have a downward tendency. In the absence of that rule there would be nothing to keep players in line. . . . It is only by forcing players to do right that the game has become so popular with the people, and so pure that ladies and gentlemen of the best classes take an interest in it."[37] Reach's paternalistic remarks are quite reminiscent of Spalding's. The owners represented reasonable, principled men, who had to force the childish players to do right. Only this would make baseball respectable amongst the finer classes of the country. As Reach said a few weeks later, "Some of them are straightforward, conscientious men, with whom it is unnecessary to make a contract. Their word alone is good, but there are a great many others whom you have to watch like a hawk in order to make them toe the mark."[38]

---

[36] "The Baseball Players' Brotherhood," *Evening Star* (Washington, D. C.), November 3, 1887, 5; "Pfeffer Not Released," *New York Times*, November 5, 1887, 5.

[37] "The Baseball Players' Brotherhood," *Evening Star* (Washington, D. C.), November 3, 1887, 5.

[38] "The Base-Ball League," *Chicago Daily Tribune*, November 17, 1887, 3.

Seemingly no nearer to its goal, the BPBP called a special session to take stock of the situation. Ward and Tim Keefe from New York, along with Arthur Irwin, Jerry Denny, Abner Dalrymple, Mike Kelly, Dan Brouthers, George Wood, and Fred Pfeffer representing the National League's other clubs, met in Cincinnati.[39] Partly, it was a meeting of convenience because the players of several clubs were crossing paths on their way to their various winter destinations, but the men also met because, as Ward put it, "the members of the brotherhood think they themselves have some knowledge of their wants and rights as players, but the league officials do not appear to look at it that way at all, in so far, although frequently importuned, they have refused us recognitions as a body." The BPBP remained focused solely on the contract language issue, with Ward stating, "No question of salary is involved in any way. No member of the brotherhood has yet signed for the season of '88, and it is probably safe to say that none will sign until the management of the league vouchsafe us some recognition . . . and from today's meeting will emanate another demand for the arrangement of such a joint conference."[40]

The players adjourned this meeting with a challenge. Ward wrote a final letter to Nick Young stating that, should the League fail to agree to a meeting prior to November 12, the Brotherhood and its 125 members would, in effect, secede from the National League on November 15. President Young cannily replied that it was impossible to meet this deadline because the League's upcoming meeting was the proper time to discuss the letter, and that meeting was on November 16.[41] Ward then moved back his demand by two days and the Brotherhood sat back to await the outcome of the owners' deliberations.[42]

---

[39] "Base-Ball and Athletics," *St. Louis Daily Globe-Democrat*, October 28, 1887, 8.
[40] "Base-Ball," *Chicago Daily Tribune*, October 28, 1887, 6.
[41] "Ball Players' Ultimatum," *New York Times*, November 6, 1887, 10.
[42] "The League and the Brotherhood," *New York Times*, November 7, 1887, 1.

The Brotherhood and Player Contracts, 1887-1888

As the meeting neared, speculation built in the sporting press. Pittsburgh, some believed, would vote recognition as a matter of self-preservation. Given the strength of the trade union movement in that city, some feared that attendance at Pittsburgh's Recreation Park would fall catastrophically because workers would avoid the games out of sympathy for the BPBP should Pittsburgh ownership vote in the negative.[43] It appears that the Pittsburgh chapter of the Knights of Labor, at least, regarded the BPBP as a fellow labor organization because two of its leaders expressed their support for the Brotherhood, along with the support of their 12,000 fellows in the Pittsburgh vicinity.[44]

These were not idle threats. The workingmen of the Smoky City were quite active in baseball patronage. Later in 1888, they discovered that one of the stockholders of the Pittsburgh team, Henry Brown, had associations with the steel mill of Singer, Nimick, & Co., which employed non-union labor. Therefore, they organized a boycott of Allegheny games until Pittsburgh severed its connection with Brown. Brown claimed he had divested himself of the stock a year previous, but it appears this assertion was untrue, and so the Amalgamated Iron and Steel Association planned to stay away from Pittsburgh's grounds at Recreation Park.[45] As one member of their association said, "I can say that scores of men in Manchester and West End, who are good attendants of the game, have quit going and it is because of Henry Brown's connection with the Pittsburg Club. Brown is still running the rolls at Singer, Nimick & Co's. mill, and has four jobs. This is not the first time he hasn't

---

[43] "Meeting of The Base-Ball League in New York Wednesday," *Chicago Daily Tribune*, November 13, 1887, 14.
[44] No title, *New York Evening World*, November 5, 1887, 1; "Baseball Notes," *New York Times*, November 13, 1887, 16.
[45] Circle, "A Pittsburg Sensation," *The Sporting Life*, July 11, 1888, 1; "The Pittsburg Boycott," *The Sporting Life*, July 18, 1888, 1.

done the square thing with us. . . . I'll venture the assertion that I know of 300 men who have quit going."[46]

Eventually, November 16 arrived, and the National League's magnates held their confab in Parlor F of New York's Fifth Avenue Hotel. As if to underscore their lack of concern for the Brotherhood, whose representatives waited at the nearby Barrett House, the owners put off the discussion of recognition until the second day. In the meantime, they did allow for an increase in the salary of umpires, lifting the $1,000 cap on umpires' salaries and increasing their pay to a maximum of $2,000 to try to secure more effective men. The League's barons also entertained some discussion of splitting the league into an Eastern and Western circuit to save on travel expenses and increase the enthusiasm created by geographic rivalries, but this talk came to naught.[47]

Finally, on November 16, the moguls sent a letter, signed by League president Nick Young, to Ward and his two Brothers at the Barrett House, Dan Brouthers and Ned Hanlon. Their lawyer, James Blackhurst, was also present. It read, "I am instructed by the League, in annual meeting convened, to state that they will be most happy to meet you and your associates of League players this evening at 8:30 o'clock, for the purpose of ascertaining the objects of the association for which you claim recognition." Once in the presence of the assembly of owners, Ward soliloquized, "Mr. Brouthers, Hanlon, and myself represent the Ball Players' Brotherhood. I am not unconscious of the fact that you have failed to designate us as such in your invitation to appear here. . . . Before we make known our mission you must recognize us as a committee from the Brotherhood."[48]

In an exchange that was rather farcical, given that everything stated was a repeat of the past two months, Giants owner John Day,

---

[46] Circle, "Pittsburg Pencilings," *The Sporting Life*, July 18, 1888, 3.
[47] "Base Ball Matters," *Chicago Daily Inter Ocean*, November 17, 1887, 2; "The Base-Ball League," *Chicago Daily Tribune*, November 17, 1887, 3.
[48] "The Men Make Their Point," *New York Times*, November 18, 1887, 2.

along with Philadelphia's president, John Rogers, asked about the goals of the BPBP and why it deserved legitimacy and recognition. Ward repeated the by now familiar litany. Al Spalding moved that the owners recognize the Brotherhood. The motion carried unanimously. So far, so good for Ward and his Brothers. They had cleared their first hurdle. Mere recognition, however, while positive, meant little as far as gaining acceptance of the new form of contract they had engineered in Cincinnati in October.[49] That would await their discussion with the committee of owners appointed to meet them.

That meeting took place deep into the night and continued the following morning. The players presented their new version of the standard contract, while the ownership committee of John Day, John Rogers, and Al Spalding examined the document and made revisions of their own. It was, in all, rather anticlimactic, considering all the verbal sparring and threats preceding the conference. The group presented its work to all the owners at 3:30 p.m. on November 17, and the group agreed to the new contract language. Both sides seemed pleased, asserting that the new contract protected their vital interests while serving to advance the game. Ward stated that the new agreement was "a fair one," and the owners pronounced the same verdict. Somewhat surprisingly, given their reluctance to even meet the Brotherhood in the first place, the *Chicago Daily Tribune* described the language of the contract as "the one drawn up and presented by the brotherhood, with but slight changes in phraseology," helping confirm the suspicion that the League's real objection had been to the Brotherhood as an organization all along. Nick Young's official statement was now to say, "It is a good thing. I think they will do their best for the interests of the league."[50] Al Spalding had a similarly revised take, stating, "I am glad they are

---

[49] Ibid.; "League and Brotherhood," *San Francisco Evening Bulletin*, November 18, 1887, 4.
[50] "Base-Ball War Averted," *Chicago Daily Tribune*, November 19, 1887, 6.

recognized, and there is a complete understanding between the league and the players. If the brotherhood lives up to the spirit of what they outlined at New York the organization will be a good thing for the players, the league, and the game."[51]

In brief, section one of the new agreement defined the parties to the agreement and section two the length of the contract, binding the player to play baseball at "reasonable times and places from April 1 to October 31." Section three required the player to obey club officers, managers, and field captains while the fourth section allowed for the disciplining of players for "dishonest play or insubordination," carelessness, or indifference, and bound the players to refrain "from any excess or dissipation." The next section provided for the blacklisting of players who broke contracts or conspired with gamblers to lose on purpose. Part six further defined the penalties for drunkenness, those being fines of $25 for the first offense, $50 for the second, $100 for the third, and a suspension for the remainder of the season for any further infractions. All these, of course, protected the owners to make sure that they received a full and sober effort from players.

Section seven offered a bit to the players, stating that teams could not implement the above penalties until providing written notice justifying their actions. Part eight meant to provide a plan to deal with cases such as those of Curry Foley or Bobby Mathews. This said that if a player became ill from "natural causes" and could not play, the club could deduct from his pay during the time lost. Injury sustained on the field in the discharge of the players' duty, however, would not result in a loss of pay, unless the team decided to release the player. If that happened, however, the release would be unconditional. Section ten, while affirming the clubs' power to fine players, capped the fines at $50 per offense.[52]

---

[51] "Interview with Ward," *Chicago Daily Tribune*, November 22, 1887, 6.
[52] "Base-Ball War Averted," *Chicago Daily Tribune*, November 19, 1887, 6.

The Brotherhood and Player Contracts, 1887-1888

While there were many more sections to the contract, twenty in all, just a few more merit description. Sections fourteen and fifteen allowed that if either party violated the agreement, the aggrieved party could terminate it. If a player violated the deal, he forfeited all future pay; if the club did so, the player could opt out of the contract. Furthermore, to deal with situations such as that of the disbanding Kansas City Cowboys in 1886, the League still held the right of reservation of players even if their team disbanded, but if the NL transferred a player to a new club, the player must receive at least the same salary as during the previous season, or else he would be free from the contract. Finally, section eighteen expanded the number of players a club could reserve to fourteen but stated that reserved players must make at least the same salary as during the previous season unless they agreed to play for less.[53] This was a new, and important, development. Heretofore, the clubs had always claimed the right to reserve players, but the rule itself had never appeared in the contract. For better or worse, Ward and the players wanted the rights and responsibilities of both parties regarding the reserve rule stated in the contract.[54]

In the end, the two sides averted a war. Both groups deserve some credit for the peaceful conclusion. The players certainly did not get all they wanted but they did succeed in getting some new language inserted into their contract. In retrospect, probably their wisest move was not to bite off more than they could chew. They had no chance of getting rid of the reserve clause, for instance, even though doing so might have benefited most of them financially, and they realized this and pulled back from making any demands on that score. They picked one goal, had the wisdom to pick an achievable goal, and carried the day, to the extent they ended up with recognition of their organization and most of what they wanted on the contract issue.

---

[53] Ibid.
[54] "Interview with Ward," *Chicago Daily Tribune*, November 22, 1887, 6.

The owners, too, made some wise moves. They now had official, standardized penalties for some of their greatest grievances with the players, especially regarding drinking. With the code for dealing with drunkenness clearly laid out in view of all, they no longer had to worry about players complaining about random or arbitrary fines on that account. They still had the blacklist available to them in extreme cases, and now they could reserve fourteen players from one season to the next. The National League also retained the right to transfer players from one team to another, should one of its teams disband or leave the league.

This is not to say that these developments pleased all owners. Arthur Soden of Boston, especially, was not happy. On recognizing the Brotherhood, Soden remarked, "They gained that point, but we never ought to have allowed it. And we would never have had to recognize them if the Westerners had kept their mouths shut and let Rogers alone." Offering a backhanded compliment to the new contract, he opined, "It is a fairly equitable one, in fact, as much so as you can make it between a responsible party and an irresponsible one. The contract don't bother me. It is not that, but now that this so-called brotherhood has gained a foothold I fear we may see trouble from it in the future." Defeated also on the question of visiting teams getting a percentage of the gate receipts or a guaranteed lump sum (Soden favored the second), he breathed defiance: "I estimate that we shall lose about $15,000 by the operation next year. However, we are not going to let that bother us. The next thing is to get together a winning team, and we intend to do that if it takes a big pile of money."[55]

Soden's views aside, both sides, consciously or not, stepped back from the abyss, realizing that baseball was doing well and that now was not the time to risk the game's reputation by engaging in brinksmanship. The players had no pressing reason to challenge owners on the salary issue because with the salary limit of 1886 now

---

[55] "Around the Bases," *Chicago Daily Tribune*, November 27, 1887, 15.

The Brotherhood and Player Contracts, 1887-1888

a dead letter, salaries were indeed rising. On the owners' side, with all teams in the league making a profit, they entertained great risk in alienating the players as a body and tempting them into disrupting a system that was making money when the only price to pay was revising the language in player contracts. Both groups proclaimed that they only had the best interests of the game at heart and only wanted what was reasonable. In November of 1887, they could agree on what was reasonable. When their next showdown occurred two years later, however, this was no longer true.

Chapter 10

The Spalding Tour and the Rowe-White Affair

BY LATE 1888, SOME NATIONAL LEAGUE OWNERS became worried that their league's business model had too many leaks. Although the game's popularity continued growing in the aggregate and overall profits were plentiful, some teams were doing a lot better than others financially. During November, therefore, National League owners secretly worked on a plan called the Brush Plan they hoped would patch the holes in their business model. The culmination of their efforts is the subject of the next chapter. While they worked, however, two other events of major importance happened simultaneously. One was baseball's second notable effort at international expansion. The other was a novel attempt at circumventing the reserve rule launched by a pair of Detroit veterans.

The men who ran baseball, like their brethren who ruled the corporate world during the Gilded Age, were always on the lookout for ways to expand. For baseball men such as Al Spalding in

The Spalding Tour and the Rowe-White Affair

Chicago or Al Reach in Philadelphia, both of whom had already branched out into the sporting goods business, a direct link existed between the fate of their businesses and the growth of baseball. The more popular the game became, the better their businesses supplying it would fare. Every time a new league organized, their companies had an opportunity to sell more of the implements of play. Bats, balls, uniforms, scorebooks, shoes, gloves, and anything else the sporting public might require were available by mail order. As the nation's transportation grid, based around the railroads, filled in and matured, it became easier for the moguls who offered sporting goods to ship customers all they needed to play the National Game.

Unlike many observers, however, whose interests and vision were local or national in character, Al Spalding had greater plans. Although he was Machiavellian in his manipulations of others, puritanical in his distaste for alcohol in baseball, and willing to bend the rules when the benefits of success seemed to outweigh the risks of discovery, he was also a cunning businessman with international plans. Like other capitalists who, fearing that the U.S. market might be nearing the saturation point, began looking abroad for further opportunities, as early as 1887, Spalding started forming plans to look for overseas markets and broaden the base of sales for his company.

Every now and then in the 1880s, someone floated plans for an international tour to popularize the game abroad. The most popular proposed destination was, unsurprisingly, the United Kingdom. Not only were baseball and cricket similar in several respects—distressingly so for those who wanted to claim purely American origins for baseball—the differences in language and cultural norms were small. The U.K. seemed, therefore, the best candidate among other nations to adopt the American game and give American businesses another market in which to offer sporting goods. American baseball players had traveled to the British Isles for this purpose as far back as 1874, but that group of ballplayers, which included Spalding, Cap Anson, and Jim O'Rourke, had had little luck persuading the British to take up baseball.

The greatest problem these plans to spread baseball encountered, besides the British attachment to cricket, was timing. Because of its northerly latitude, a baseball tour in Britain would likely not do well during the winter months when weather conditions would be hostile to players and spectators alike. Therefore, a tour of any duration needed to take place during the summer. This would interfere with the championship schedule in the United States, and no team would surrender the sure money it realized from healthy attendance in the U.S. for the potential profits, uncertain at best, of a trip across the Atlantic. Not to mention, the touring team would need the permission of its fellow league members to suspend the normal schedule for such a trip, another impossibility. Therefore, one other proposal involved taking two teams of amateurs, possibly made up of college students, to tour in Britain. Not only would their schedules allow for summer travel but because college students largely came from the ranks of the well-to-do in the 1880s, the social skills and standing of college students would serve ambassadorial functions as well.[1]

With Great Britain therefore an unlikely destination, at least for a team of major league players, the answer to this conundrum, some realized, was to tour in the Southern Hemisphere over the winter instead. Speculation about such a tour centered on Australia because it offered nearly all the same advantages, in terms of language and culture, which a trip to Great Britain did. The population of Australia was much sparser than in the British Isles, it was true, so such a trip required much more travel time between games, but by the later 1880s most baseball observers had decided that the road to popularizing baseball internationally began Down Under.

---

[1] Henry Chadwick, "It Might Pay, After All," *The Sporting Life*, April 25, 1888, 1.

The Spalding Tour and the Rowe-White Affair

Once this became accepted wisdom, the question was whether such a tour would pay. The odds seemed against it. Australians had no prior experience with baseball. To many it seemed doubtful that they would pay to watch Americans play a game with which they were unfamiliar. Besides the logistical issues of planning such a tour, this question regarding profitability was the rock upon which all schemes to tour internationally foundered. Al Spalding, however, believed he had a plan that would untie this Gordian Knot. Because he was a participant in the British tour of 1874, he knew that immediate financial reward was unlikely. Realizing this, when he explained his plans to Harry Palmer, he said, "In my judgment such a trip would prove a losing venture to any man who undertook the journey with any expectation of making money out of the gate receipts of his games." Therefore, rather than planning the tour with the thought of immediate profit, Spalding stated, "In undertaking such a trip I do so more for the purpose of extending my sporting goods business to that quarter of the globe and creating a market for goods there, rather than with any idea of realizing any profit from the work of the teams I take with me."[2]

---

[2] Harry Palmer, "To Australia," *The Sporting Life*, March 28, 1888, 1. We must consider material trying to evaluate the Spalding Tour carefully. Harry Palmer, Chicago correspondent for *The Sporting Life* and Spalding's right-hand newspaper man, accompanied the tour and wrote most of the material concerning it for that paper. His writing was not blindly laudatory, but he tended to look on the brighter side of things. *The Sporting News*, in contrast, did its best to diminish Spalding's attempt and tear down his achievements, referring to the tourists as the "Chicago Fakirs." Spalding had recently declined to renew his advertising with *The Sporting News*, so that paper decided to hold a grudge in retaliation. When its correspondent interviewed James Hart, Spalding's financial manager for the trip, and Hart claimed the tour had brought in $10,000 in exhibition games before leaving the United States, the subtitle of the section was "Hart's Blarney." Likewise, it titled other parts of its account "Jim Hart of Milwaukee Doing Spalding's Dirty Work" and "They Try to Skin the Ladies of San Francisco," and wrote, "I can not tell you with what disgust the people of San Francisco look upon the recent exhibition games here by the Chicago and All-America teams." Gold Pen, "The Chicago Fakirs," *The Sporting News*, November 17, 1888, 2. *The Sporting News* also referred to Harry Palmer as

Spalding deemed the time was right, stating, "We have shipped a few goods to Australia during the past three years, and the trade from there has been growing so steadily that I feel confident of being able to build up a business there, as the result of my contemplated venture, that will, in the end, repay me." When reminded of the enormous financial outlay to tour across the Pacific with a party of twenty-two ballplayers, Spalding made clear he harbored no illusions about what he was getting into: "It will take at the correct calculation $30,000, and that amount of money will be deposited in bank for expenses before we leave here." Furthermore, Spalding said to Palmer, "I shall be perfectly willing . . . to spend a few thousand dollars to the end of establishing branch houses in Sydney and Melbourne, and that is principally what takes me there."[3]

In March of 1888, Spalding began contemplating what players to take on a tour, but true to his belief in recruiting "respectable" people as patrons for his games, he said,

> every player we take with us must be not only a ball player, but a gentleman in appearance, intelligence, and address. Full dress suits will, I fancy, be almost as requisite to each player as his base ball uniform will be, for I intend to have our party received in royal style at Sydney and at Melbourne, and they will doubtless be generously entertained by many people of high social and official position during our stay.[4]

Realizing the value of publicity, Spalding arranged for an October tour throughout the western U.S. to increase the hype. On his way to Australia, he planned contests in Milwaukee, St. Paul, Minneapolis, Des Moines, Omaha, Kansas City, Topeka, Denver, Leadville, Colorado Springs, Cheyenne, Salt Lake, Sacramento, and

---

Spalding's "bum polisher." I have done my best to pick out the statements that are relatively free of bias when writing about the tour.
[3] Harry Palmer, "To Australia," *The Sporting Life*, March 28, 1888, 1.
[4] Ibid.

The Spalding Tour and the Rowe-White Affair

San Francisco. The actual tour played in many of those locations, although not all of them. Before setting forth Spalding crowed, "On the trip, you may rest assured, that the arrival and departure of our party at each point I have named will be a not-to-be-forgotten event, while the series of games we shall play in 'Frisco, just before leaving, I anticipate, will be the biggest events in base ball that have yet taken place on the slope." Following their time in San Francisco, the tour would call on King Kalakaua in the Sandwich Islands (Hawaii) before arriving in Melbourne. Once there, "The boys will be able to tire themselves out, if they choose, at kangaroo shooting."[5]

From there, the American contingent would play games in every Australian town that promised even a moderate audience. The original itinerary called for games in Adalaide, Burabura, Gelong, Ballarat, Sandhurst, Waga, Orange, Bathurst, Sydney, New Castle, and Brisbane, plus Launceston and Hobartown in Tasmania and Auckland, Thames, Hokaika, Christ's Church, Wellington, and Dunedin in New Zealand. Like the proposed American schedule, the teams did not make it to every town on that list but did play in several Australian locations. Spalding's original plan called for a return to San Francisco after this grand tour, although later he changed the tour into something far longer and more ambitious than he was willing to discuss in March.

Spalding predicted that, even if the tour was not an immediate financial success, the game itself would take root in Australia much more easily than it had in Britain. He said Australians would embrace baseball "like a duck to water. Australians have all of that love for outdoor sports and athletics which characterizes the English people, coupled with the push and enterprise of the Americans."[6] There were a few glimmers of baseball activity in Australia on

---

[5] Ibid. In the 1880s Americans sometimes referred to California as the Far Slope, or words to that effect.
[6] Ibid.

which to base such rosy predictions. Melbourne had a baseball club, although it limited its membership to Americans only and had been active just a single year, but the U.S. Consul-General to Australia, W. J. Morgan, was an honorary member, as were "a number of other prominent citizens of America."[7]

Joining Palmer in praising the potential of Spalding's venture, and joining Spalding in assigning certain national characteristics to all Australians, Henry Chadwick was "confident that Mr. Spalding will find large profit in it; not, perhaps, in the way of gate receipts, but certainly in the wider extension of his sporting goods business. With characteristic Western pluck and energy, however, he is going to take the chances of success or failure in his business venture, and I predict for him a noteworthy success." Chadwick was confident an Australian trip would succeed where the trip to Great Britain in 1874 failed because "he is now, too, going to a very different country, and among a people, who, despite of certain inherited colonial tendencies, have more of the characteristics of our own people, in certain respects, than their old-country progenitors have; and there is not likely to be such national prejudice met with in Australia by a party of American base ball players in 1889 as the visitors to England in 1874 encountered."[8] Spalding later asked Chadwick, who was baseball's greatest living historian, to accompany the expedition and write about the grand adventure, but the Old Brooklynite declined on account of age and other duties. One of these other duties, we should remember, included working on Spalding's yearly baseball publication, so it is no surprise that Chadwick was an enthusiastic supporter of the whole plan.[9]

Not all were sanguine of success, however. One Californian sportswriter who professed to have met many Australians in the Golden State did not like the odds: "We feel sorry for Al, so far as

---

[7] H. G. Kritch, "A Ball Club in Australia," *The Sporting Life*, March 28, 1888, 5.
[8] Henry Chadwick, "Chadwick's Chat," *The Sporting Life*, April 11, 1888, 4.
[9] Henry Chadwick, "The Australian Trip," *The Sporting Life*, September 12, 1888, 7.

the financial part of the undertaking is concerned. Almost universally do they express themselves as wedded to cricket and lacrosse, affect to despise base ball, and in prejudice out-English even a Londoner."[10] The Australian sports editor for the *Referee* and *Sunday Times*, Neville Forder, offered the same prognosis. Asked by James Hart, one of Spalding's business managers, if such a trip would pay in Australia's larger cities, Forder thought not. He admitted that some had tried organizing baseball clubs in Australia, but "our people are educated up to cricket, and can see no fun in the quadrangular game.... Your runners and boxers do very well here, and are generally very well treated, if they are white.... So you see we support good goods, but base ball is not our game."[11]

Despite the naysayers, Spalding made his grand excursion. He could not pass up such a visible opportunity to promote baseball, further popularize his name, and advance his business interests. Proclaiming his intent to bring America's game to the "crowned heads, nobles, and peasantry of the Old World," Spalding decided to match his Chicago team, headed by first baseman Cap Anson and centerfielder Jimmy Ryan, against a second team featuring players recruited from other National League and American Association clubs. The most visible player among this second group was Brotherhood president John Ward of the New York Giants.[12]

Spalding billed his second squad as the "All-America Team," and it was somewhat akin to an all-star team, although the comparison is not exact. The members of the All-Americas were good players; after all, Spalding wanted competitive games between closely matched teams to help stimulate interest in his tour. He also favored speedy, athletic men in his choice of players for the All-America team, believing their athletic skill would appeal to foreign audiences. However, his other primary criterion for selection was

---

[10] Waller Wallace, "California Cullings," *The Sporting Life*, May 2, 1888, 7.
[11] Neville Forder, "Base Ball in Australia," *The Sporting Life*, May 16, 1888, 1.
[12] Levine, *A.G. Spalding and the Rise of Baseball*, 103.

the deportment and reputation of the men. Knowing that the tour would involve diplomatic responsibilities as well as athletic ones, he recruited players who looked as good at a formal dinner as they did on the diamond.[13]

It is not necessary here to discuss all the details of Spalding's Australia trip because literature already exists about it. A few things merit further description, however, because they provide more insight into the milieu of the 1880s and demonstrate how the tour affected the Brotherhood. One of the most notable was the membership of the teams. With all the issues between owners and players that took place the previous winter, the men who were the acknowledged leaders on each side, Al Spalding and John Ward, were not even in the United States during the winter of 1888. It is possible that this was by Spalding's design. Having the National League's most articulate and accomplished enemy out of the country, and thus conveniently unavailable to confer with his Brothers, may well have been part of Spalding's plan when he invited Ward. That Spalding's fellow owners adopted the Brush Classification Scheme discussed in the next chapter in Ward's absence might not have been a coincidence.

Taking Ward was a double-edged sword, however. The trip to Australia (and eventually, beyond) involved a lengthy sea voyage with few responsibilities along the way, giving a man of Ward's intellectual stature abundant time to think, plan, and evaluate what the Brotherhood might do in the future. Ward's only real responsibility, besides the social gatherings planned for the expedition, was captaining the All-America team. Another Brotherhood officer, Ned Hanlon, also joined the tour.

The situation with Ward and Hanlon aside, Spalding seemed to sense that it was time for a big move. He had stated many times in

---

[13] For more on the importance of athleticism and speed in baseball in these years, see chapters three and four of Rob Bauer, *Outside the Lines of Gilded Age Baseball: Alcohol, Fitness, and Cheating in 1880s Baseball*.

The Spalding Tour and the Rowe-White Affair

public that the purpose of the Australia tour was promotion of the game and his business—this was no secret to anyone who read sports newspapers. Spalding had ventured a great deal to put the trip together, making contracts with many of the better players in baseball and creating a vast array of promotional materials including wall paper, lithographs, printed histories of each player, wood cuts for use in newspapers, and more. He planned to cover all traveling expenses as well, although he did not offer much remuneration beyond expenses, the contract calling for each player to receive fifty dollars per week. Perhaps this turned off some potential players who might have joined. Charlie Comiskey, first baseman and captain of the St. Louis Browns, objected on these grounds, according to some sources. (Other sources, however, including Spalding himself in a letter to Henry Chadwick, stated that Comiskey declined so he could manage business interests.) Other players who also turned down invitations did so from a mix of motivations. Still, an international vacation lasting several months with the occasional baseball game thrown in, all expenses paid, was an opportunity occurring once in a lifetime, and most men took Spalding up on his offer.[14] Later, Spalding decided to offer $5 to each player on the winning team for each game to ensure that both teams played their best, rather than going through the motions.[15]

Spalding hoped for diplomatic recognition from outgoing president Grover Cleveland, but despite meeting the president at the White House, and the love Mr. and Mrs. Cleveland professed for baseball, such was not forthcoming.[16] Spalding's Tourists, as most observers named them, steamed around the world nonetheless after Spalding decided to extend his trip to take in such expected English-

---

[14] "The Base Ball Event of the Century," *The Sporting Life*, October 17, 1888, 2; Henry Chadwick, "Chadwick's Chat," *The Sporting Life*, October 17, 1888, 5.
[15] John Montgomery Ward, "Across the Continent," *Chicago Daily Tribune*, November 11, 1888, 25.
[16] Bob Larner, "Washington Whispers," Philadelphia, *The Sporting Life*, June 6, 1888, 9.

speaking locations as Great Britain and Australia, but also more exotic locales such as Egypt, India, and Ceylon. An outbreak of disease in Calcutta, along with a tight schedule, cancelled the planned stop in India, but the teams did pause in Egypt and played a game of ball on the sands near the Great Pyramids. The tourists even climbed the Great Pyramids and posed for a photograph draped all over the Great Sphinx like Yankee tinsel. This act, however, along with insulting and obviously futile attempts to loft baseballs over the ancient tombs of the pharaohs, probably cancelled out whatever curiosity they might have aroused amongst the Egyptian population.

Before departing from Giza, however, three players from the All-America team, Ward, Jim Fogarty, and Jim Manning, climbed to the apex of one of the Great Pyramids and back down in less than ten minutes. While the agile trio performed this feat of endurance, some of the remaining players held a contest to see which of them could hit the eye of the Sphinx with a thrown ball first. This led to a rebuke from one of the Chicago newspapermen accompanying the tour, who wrote, "When Napoleon was in Egypt he stood in awed silence before the solemn majesty of the forty-century old Sphinx. The members of the Chicago club, when brought into the presence of this impassive mystery of the desert, threw hard balls at it and hit it in the eye. The Sphinx has seen and suffered much. . . . But never . . . has she been hit in the eye . . . by a Chicago ball-player." The writer hoped the Chicago players would shape up before they reached Europe, so that "the kindly offices of the Secretary of State will not have to be invoked in a month or so to rescue from a French or English dungeon a merry Chicagoan who has been pelting the image of Napoleon or of Nelson."[17] France was in the middle of the

---

[17] No title, *Chicago Daily Tribune*, February 11, 1889, 4. Technically, this statement is incorrect because the only player to hit the eye of the Sphinx with his throw was Jim Fogarty of the All-America team, according to Harry Palmer. Palmer was, by 1889, also the head baseball editor for the *Chicago Daily Tribune*.

The Spalding Tour and the Rowe-White Affair

Boulanger Affair, after all, and when Chicago's Cap Anson heard of it, he remarked that, "he could furnish President Carnot with a Cabinet which would knock Boulanger out of the box in a single inning."[18]

In addition to Anson's comment regarding France's political issues, the tour was not immune to other political tensions involving Europeans. The Americans did do some pelting in France, but in the form of throwing flowers at masqueraders in Nice's Battle of the Flowers. It appears they took especial aim at the heir to the throne of England, the Prince of Wales, but "the Prince, of course, did not understand that there was really a little American opposition to royalty concealed in the flowery weapons and looked upon it as a new exhibition of the queer ways of the people across the sea. When one especially big bunch fired by Healy hit the royal rider squarely on the nose, he bowed in acknowledgment of the precision of the shot."[19]

What the prince could not have known was that pitcher John Healy was a fervent patriot for Irish independence, and thus took special pride in his feat: "Healy, whose special mission on the trip is the liberation of Ireland, uttered an exultant cry at his success. The Prince frowned at this, but speedily recovered his equanimity, lifted his hat, and fired a bunch of violets in return. The aim was faulty, but the boys secured the violets. Healy still has his as token that Ireland will yet be free."[20] The players later atoned for the flowery barrage when they interrupted their March 12 game in Kennington Oval to cheer the Prince on his arrival in the fourth inning.[21]

In contrast to their experience in Egypt, the tourists were less fortunate, historic monument-wise, in Italy. For a moment, Spalding

---

[18] John Montgomery Ward, "Base-Ball Tourists at Naples," *Chicago Daily Tribune*, February 17, 1889, 11.
[19] "Pelting a Prince with Flowers," *Chicago Daily Tribune*, March 1, 1889, 1.
[20] Harry Palmer, "The Great Trip," *The Sporting Life*, March 6, 1889, 2.
[21] "First Game of the American Ball Players," *New York Times*, March 13, 1889, 1.

entertained hopes that the tourists would have an opportunity to play in Rome's Colosseum. He reportedly even offered Italian officials $5,000 for the privilege. His efforts did not come to fruition, however, because the Italian authorities would not stand for it, nor was he able to secure an exhibition of baseball for the pope, Leo XIII, when His Holiness pled illness. Denying the truth regarding this diplomatic setback, the *Chicago Daily Inter Ocean* chose to blame the tourists' failure to assume the mantle of the ancient gladiators on the faulty state of the spectator galleries in the Colosseum instead.[22]

Another thing the tour demonstrated was the extent of the social Darwinism-inspired racism existing in the United States. Racism's existence, and the extent of its popularity in the 1880s, is no secret. I see no need to repeat every instance that surfaced on the trip. Still, a few examples are in order. Some commentators, purposely forgetting that the trip's itinerary mainly consisted of coastal cities, wrote about the dangers posed by the aboriginal Australians: "Base ball in the bush! The American national game played by its ablest exponents before the Zulus, the bushmen and kangaroos of Australia! . . . They will be in danger from the aggressive female population from the time they first appear in their snow-white jersey suits in all the vigor of their virile powers." The greatest danger was that "travelers who have traversed the wilds of the inland continent say that one of the favorite ways of expressing love practiced by the dark-skinned but intensely affectionate maiden of the bush is to offer her accepted lover as a toothsome tid-bit to her cannibalistic chieftain father."[23]

---

[22] Levine, *A.G. Spalding and the Rise of Baseball*, 101, 104-105; "Honored Ball Players," *Chicago Daily Inter Ocean*, February 14, 1889, 2; John Thorn, *Baseball in the Garden of Eden: The Secret History of the Early Game*, (New York: Simon & Schuster, 2011): 233.

[23] "Base Ball in Australia," *Rocky Mountain News* (Denver), October 28, 1888, 1. The paper's editor did make a note that Zulus did not live in Australia but then flippantly added that the word worked well enough to describe the native Australians who did.

The Spalding Tour and the Rowe-White Affair

In fact, the tourists themselves did not even make it out of the United States before some began demonstrating their own racism. In Omaha, on their way to San Francisco, the clubs acquired a "mascot" for their trip, mascot in this case referring to a young black man named Clarence Duval. Duval, an extra in a traveling opera company, had been the White Stockings' mascot during part of the 1888 season before deserting the team in New York during an August road trip. He got to Omaha with this opera company but then lost his position in the troupe, and so he reunited with his old club when given the opportunity. While Anson described Duval as "a little darkey that I had met some time before while in Philadelphia, a singer and dancer of no mean ability, and a little coon whose skill in handling the baton would have put to the blush many a bandmaster of national reputation," he also denigrated the young man by saying "outside of his dancing and his power of mimicry he was, however, a 'no account nigger,' and more than once did I wish that he had been left behind." Duval may have wished the same when, in Egypt, players dressed him in catcher's gear and led him, roped at the neck, through the Cairo rail station.[24] An interesting coda to the story of Clarence Duval is the fact that, when the Players League set up shop for the 1890 season, Duval jumped ship from the Chicago White Stockings and signed on as mascot with the Chicago Pirates of the Players League.[25]

While in San Francisco waiting to embark for the antipodes, one of the tour's chroniclers, Harry Palmer, visited San Francisco's Chinatown along with various players. In describing the experience, he wrote, "I am safe in saying that no pen, however clever, could adequately depict the revolting and fascinatingly hideous sights we witnessed. The illustrations of the vice, crime and bestiality, so prevalent in the Chinese quarters of this city, which have appeared

---

[24] Thorn, *Baseball in the Garden of Eden*, 231-232; Levine, *AG Spalding and the Rise of Baseball*, 101-102.
[25] Levine, *AG Spalding and the Rise of Baseball*, 60, 104.

in our illustrated publications from time to time, have not been overdrawn or exaggerated." Palmer went on to describe how the Chinese lived in buildings with 400-600 residents "which could not accommodate more than 30 or 40 Americans comfortably," thus playing upon fears of a "Yellow Peril" of Asians taking over the West Coast of the United States. Also echoing the fear that Asians would never assimilate into American society, Palmer wrote, "The streets swarm with Mongolians. They have run all white people out of the district and have established their own government, their own mercantile houses, their own water works, their own courts, until, although they are under the surveillance of the city authorities, they nevertheless, to a great extent, live independently of the municipal laws."[26]

Despite this, Palmer and the rest of the tourists risked an expedition "into vile-smelling lodging houses; into opium joints, thick with the sickening vapors that issued from the over-crowded compartments, down through underground passage-ways . . . into Joss houses, with their hideous idols. . . . Our little party threaded its way, until we grew dizzy from the overpowering odors and anxious again to breath the air of a Christianized and civilized community." Only the accompanying law enforcement officers emboldened the ballplayers enough to risk such a journey. This led Palmer to conclude his description Chinatown by writing, "No religion save idolatry is known in Chinatown. Virtue has never had an abiding place there. The people have brought the heathenish customs and horrible practices of their barbarous country with them to San Francisco, and cling to them with a tenacity that shows the hopelessness of their conforming to our views of life and religion, or of their ever becoming desirable citizens."[27]

Following their foray into the warrens of Chinatown, the men eventually raised anchor for Australia. Along the way, Spalding

---

[26] Harry Palmer, "The Great Trip," *The Sporting Life*, November 21, 1888, 4.
[27] Ibid.

The Spalding Tour and the Rowe-White Affair

decided to inform them that he planned to extend the trip. The teams would still play in Australia, but now they would also continue all the way around the world, visiting Asia, Africa, and Europe before returning to the U.S. Wisely, Spalding did not broach this plan to the players until the sea voyage was underway; after an incident concerning Mike Kelly, who originally agreed to go but later went back on his decision, Spalding understandably was wary about anyone else getting cold feet at the last moment. Although the players were, almost to a man, in favor of the change, a concern arose that modifying the itinerary was a breach of contract on Spalding's part because the contract only engaged the players to go to Australia and play baseball there. Ever the sly fox, Spalding escaped this pitfall by pointing out that the wording of the contracts did not specify the route by which the party would return to the U.S.[28]

The trip to Australia called for a stopover in the Sandwich Islands, today known as Hawaii. This provided plentiful opportunities to demonstrate more of the racism and prejudice common to the late-nineteenth century. Led by their baton-wielding young mascot, Clarence Duval, newly attired in "a scarlet jacket, khaki pants, black boots, and a braided cap," the men paraded through Honolulu to King Kalakaua's palace. Their marching tune was an interesting choice, "Marching Through Georgia," as they sought to present themselves as conquering heroes in imitation of General Sherman's Yankee troops in the Civil War. While both John Ward and Harry Palmer found the Hawaiian monarch an agreeable and dignified leader, Cap Anson noted, "The monarch of the Sandwich Islands needs exercise. His flesh is soft and I don't believe he could do a hundred yards in less than two minutes."[29]

---

[28] Mark Lamster, *Spalding's World Tour: The Epic Adventure That Took Baseball Around the Globe—and Made it America's Game* (New York: Public Affairs, 2006): 98-99.
[29] Ibid, 106.

The teams planned to play an exhibition for the people of Honolulu, but because the next day was Sunday, laws forced upon the Hawaiians by American missionaries prevented such a desecration of the Sabbath. The king, who wanted to see baseball and was constantly at odds with the missionaries because of their interference with traditional Hawaiian culture, therefore requested the men attend a luau instead. Newton MacMillan, another reporter accompanying the trip on behalf of the *Chicago Daily Inter Ocean* and *New York Sun*, described the luau as "a barbaric festival, fraught with that pagan abandon which obtained in the Sandwich Islands before the day when the good missionaries came and converted their Hawaiians from their wickedness and cannibalism." The fact that MacMillan described the relationship of the missionaries to the native people by writing "their Hawaiians" is a good indication of the lack of cultural and racial tolerance existing toward darker-skinned people in 1888.[30]

This was not the end of things in Hawaii. King Kalakaua also scheduled a performance of the hula dance for Spalding's tourists, "a dance considered so pagan and libidinous that it had been banned by the forces of missionary propriety." The group also forced Clarence Duval to perform "plantation dances" for its entertainment. The missionary authorities overruled the king's decision to hold a hula dance, however, reasoning that, "a luau on the Sabbath was already a blasphemy; a hula dance would be untenable." While King Kalakaua officially announced that the tourists could see the hula on their next stop in Honolulu, in secret, he arranged private performances for each player in the queen's royal gardens.[31]

Finally, when referring to the Spalding Tour, both participants and press described its purpose using the racist, social Darwinism-influenced language of the time. One reporter, after viewing the incident with Duval in Cairo, remarked, "Could a disciple of Darwin

---

[30] Ibid, 112.
[31] Ibid, 112-113.

have seen the mascot in his impromptu makeup, his host would have bounded with delightful visions of the missing link." For Spalding, baseball epitomized "All those essentials of manliness, courage, nerve, pluck and endurance, characteristic of the Anglo-Saxon race," while some in the press described the achievement by stating, "a country that holds liberty dear must have . . . men of athletic spirit" who make "a race fit for peace and war."[32]

Despite such sordid racism, the tourists returned home in April of 1889 to a rousing reception that included the now-famous dinner at Delmonico's in New York City, considered among the city's most fashionable restaurants. This dinner, attended by Wall Street financiers, sundry baseball dignitaries, and other personages as luminous as Teddy Roosevelt and Mark Twain, was notable for more than just the guest list and the quantity of food, which the waiters naturally served in nine courses. Speeches abounded; Spalding, along with his two captains, Anson and Ward, described the tour, Ward displaying his "singularly correct knowledge of the English language." While, predictably, listeners considered Twain's speech the oratorical highlight of the evening, even it paled in drama compared to a historic pronouncement from former National League president A. G. Mills. Mills took the podium and announced, by virtue of patriotism and research, that baseball was a distinctly American game, devoid of roots in any foreign land or games. Thunderous applause greeted the verdict along with a rhythmic pounding of the tables to chants of "No rounders! No rounders!" Some consider this dinner, flooded with patriotism and prestige as it was, the high point of nineteenth-century baseball.[33]

While this grand tour may not have resulted in other nations immediately embracing America's national pastime, any more than

---

[32] Levine, *AG Spalding and the Rise of Baseball*, 103-104, 107.
[33] Thorn, *Baseball in the Garden of Eden*, 234-236. Rounders is an English game that bears certain resemblances to baseball. At that time, many debated whether baseball's origins were as a game branching from rounders at some time in the past or if it was a truly American creation.

Spalding's discovery of the rickshaw in Ceylon produced the American rickshaw company he considered founding on his return, in all, 1889 promised to be a good year for baseball's leading men. The success of Spalding's tour and baseball's seemingly exponential growth in popularity, exemplified by incoming president Benjamin Harrison's display of a scorecard on the White House mantel, all forecast a rosy future. (Some, however, questioned the new president's commitment to baseball because when Spalding and his tourists called on him after returning to the U.S., Harrison gave them a cold shoulder according to some accounts.)[34] More than ever, baseball aligned itself with patriotism, late-nineteenth century feelings of the nation's Manifest Destiny, and the American Way. Each November, on Election Day, the New York and Brooklyn nines squared off in celebration of the Republic to remind the country of this fact, and Spalding's tour only reinforced such feelings.[35]

This does not mean, however, that all was perfect during Spalding's absence. In addition to the usual disagreements between players and their teams regarding salary stemming from the Brush Plan, a serious situation arose in December. When the Detroit Wolverines disbanded, the team commenced selling its men to the highest bidders around the National League. In a move that sent a thunderclap throughout baseball, two players decided to toss a monkey wrench into the operation. Third baseman Deacon White, rumored on his way to Boston, did not want to go to the Hub City because of a past grievance with the management there. Detroit also wanted to sell White's teammate Jack Rowe to Pittsburgh, and Rowe likewise claimed an objection. Instead of consenting to their sale and transfer, therefore, White and Rowe decided to pool their resources and buy a controlling interest in the Buffalo franchise of

---

[34] Levine, *AG Spalding and the Rise of Baseball*, 104; Freeman, "The Surprising Cowboys," *The Sporting Life*, May 8, 1889, 1.
[35] To give just one example, see "A November Game," *The Sporting Life*, November 10, 1886, 3.

The Spalding Tour and the Rowe-White Affair

the International League. Both had played in Buffalo prior to joining Detroit, Buffalo having held a National League franchise in 1885, so their plan was to become owners in Buffalo and then play for the team they now owned. To justify the legality of the move, the two men cited that they had signed a contract with Detroit and fulfilled it, so Detroit could no longer have a claim on them, especially considering the team no longer existed and had sold its franchise to Cleveland.[36]

Predictably, the National League responded with the blacklist, claiming that because the International League was a party to the National Agreement, no International League members could employ or play against the blacklisted men. Any team doing so risked expulsion from the National Agreement. Still more infuriating to the two players, the National League claimed that Detroit was still a member until it formally resigned at the League's spring meeting, citing that the club had voted at all meetings held since the conclusion of the season. Former Wolverines president Fred Stearns offered the meager consolation, "They can own the club and manage it jointly, but they cannot play until they have the consent of the representatives of the stockholders of the old Detroit Club." White responded by stating, "I signed a contract with the Detroit Club to play ball for them from April to November, 1888, and have carried out that contract.... I am aware that in the League I should be obliged to go where I was sent, but I am not in the League now. I shall play ball at Buffalo." White also stated that, should the National League attempt to blacklist him, "We shall sue the clubs refusing for conspiring to prevent us from earning a living. Our lawyers say that the reserve clause of the League and the claimed right to sell a player will not stand, and most of the League magnates privately admit as much."[37]

---

[36] "Pugnacious Ball Players," *New York Times*, December 20, 1888, 2.
[37] Ibid.

The Buffalo Two appeared set on their course, and they almost became the Buffalo Three when a former teammate in Detroit, Charlie Bennett, considered joining them. After a stormy negotiating session with Boston, Bennett said, "They must come to my terms or I don't go. If I hold out until after the Detroit League Club expires I shall be a free man and can go where I please. I should like to join the boys in Buffalo or play here for Leadley."[38] Baseball's supporters in Detroit had reorganized with a new group of players and joined the International League, and Leadley was the manager of this new Detroit team. This further clouded the National League's position because it claimed Detroit was still a member, but the National Agreement prohibited the establishment of any new team within a five-mile radius of an existing one. The League countered that if the existing team gave its permission and waived the rule, this was acceptable. This led Dave Rowe, Jack's brother, to ask, "Would Nick Young approve the contract of any player of the old Detroit Club with that club for next season, if sent by that defunct organization? . . . What *is* a club if it is not their franchise? When a club is admitted, *that* gives them a franchise. If they dispose of that to another party, in another city, and another League takes possession, it looks reasonable to suppose there is a National League vacancy in that town."[39]

White also used one of the Brotherhood's key arguments when he framed his move as a challenge to the practice of buying and selling players rather than the reserve rule: "The reserve rule is all right. It is the bulwark of the National game. What I protest against is the selling of a player without his knowledge or consent. I am quite willing to break up that custom." He believed the League's claim to this power would fail in the courts, stating, "If in law the Detroit Club can send me to Boston, it can also send me to New Zealand. According to the contract, I simply give the Detroit Club

---

[38] "Detroit Dotlets," *The Sporting Life*, December 26, 1888, 1.
[39] T. T. T., "Baltimore Bulletin," *The Sporting Life*, January 20, 1889, 5.

the right to reserve my play in Detroit, not in Boston. The reserve rule, to the extent I have set forth, is all right and should be respected, but it never contemplated the buying and selling of players." He further charged that Boston had broken faith on three separate occasions in its efforts to sign White and others: "That club first broke the National Agreement by negotiating with players previous to October 20, and then broke faith with Mr. Stearns and the Detroit Club by agreeing to deprive the latter of any purchase money agreed on for the players to be transferred, and lastly broke faith with the players in failing to carry out an agreement it made with them."[40]

The incident White referred to was when Boston sent a man to act as its representative in negotiating with the players when Detroit played a late-season series in Washington on October 11-13. The Triumvirs wanted half a dozen Detroit players as a group, fearing that they might fall into the hands of their competitors one by one if Boston did not acquire the whole group preemptively, just as Brooklyn's Charles Byrne had done with the New York Metropolitans the previous off-season. The Detroit players claimed they reached a verbal agreement with Boston's representative, in front of several witnesses, but that Boston later reneged on the deal. The Beaneaters then proceeded to try to sign the players separately to cover up their deception. White closed his case by stating, "My contract with the Detroit Club expired last November. I fulfilled my part of that contract to the letter. There was nothing said in that contract about letting them transfer me to any place they saw fit, and there is no law that allows a man who has a contract with me for one year to say what I shall do the next year."[41]

Bennett eventually decided not to cast his lot with Rowe and White after all and signed with Boston in late January. Some hoped that would break the logjam because Boston declared it no longer

---

[40] "A Revolt," *The Sporting Life*, December 26, 1888, 2.
[41] "Plain Talk," *The Sporting Life*, December 26, 1888, 3.

had any interest in White, which cleared the path for Pittsburgh to sign both. Rowe and White stuck to their plans. They were not angry with Pittsburgh in particular, only the general way in which teams bought and sold players. When Pittsburgh President Nimick went to meet with them in February, the three had a friendly conversation, but Rowe and White maintained their desire to manage Buffalo rather than play in the Smoky City.[42]

Complicating matters was the debate swirling around the future of the game in early 1889. By this time, all kinds of rumors had Brooklyn and Cincinnati joining the National League by 1890. Should that happen, the American Association would need two new teams and Buffalo was on the Association's short list of replacements. The potential conflicts for the National Agreement, of having two men own a team in one major league and play for a team in the other, are certainly interesting, not least for the potential conflicts of interest that might create.

The controversy dragged on into the spring. The League's stated intent was to accept Detroit's official resignation at its spring meeting in March. In the meantime, however, it realized that if any Detroit players had not accepted new offers when the team reserving them ceased to exist, the men would be free to sign wherever they wished, and White and Rowe could then carry out their plan. To circumvent this inconvenient truth, the League turned to paperwork shenanigans: "After careful consideration of the case of Rowe and White it was determined not to accept the Detroit Club's resignation but to place the same in President Young's hands, subject to his acceptance at the proper time—which means when Rowe and White come to terms."[43]

Detroit, meanwhile, was getting rather desperate. Perhaps concerned it would never see a penny for Rowe and White any other

---

[42] "Rowe and White's Position," *The Sporting News*, February 9, 1889, 1.
[43] "The League," *The Sporting Life*, March 13, 1889, 3. Editor Francis Richter, who attended the National League's spring meeting, presumably is the author of this piece.

The Spalding Tour and the Rowe-White Affair

way, it considered offering the men some of the purchase price offered by Pittsburgh, reasoning that getting less than everything was better than seeing the men retire from major league baseball and get nothing. This would probably incur the anger of Detroit's former brethren in the National League, of course, but because Detroit was only in the League on a dubious technicality at this point anyway, that seemed the lesser of two evils.[44] As a result, the team tried to tempt the recalcitrant duo into a compromise whereby they would play for Pittsburgh but pocket $2,000 of the sale price. The men held out for $3,000 at first, and in addition made a provisional arrangement that Deacon White's brother, former major league pitcher Will White, would manage the Buffalo team in their stead should they go to the Smoky City.[45]

Neither side budged from their positions until July. Finally, in desperate need of reinforcements because of injury, Pittsburgh signed the pair for the remainder of the season at a salary of $2,500 each, and paid $8,000 to Detroit, or what remained of Detroit, as well.[46] The two men lost their bid for independent status but got respectable paychecks all the same. It is also possible that Brotherhood president John Ward helped persuade them to sign, knowing that the players would need all the public goodwill they could muster in their upcoming showdown with the National League.

It is difficult to tell if he timed everything to perfection, and if it was all part of one grand plan, but he may have. Just as Al Spalding and his two teams embarked on their world tour, National League owners put the finishing touches on the next chapter's subject, the Brush Plan. This plan rocked baseball by implementing a universal salary scheme in the National League. Although contemporaries attributed the plan to owner John Brush of Indianapolis, some

---

[44] Circle, "Pittsburg Pencilings," *The Sporting Life*, March 20, 1889, 5.
[45] "Pittsburg News," *The Sporting Life*, April 24, 1889, 1; "Condensed Dispatches," *The Sporting Life*, April 24, 1889, 1.
[46] "Pittsburgh Cranks Disgusted," *Chicago Daily Tribune*, July 14, 1889, 12.

baseball historians suspect Al Spalding was the true architect. If this is true, Spalding's timing could not have been better personally or worse for the Brotherhood. Even as his fellow owners penned the plan's final text, his ship left San Francisco harbor with the BPBP's president on board. They left one day late. Had weather, or any other accident, delayed the trip even one more day, John Ward would have known about the new salary classification plan, probably would have stayed behind, and baseball history might have turned out quite differently. The delay only lasted for one day, however, Ward sailed with the expedition, and he did not find out about what took place in his absence until months later.

Chapter 11

The Brotherhood and the Brush Classification Scheme

While the 1888 season wore away into late September, we could forgive a baseball observer for forgetting about the Brotherhood of Professional Baseball Players. The BPBP had maintained strict silence ever since its June meetings regarding the salary limit and the language of player contracts. The two national sporting papers of the day, *The Sporting Life* and *The Sporting News*, rarely mentioned the organization, and the group took no action worthy of notice while the season meandered through the summer months. Of course, this was because the members of the BPBP were busy playing baseball and it was difficult to get enough delegates to the same place at the same time to hold deliberations.

The first month of the off-season was likewise subdued. Two members of the Brotherhood's leadership, John Ward and Ned Hanlon, were involved in Spalding's world tour and were about to depart the United States. Some believed, therefore, that the organization would prove quiescent in whatever might happen that winter. Unlike the year before, it made no movement to send a delegation to the National League's winter meeting or to request a hearing on any major issue because the BPBP believed its efforts at the last League meeting had produced a satisfactory settlement. As of November, the organization saw no need to involve itself in the National League's councils. It set its next meeting for early December.

Both these beliefs, that the Brotherhood would prove malleable without Ward and Hanlon and that relations between the BPBP and the League were now harmonious, were incorrect. The Brotherhood might have believed it had pacified its relations with the League, but behind closed doors, the League's owners concocted a new scheme that would, ultimately, transform and reconfigure the landscape of baseball in ways that few foresaw in November of 1888. Likewise, if the League's owners believed that they could walk over the Brotherhood without Ward and Hanlon in the picture, they also calculated poorly. They failed to grasp the democratic nature of the BPBP. True, its president was tossing the sphere in Australia, but the Brotherhood's affairs meanwhile rested in the capable hands of its executive committee. Still, most members kept a low profile even when the National League unveiled its plans, "sawing much wood" in the parlance of the 1880s.

It did not take long for the National League to create a general conflagration. At its yearly winter meeting, held in late November at the Fifth Avenue Hotel in New York City, it announced a new plan that would put baseball into an uproar for more than two years. After National League owners emerged from their council, president Nick Young read the new salary plan to the assembled reporters anxious to hear about any changes planned for 1889:

> The compensation for all League players for services as players shall be limited, regulated, and determined by the classification and grade to which such players may be

The Brotherhood and the Brush Classification Scheme

> assigned by the Secretary of the League, after the termination of the championship season, as follows:
>
> Class A, compensation $2,500; Class B, compensation $2,250; Class C, compensation $2,000; Class D, compensation $1,750; Class E, maximum compensation $1,500. But this section shall not prohibit the payment of extra compensation for the services of one person to each club as field Captain or team manager.
>
> In determining such assignment, batting, fielding, baserunning, battery work, earnest team work, and exemplary conduct, both on and off the field, at all times, shall be considered as a basis for classification.[1]

Young continued, describing the technical aspects of the plan, but it was clear enough what had happened. The barons had broken their agreement made just one year before and declared war on the Brotherhood. Furthermore, when it came to player compensation, National League owners had determined to turn back the clock to 1886, at least for average players.

Logically enough, people immediately questioned if this new plan would be like the salary limit adopted in 1886; that is, would owners live up to the letter of their law, or would they sidestep this agreement with the same tactics used to punch holes in their last effort of this kind? Regardless, like Julius Caesar crossing the Rubicon, the National League owners were ready to toss the dice, and the series of events that followed remade the entire landscape of professional baseball.

Incredibly, Young argued that this new plan was beneficial for the players. He claimed, "It will not affect rising and ambitious players. But it places a premium on honest and efficient work on the

---

[1] "Bombshell in Baseball," *New York Times*, November 23, 1888, 2.

ball field, and requires good general deportment off the diamond. It will prevent players drawing large salaries because of their previous records.... Intelligent players will recognize it and it depends upon their own exertions whether they shall be benefited by it." When someone asked how Young would determine in what class each player belonged, he stated, "I will consult certain persons and we will form a sort of civil service commission and pass upon the merits of the respective players. During the playing season I will make arrangements to obtain reliable reports of the playing and deportment of the players. In other words, I will establish something in the nature of a secret service department."[2]

While Young refused to call it a spy system, one wonders how else he would obtain reliable reports on the deportment of the players without someone spying on them. Furthermore, leaving aside such potentially sinister motivations and simply examining the workability of such a plan, many potential pitfalls creating legitimate cause for complaint are plain. How could any observer rate "earnest team work" or "exemplary conduct" in any reliably standardized way? Personal bias or honest differences of opinion over what was "earnest" made any consistency impossible.

Observers also noted the risk of what contemporaries called record playing. That meant that fielders would not take difficult chances to get to certain balls out of fear the official scorer would charge them with an error if they failed to field the ball cleanly. Instead, they would let the ball go by to avoid hurting their fielding record with an error that the classification committee might use against them.

Finally, Young's remark about players not drawing a large salary based on their previous record was puzzling. If the classification committee was not going to base its conclusions on previous performance, what would it use instead, short of intangible

---

[2] R. M. Larner, "The Players and the New Limit Rule," *The Sporting Life*, November 28, 1888, 1.

The Brotherhood and the Brush Classification Scheme

and unquantifiable things such as teamwork? This includes the situation of how to classify men who played in the minor leagues the previous season and had no record against major league competition on which to draw.

Additionally, Young tried to evade accusations that the League had broken faith with the Brotherhood. He pointed out that this scheme did not apply to anyone who signed a contract before December 15, which was about three weeks away. Young said, "The provisions of the existing contract will be carried out to the letter. This new rule is intended to apply only to future agreements. Those players held in reserve for next season cannot be classified at any salary below that which they received during the past season, as shown by existing contracts."[3] Even if this were true, this would eliminate all leverage for players negotiating for an increase in salary for 1889. Ownership could simply make a take-it-or-leave-it offer when the only other option was the salary classification scheme.

One final thing worth noting was the composition of the vote on the Brush Plan's adoption. Six clubs voted in favor, while only Arthur Soden of Boston and John Day of New York responded in the negative. The League's bylaws required a two-thirds majority for passage, which meant six votes out of eight, so the plan passed with the bare minimum of support. Day's vote is not surprising. He was on good terms with most of his players and believed in compensating them better than most. Apparently, he judged that keeping them happy, pleased to play in New York, and thus more likely to perform at their best because of having some loyalty to their organization was more important than saving a couple hundred dollars here and there. When asked if the scheme would affect the salary he planned to offer his players, he said, "Not in the least. There will be few of my men that will not receive the same salary next year that they received last season." In Day's eyes the only

---

[3] Ibid.

merits of the Brush Plan were, first, that it prevented players from complaining their way out of town because if released from their present contract, they would be subject to the classification scheme. He also believed it would help rein in the money paid to unproven players.[4]

Soden's "nay" vote appears surprising given his reputation for stinginess. The explanation for his behavior lies in the fact that Boston had enjoyed huge patronage in 1887 and 1888 thanks to purchasing King Kelly and John Clarkson from Chicago. With its recent raiding of Detroit's larder to sign some of the Wolverines' players for 1889, Soden had no reason to expect anything different in the coming campaign. The team was flush and could carry a large payroll to contend for the pennant while still making heaps of money anyway. Boston, therefore, gained a competitive advantage over others by paying big prices for crack players and thereby forcing up the cost of players generally. Boston could pay a lot more than most of its competitors could, and when their opponents dropped out of the bidding due to lack of funds, the Triumvirs could swoop in and sign their man.

The sportswriters covering the game knew this, too. Frequently, they lashed out at the business practices of Boston, along with Brooklyn and occasionally New York, for the inflationary tendencies of those practices.[5] When Soden said to Tim Keefe, "We are going to have that championship in Boston if it costs $100,000. If we want a player we don't care what it will cost to get him, we'll pay it," *The Sporting Life* editorialized, "Their plunging tactics more than any other one thing are responsible for the reckless extravagance prevalent the last few years, which made the new League salary limit rule and classification scheme imperative."[6] A. G. Ovens of Indianapolis wrote, "Some of these players have gone

---

[4] "New York's Idea," *The Sporting Life*, December 5, 1888, 1.
[5] "The League Meeting," *The Sporting Life*, November 28, 1888, 2.
[6] No title, *The Sporting Life*, December 19, 1888, 2.

The Brotherhood and the Brush Classification Scheme

to Boston and will continue to draw salaries greatly in excess of what they can earn. They are worth no more to Boston, as far as they are individually concerned, than they were to Detroit, but the former city, by reason of its population and that fact that it is a great ball town, can afford to pay them what they demand." The result was clear: "For years four, if not five, clubs have been run practically at a loss for the sake and benefit of the first-named three [Boston, Chicago, and New York]. Year by year the matter was growing worse and it was only a question of time when such cities as Indianapolis, Washington, Cleveland and even Pittsburg would be forced to the wall." While Ovens exaggerated the penury of a few of these franchises, he expressed the general views of many within the baseball fraternity.[7]

It is curious, then, that baseball observers blamed Boston and Brooklyn for inflating salaries, but the owners decided that the only way to deal with the issue was to punish the players. If the purchasing tactics of a few teams were to blame, it made more sense to devise a plan to redistribute revenue from the wealthier teams to the poorer ones or to curtail the purchasing of players. These approaches, or another direct disincentive to purchasing men for large sums, would address the problem more directly than the Brush Plan. Out west in Kansas City, the team's president proposed an interesting measure along these lines for the American Association. His idea was that all teams in the Association would form a joint stock company, with the more valuable teams owning more shares, and that whatever profits the company made, it could pay teams proportional to their number of shares.[8] This failed to gain traction, however. Therefore, in the absence of any alternate plan, the players saw the Brush Plan for what it was—a direct threat. They were trying to earn the best salary that the market would bear. Instead of

---

[7] A. G. Ovens, "Indianapolis Mention," *The Sporting Life*, December 5, 1888, 5.
[8] Freeman, "Speas' Specific," *The Sporting Life*, February 27, 1889, 2.

penalizing the teams engaging in inflationary business practices, the National League chose price controls instead.

Grandfatherly Henry Chadwick was one of the few to make this connection. Chadwick believed that controlling salaries was important but that this was the wrong way to do it. He wrote that a plan regarding salaries, "Is not to be done in a hurry, or without due preparation. Besides which, the system itself is based upon a weakness which will at all times threaten its failure, and that is that it does not do away with the existing unhealthy competition for players' services, which, while it remains in force, will always prove an obstacle to the success of any interference with salaries."[9]

Despite such reasoned and rational protests, countering business practices like Boston's appears the motivating factor for the rest of the League in adopting the plan. The four National League cities of smaller market size, Indianapolis, Cleveland, Pittsburgh, and Washington, knew that to keep up and secure their share of talent to contend against teams like Boston and New York they needed some rule to counteract this reality of the free market. They managed to talk Chicago and Philadelphia into approving their plan, giving them the six votes needed for passage.[10]

In addition to the hope of leveling the financial playing field, National League owners also hoped this plan would help them defeat that persistent bugbear, alcohol. Despite the graded system of fines in their contract with the BPBP for 1888, this problem had not abated sufficiently in their eyes. League owners hoped that a salary plan accounting for off-field conduct would provide a stronger incentive for recalcitrant drinkers to brace up. It would also help them shift the blame and, presumably, the animosity of the drinker at the same time. Instead of a club leveling fines directly on its players, the team could shift the blame for a reduction in salary to

---

[9] Henry Chadwick, "Chadwick's Chat," *The Sporting Life*, December 19, 1888, 3.
[10] "Classification and Limit," *The Sporting Life*, December 5, 1888, 1.

The Brotherhood and the Brush Classification Scheme

the more impersonal League Office that was responsible for the classifications. The National League even wrote this into the plan, with teams now reporting violations directly to Nick Young.[11] One writer described the situation by stating, "The drinking habits of a player will be a fatal obstacle to his reaching class A. Temperate habits will be the first qualification for this class. . . . Professional base ball has been disgraced long enough by excessive drinkers." The Brush Plan's supporters hoped that "to be classified in class A at the close of the season will be his goal, and better exhibitions of ball playing may be expected as a consequence of this action on the part of the League."[12]

One other notable aspect of the Brush Plan was that player grades were a secret. A team would know where its own men stood because it had to pay them appropriately, but one club would not know the grades of players on other teams. Nothing prevented the players from revealing their status if they wanted to, but the grades would not be public knowledge otherwise. Cynics must have smiled, however, when Washington sportswriter Bob Larner spoke with Young and reported, "'Class A' will not be heavily stocked at the beginning, and many players who are perhaps counting upon being at the top of the ladder, are more apt to find themselves in the middle or near the bottom."[13]

One of the Brotherhood's officers still in the United States, New York pitcher and Brotherhood Secretary-Treasurer Tim Keefe, seemed to have some of these questions in mind when asked his views on the League's move:

> Though I cannot say definitely what shape the action of the brotherhood will take, depend upon it we are not going to sit idly by and allow the league to deal as unfairly by us and in

---

[11] No title, *The Sporting Life*, March 27, 1889, 4.
[12] "Classification and Limit," *The Sporting Life*, December 5, 1888, 1.
[13] R. M. Larner, "The League Law," *The Sporting Life*, December 19, 1888, 1.

as bad faith as has been the case. They broke faith with us last year, when they promised to abolish the $2,000 limit clause and did not. At that time, when we asked Mr. Rogers why the league acted thus, he tried to throw the blame upon the American Association. When we came to investigate we found, through Mr. Brunell, that Mr. Rogers was to blame. The action of the league this year is in direct violation of our contract clause, which states that a player, when reserved, shall not receive less than he received the previous season. It is certainly time to act. There will be plenty of fun ahead for the league. Why, it is the old $2,000 limit business over again.[14]

Many doubted that this new system would turn out any different from the 1886 rule and reminded observers of the National League's breach of faith. After reviewing how every team had circumvented the old limit rule, the *Chicago Daily Tribune* wrote that the League meant to establish a pure baseball trust with complete control over the players and pointed out, "Last winter the league agreed to a new form of contract submitted by the brotherhood of professional baseball players. One stipulation in that contract is that a player shall not be reserved at a less salary than he received under his last year's contract. . . . The league will be compelled to either break the new law or overlook the clause by which it retains control of the players."[15]

Other members of the Brotherhood did not need Ward to speak for them, either. Arthur Irwin, field captain of the Philadelphia Quakers and a man universally regarded for his heady play on the field, offered the first hints that the BPBP might have some hole cards of its own when he told Boston sportswriter William Sullivan,

---

[14] "Concerning the League Meeting," *Chicago Daily Tribune*, November 25, 1888, 10.
[15] "How Base-Ball is Run," *Chicago Daily Tribune*, November 25, 1888, 10.

The Brotherhood and the Brush Classification Scheme

"If this business is enforced and lived up to and ball players' salaries are all kept down to $2,500 a year, the eight League clubs will be owned and run by new men to the base ball world in two years." Irwin proceeded to drop a few more hints:

> Supposing all the League players sign an agreement to stick together, and they are divided into eight teams, which are put into the eight League cities. Now don't think that can't be done, because it can. Let me tell you something that perhaps you don't know. We knew what we were about when we made our kick for the Brotherhood contract. I know some one may cry 'Chestnut' when I say that there were men behind us with money at that time, ready to take up our cause. Did you know that Erastus Wiman, the New York millionaire, informed us that if we would furnish him with the players for eight League clubs he would see that the money was forthcoming to run them? Every one knows what Erastus Wiman is.[16]

In St. Louis, sportswriter Joe Pritchard also had an inkling that all was not as it seemed. He thought the BPBP was "possessed of a great deal more strength than most people think for." Furthermore, "If the League moguls refuse to listen to their appeals the members of the Brotherhood then will strike for their rights, and if they are forced to do such a thing they will establish clubs in the various cities now under control of the National League and call the new circuit the Union League." One Brotherhood member told Pritchard, "I know just about what my services are worth to my club, and this amount I shall expect to get. If the bosses attempt to bulldoze us into signing, I am of the opinion that they will find they have bit off more than they can chew. . . . The Brotherhood is not saying much, but its

---

[16] Mugwump, "Hub Happenings," *The Sporting Life*, December 5, 1888, 1.

members are doing considerable thinking, and they will act, and act promptly, too, when they see fit."[17]

Even as Irwin was breathing fire, however, Tim Keefe, after stewing over things, was retracting his claws. He confirmed the truth of what Irwin said but then remarked he might have responded a bit hastily. He said he believed Young's statements about not breaking the deal with the Brotherhood and that their agreement still held for men already under reserve, stating that the initial reports he had read were incomplete and misleading. Keefe also acknowledged that a prime motivation for the plan was to keep players from complaining their way out of town to get more money elsewhere, although he declined to say whether he found this mollifying.[18] Was Keefe sincere, or merely trying to muddle the situation by throwing out false leads as to the BPBP's intentions? Throwing up a smokescreen seems most likely.

To add to the confusion, Erastus Wiman denied being in league with the Brotherhood, although he admitted he had spoken with it and been part of its councils in the past. Interviewed by New York writer George Stackhouse, he said, "I am out of base ball. Some time ago, probably a year or more, I might have done so, but not now. At that time I had the old Metropolitan Club on my hands, and acknowledge that I did consider such a scheme. Ward came to me and made such a proposition and I thought favorably of it at the time. Now such a thing is out of the question."[19]

Further clouding matters was that the implementation of the new plan seemed to work differently depending on who interpreted it. The League claimed it was not breaking faith with the Brotherhood, but at the same time, as Nick Young said on December 15, "The new classification rule takes effect on and after to-day and all players who are not under contractual obligation now will have to

---

[17] Joe Pritchard, "St. Louis Siftings," *The Sporting Life*, December 5, 1888, 5.
[18] Mugwump, "Hub Happenings," *The Sporting Life*, December 5, 1888, 1.
[19] George Stackhouse, "New York News," *The Sporting Life*, December 12, 1888, 4.

be graded in accordance with the provision of the law." Both these things could not be true at the same time. Some teams in the National League seemed confused about their own rule as well. By December 15, only two of them, Washington and Indianapolis, had sent Young their list of which players needed classification and which had come to an agreement.[20] The Indianapolis classification list included its entire roster, with the exception of captain Jack Glasscock and one other marginal player, because, in a perversion of the intent of the rule that should not have been difficult to see coming, Indianapolis management had refused to negotiate with any players, so they would have to fall into the classification system no matter what.[21]

One final notable aspect of the Brush Plan was its intent to divide the players against themselves. If a player had average talent and respectable habits, his salary under the Brush Plan was unlikely to vary significantly from what he would make with no plan in place. Owners said so constantly in their attempts to persuade the public that they did not intend their plan to hurt the players. The only players hurt badly would be those who made more than $2,500 per year and those who drank and partied frequently. The League's owners hoped to turn this large body of average players against their own leadership by trying to demonstrate to the average players that their interests were not the same as those of well-off players such as Ward who claimed to speak for them. This part of the Brush Plan did not work, however, partly because the players showed loyalty to the BPBP and partly because many baseball players hoped they might one day end up playing in a city such as New York and earning a larger paycheck.

Clearly, baseball players did not like the Brush Plan, even while they contemplated what they might attempt to do about it. What, however, of the sporting press? How did it respond to the National

---

[20] R. M. Larner, "The League Law," *The Sporting Life*, December 19, 1888, 1.
[21] A. G. Ovens, "Indianapolis Affairs," *The Sporting Life*, December 19, 1888, 1.

League promulgating this radical plan? This was a critical point because if the players were to attempt any large-scale protest, having the press on their side was of great value. Because newspapers were the only source of news for most cranks, what writers had to say was crucial. The Brotherhood could not get the public on its side unless the press was on its side.

The sundry newspapers reporting on the scheme had a predictable mix of reactions, although a majority favored the National League's move. For its supporters, a few considerations seemed most meritorious. Some, like the *Philadelphia Item*, believed that the plan benefited most of the players because more stability in finances would remedy the evil of teams dropping out of leagues during or after the season. In fact, some minor league teams had gone bankrupt and disbanded in 1888, in addition to Detroit leaving the National League. Therefore, an overall drop in team expenses meant greater stability in the job market. Others, such as the *Philadelphia North American*, cited a similar reason, that uniform salaries would go far toward allowing the clubs to compete on an even basis. Teams from smaller markets selling the releases of men they could no longer afford would be a thing of the past.[22]

Few papers were so blunt as to simply write that ballplayers were overpaid and deserved less money, but a few did, such as the *New York World*, which opined, "This new salary limit will reduce the aristocratic base ball player to the level of lawyers and doctors and journalists. The boss barons will be made a little richer, but the country can stand it." Likewise, the *Washington Capital* stated paternalistically and falsely, "The men will be better off under the change, as the smaller salaries will tend to make them more saving. As it is now, the high salaries paid serve no other purpose, except in

---

[22] *The Sporting Life* reprinted the responses from these various newspapers in "The Salary Limit," *The Sporting Life*, December 5, 1888, 3.

a very few instances, than to supply funds to be squandered in the various excesses of life."²³

This last point was certainly in keeping with the times. In the 1880s, social Darwinism was powerful, with its belief that it was useless to help poor people or people of bad habits because they would only squander whatever help they received. In the eyes of social Darwinists, their poverty was proof that they were unable to do better. This viewpoint came in different shadings, however, with some willing to allow that the poor could improve their situation but only through acquiring the moral habits of their social betters.

Nick Young often struck this tone upon receipt of letters from players appealing to him. Whenever a player petitioned him, Young's responses typically evaded the request but advised the petitioner to upgrade his moral habits. For instance, when one player sent him a letter describing his qualifications for a spot in the National League (an inappropriate request because Young had no power to sign players), Young responded by writing, "You say you drink very little. Why not commence at once, and say 'I never drink.' The hardest drinker commenced by drinking very little. It is very important that men who aspire to be ball players should be temperate in all things, to put them in the best possible physical condition."²⁴ This is not to say Young was incorrect in his views on drinking. Many players tarnished potentially fine careers through an overfondness for intoxicating beverages. The significance is that rather than simply responding to the question posed, which he could have done by replying that such a request was outside of his powers to grant, Young chose to include an unsolicited lecture on morality as well.

The plan's opponents likewise took various grounds for their disagreement. The *New York Sun* was among the few simply stating that players deserved what they could get, just like any other worker

---

²³ Ibid.
²⁴ R. M. Larner, "Appeals to Young," *The Sporting Life*, January 30, 1889, 1.

or business owner: "Buck [Ewing] and his brothers are eminently good laborers, and they are worthy of their hire. Why shouldn't they have it?" Others, such as the *Cincinnati Enquirer*, believed that teams would find every way imaginable to subvert the new rule and find loopholes just as everyone had done in 1886. That paper even quoted Cincinnati Red Stockings president Aaron Stern as opposed to the American Association copying the League: "I believe in every club being master of its own affairs. I want to be able to do business with my men in my own style. I think I am able to judge what their services are worth without having someone to classify them for me." Stern also believed that this classification system would drastically increase record playing, both in the field and at bat. This complaint was probably the most common of all. Many observers, like the *St. Louis Globe-Democrat*, thought players would play for their statistics, since statistics were the only fair criterion for judgment, and that teamwork and strategy inevitably would suffer as a result.[25]

From Washington, Bob Larner called the new plan "undoubtedly a sensible and businesslike proceeding" that would reverse the current situation in which "the life blood has been slowly, but steadily ebbing from base ball for several years past." He wrote that the star players would no doubt complain, "But when they stop to consider the situation in a calm, reasonable spirit they will probably appreciate the policy." Larner also tried to assuage worries about the feasibility of a classification system that included intangible factors by stating that Nick Young "has the confidence of players, managers and the public, and there is no doubt but he will do his work well, and at the same time earn the merited advance in his salary."[26]

O. P. Caylor saw some merit in the plan but believed the teams should have graded salaries between $1,000 and $3,000, with jumps

---

[25] "The Salary Limit," *The Sporting Life*, December 5, 1888, 3.
[26] Bob Larner, "Washington Whispers," *The Sporting Life*, November 28, 1888, 6.

The Brotherhood and the Brush Classification Scheme

of $500 in between. In addition, he thought that continuous and quality service with the same team should entitle a player to improve his standing by one grade every three years, even if the man's performance stayed steady and his classification was otherwise unchanged. If a team did not want to pay the increase, it should let the player go. Caylor also called for the BPBP to offer a compromise plan if it was unhappy, believing that such a compromise had a chance of acceptance.

The backbone of Caylor's commentary was that the Brush Plan gave no reward for long and faithful service on the part of individual players. All observers agreed that one reason salaries had risen in recent years was that talented but discontented players felt they could make more elsewhere, thus putting pressure on their teams to move them or else risk an uninspired performance by a petulant player. As is, the Brush Plan would only provide more reasons for dissatisfaction, leading to lackluster play on the field. If veterans of long experience and loyalty saw younger, unproven men getting as much or more compensation than they did, it would not provide much incentive for loyalty to the ball club.[27]

When making such comments, Caylor had in mind the situation in his former home, Cincinnati. There, the Red Stockings signed young outfielder "Bug" Holliday and, being an American Association team, could sign Holliday for whatever they saw fit to pay him. Apparently, the team saw fit to pay Holliday quite a bit (the rumored value of the contract being $2,800) because the signing caused three of Cincinnati's talented veterans, John Reilly, Bid McPhee, and Hick Carpenter, to hold out for greater pay.[28] A graded salary plan would result in the same situation, Caylor thought, the only difference being that the salaries producing the jealousy would be a bit lower.

---

[27] O. P. Caylor, "Caylor's Comment," *The Sporting Life*, January 23, 1889, 4.
[28] No title, *The Sporting Life*, February 6, 1889, 2.

It turned out that Holliday was the best hitter on the Reds in 1889, but young players did not usually have such spectacular debuts, and no one could predict this ahead of time. Carpenter and McPhee came to terms with Sterns before too many suns had set, but Reilly proved more stubborn. When interviewed, Reilly confirmed the reason for his holdout, stating, "Mr. Stern pays Holliday a large salary, and I think I can reasonably ask for as much as he is to receive. I have been with the Cincinnati Club for a number of seasons, and I feel that I have always given satisfaction and have improved each year in my work."[29] Reilly, because of his past efforts in Cincinnati, had support: "The argument made by Long John is that if 'Bug' Holliday is worth $2,800 to the Cincinnati team, he is surely entitled to as much. . . . If there is one man in the Cincinnati team whose whole soul is in its success that man is Reilly. He is one of your mortals who mourns over a lost game like a man who has buried a friend."[30]

In Baltimore, Albert Mott was not sanguine of the plan's chances. He wrote that the Brush Plan "has the fatal defect of depending entirely for its success upon the good faith of a miscellaneous assembly of human beings, with the usual human traits, among which it may be safely depended upon they possess at least a modest avarice and a laudable rivalry." Mott predicted,

> when fate, luck or the fortunes of the field combine with private proddings of patrons and public impaling by the press, the temptation to evade the law becomes too strong for fallible human nature, and the result is a breach of the rule such as to ultimately cause it to become a dead letter. Unhealthy sentiment may ascribe a more lofty code of morals to "magnates" than to the balance of the human race, but unfortunately for the welfare of the game, they have

---

[29] John Reilly, "Reilly's Ultimatum," *The Sporting Life*, February 13, 1889, 2.
[30] Ren Mulford, Jr., "Cincinnati Chips," *The Sporting Life*, February 13, 1889, 5.

The Brotherhood and the Brush Classification Scheme

always shown themselves to be possessed of the average failings.[31]

As if to confirm the worst fears of the critics, even before December was over, various teams behaved in ways suggesting they were not following the letter of their own law:

It is understood that several of the New York, Boston and Philadelphia players have already made acceptable terms with their respective managers, but their contracts have not been formally announced. Such proceedings are calculated to create dissatisfaction in various quarters and open the door to allegations of favoritism in allowing players and managers to dicker about terms after the 15th.[32]

This suspicion thickened when, in early February, the New York Giants announced that Roger Connor, Mickey Welch, Jim O'Rourke, Danny Richardson, Art Whitney, Gil Hatfield, Will George, Bill Brown, Mike Slattery, George Gore, and Ledell Titcomb had signed, with Tim Keefe and Buck Ewing on the verge. The December 15th deadline was long gone, but because the men signed without much discussion or complaint, observers understandably surmised that something might be afoot.[33]

It also turned out Keefe was not ready to sign. He chose to hold out instead. Making a mockery of the Brush Plan, he held out all the way into May, signing after the season began. He timed everything perfectly. By the time the season opened, several New York pitchers could not perform because of injury. Things were so bad that catcher Buck Ewing had to pitch a game, against the now-formidable

---

[31] T. T. T., "Baltimore Bulletin," *The Sporting Life*, December 26, 1888, 5.
[32] R. M. Larner, "Washington Whispers," *The Sporting Life*, December 26, 1888, 1.
[33] R. M. Larner, "From League Headquarters," *The Sporting Life*, February 13, 1889, 1.

Boston Beaneaters, at that. While Ewing did admirably, showing a terrific fastball, at this point New York owner John Day saw no choice but to give in and sign Keefe on Keefe's terms, which were a salary of $4,500.[34]

Of course, several players kicked against their classification and refused to accept the terms offered at first. Washington's ace pitcher, "Grasshopper" Jim Whitney, was among them, aggrieved despite his Class A ranking because it would violate his contract and pay a lesser salary than he had earned in 1888. The Grasshopper, despite a losing record for his career, was a terrific pitcher. He led the National League in fewest walks allowed per nine innings in five consecutive seasons, 1883-1887, and led the NL in ratio of strikeouts to walks four different times. The first eight years of his career were possibly of Hall of Fame-caliber. Therefore, while most sportswriters were praising the effort to bring salaries down, many sympathized with Whitney as a man who deserved better.[35] Whitney did manage to complain his way out of Washington when the Nationals traded him to Indianapolis in exchange for another pitcher, John Healy, but Whitney still had to sign for the figure at which Nick Young slotted him.[36]

Confusing the situation was the matter of the lingering effects of the salary limit of 1886. Recall that, to work around the $2,000 limit, teams often offered players $2,000 in their baseball contract but then supplemented that amount with personal service contracts. Jack Glasscock of Indianapolis was one player affected by this situation. In 1888, his baseball contract and supplemental contract together paid him $3,000. Indianapolis offered him a straight $2,500 for 1889 (along with an extra stipend for being team captain, which the Brush Plan allowed), a clear decrease over the previous year. Yet, the Hoosiers had the audacity to claim they were giving their infielder a

---

[34] W. I. Harris, "New York News," *The Sporting Life*, May 15, 1889, 5.
[35] R. M. Larner, "Washington Whispers," *The Sporting Life*, February 6, 1889, 6; Sam, "The Washingtonians," *The Sporting News*, February 9, 1889, 3.
[36] "Signed with the Hoosiers," *Pittsburg Dispatch*, April 6, 1889, 6.

The Brotherhood and the Brush Classification Scheme

raise because his baseball contract stood $500 higher than in 1888. Glasscock did not see things in that light, feeling this was an act of bad faith given the provision in the National League's deal with the Brotherhood on contracts disallowing the unilateral reduction of a player's salary. He decided not to sign his contract, hoping the Brotherhood would take up his cause.[37] Glasscock later relented, however.

Indianapolis was also involved in another interesting situation that the Brush Plan did not address when it moved to sign pitcher Charlie Getzein in early March. Getzein had not signed by December 15 but because he had formerly been with Detroit, which disbanded over the winter, it was impossible for him to have done so. He believed he should be exempt from classification because the team that would have classified him no longer existed. He could not sign with his old team, but that team had not sent him somewhere else in time to negotiate by the December deadline, so Getzein understandably felt aggrieved.[38] He signed with Indianapolis in late March, lacking a better option, but without undue complaining.[39] This caused one paper to offer, "It is no sure thing that Detroit did not divide the purchase money with Getzein. At any rate, he became well satisfied with Indianapolis very suddenly."[40]

As mentioned previously, players with limited major league experience proved difficult to classify because they had a limited record of performance against major league competition and little reputation, for good or ill, in terms of deportment. Such was true of Chicago White Stockings outfielder Hugh Duffy. An eventual Hall of Famer, Duffy was a rookie in 1888 with 298 major league at bats. He had had a nice year however, with a .282 batting average, he possessed a reputation as a solid defensive player, and did not have

---

[37] Pickwick, "Jack Glasscock Talks," *The Sporting Life*, February 27, 1889, 1.
[38] Lew, "Getzein of Detroit," *The Sporting News*, March 9, 1889, 3.
[39] "Getzein Has Accepted the Terms," *Chicago Daily Tribune*, March 24, 1889, 6.
[40] "Notes and Comments," *The Sporting Life*, April 3, 1889, 4.

an unsavory record regarding alcohol or behavior. When he found out Nick Young rated him in Class C and he would therefore get $2,000 just as he had the year before, Duffy felt underappreciated and inclined to protest. Chicago management agreed with his own assessment of his greater worth, seeing that the team turned down a reported offer of $8,000 for his sale over the winter.[41]

One reason Chicago offered for its behavior in the Duffy case was that, because Nick Young put Duffy in Class C, it had no say in the matter. This was not always true, however, because the classification scheme was malleable when the situation required it. At least, it was for Philadelphia Quakers first baseman Sid Farrar. Farrar, slotted into Class C at first, held out because he believed he deserved better. As April moved along and opening day approached with Farrar still not in the fold, Quakers management started getting desperate: "Col. Rogers and Manager Wright then promised to use their united influences with President Nick Young to have Farrar placed in Class B this year. This won Sidney over and he signed." Farrar himself said, "If the club wants to pay me $2,250 you can bet Old Nick will put me in Class B."[42]

As for Chicago owner Al Spalding, recently returned from his foray around the world, his attitude toward the Brush Plan depended upon when you asked him the question. When he "first" heard about the scheme on his tour, he stated he disliked it. Once back in Chicago, however, and with no further need to keep the Chicago and All-America teams happy and well-disposed toward him personally, his views underwent a radical change, and he stated his intent to support the new scheme fully. (As mentioned earlier, some historians believe he was the true architect of the Brush Plan all along. Given that nothing happened in the National League without his blessing, it seems almost inconceivable that his fellow owners

---

[41] Ibid.
[42] "Sid Farrar Signs," *The Sporting News*, April 13, 1889, 1.

The Brotherhood and the Brush Classification Scheme

would have taken such a drastic measure without his knowledge and approval.)

Besides these various reactions, most of which were predictable, one other aspect of the Brush Plan deserves mention. One final problem with this plan was that, when implemented, it did not always reward players for being good baseball players, which is, in the end, what wins games. This forced teams into poor economic choices at times. For instance, Nick Young classified Boston's John Morrill, a man acknowledged by all observers as a gentleman, in Class A. Jerry Denny of Indianapolis ended up in Class B. Yet, Denny was a far more effective baseball player than Morrill by 1889. About to turn thirty-four years old, Morrill was coming off a dismal season in which he hit .198, posting an OPS+ of 79 and 1.4 WAR, his WAR landing that high only because of his defensive skill. Denny, in contrast, was still in the prime of his career, had just finished a nice season with a 115 OPS+ and a WAR of 2.4, and he was the acknowledged king of defensive third basemen. However, he drank from time to time, while Morrill never did. Despite this, Denny was still more valuable than Morrill was. The difference in contributions on the field was even greater during the 1889 season. Morrill, on his last legs as an active player, limped home with 0.1 WAR and retired (other than two games the next season) after playing in only 44 games for Washington. (He was still with Boston when Young decided his classification, but Boston transferred him to the Nationals before the season began.) Denny, meanwhile, essentially reproduced his 1888 season, posting 2.3 WAR for Indianapolis.

Observers at the time did not necessarily see things this way, however. Ignoring the statistics, many heralded Morrill's move to Washington as a masterstroke that might finally elevate the Nationals to respectability in the National League: "Every body knows that under so capable, efficient and practically experienced manager and Captain as John Morrill is known to be, the Washington Club, will make things mighty interesting in the League this season. . . . In Morrill the club gets a man who is known throughout the land, as a manager who possesses the requisite qualifications, and as an honorable and upright player."[43]

Even though Washington acquired shortstop Sam Wise from Boston along with Morrill, and catcher Tom Daly from Chicago as well after Al Spalding released Daly in anger over his drinking on the Spalding Tour, it still did not help the Nationals play better baseball. In fact, they were worse in 1889 than they had been in 1888, their win total falling from 48 to 41, and by midseason Morrill had to step down as manager with the club standing at 13-38. When the club started slowly and he finally realized Morrill was not the answer, a writer lamented, "John Morrill, as captain, was expected to infuse new life and vigor into their movements, and many of the wise men interested in the game put them down for sixth or seventh place sure. Some were enthusiastic enough to predict that they would wind up fifth or better." Instead, by June, "he is exceedingly weak at the bat, and while I know that he does the best he can under all circumstances, I am convinced that his best days on the ball field have passed."[44]

This is but one example of how the Brush Plan did not always reward players for being good players and could even hurt teams economically at times. It forced Washington to pay Morrill much more than the value he produced. The plan's supporters claimed the it would inspire players to greater performance, but as the situation played out, that was not the purpose, only an incidental benefit the League hoped it might realize. The real purpose was to inspire players to better personal habits. Recall that Nick Young had said, "Intelligent players will recognize it and it depends upon their own exertions whether they shall be benefited by it." Yet, if classification depended as much or more on a man's deportment as it did on his performance, this diluted or eliminated the incentive to greater

---

[43] Sam, "Joy in Washington," *The Sporting News*, April 13, 1886, 3.
[44] R. M. Larner, "Senators Scorched," *The Sporting Life*, June 5, 1889, 2.

exertion. Clearly, the exertion the National League had in mind was that players not exert themselves in having a good time during the late hours.

This is not really a surprise, however, and it fits perfectly with the National League's record of relating to its players all through the later 1880s. As was true regarding player fitness, gambling, or violence in baseball, League owners did not much care how they made money, so long as they made money. Spalding and others expressed, frequently, a desire to elevate baseball's image amongst the "better class" of people and believed that finding more moral players or, failing that, upgrading the morals of existing players was the surest path to this goal. Of course, players who drank less would most likely play better, and the team would win more games if that happened, but winning was not as important as profiting. This behavior also demonstrates the paternalistic attitude baseball owners so often took toward their players. If the players would not shape up on their own, the League must make them. Most were no better than irresponsible children, so in its own eyes the League was doing them a favor by reducing their pay and preventing them from wasting their own money.[45]

On the surface, despite a few little arguments, things seemed serene for the National League in mid-March of 1889. The opening of the season was near, enthusiasm amongst the fans was on the rise, some teams had assembled their men already to get in shape for the coming campaign, and most NL players had not publicly protested their contract situation. True, there were still a few holdouts and complaints, the League had not yet resolved the Rowe-White matter, and a few legal questions hung in the air regarding the Brush Plan, such as whether some teams, New York for instance, had evaded it.

---

[45] For the full description of player drinking, training, and other personal habits, see Rob Bauer, *Outside the Lines of Gilded Age Baseball: Alcohol, Fitness, and Cheating in 1880s Baseball.*

Still, by the standards of most off-seasons in 1880s baseball, this was not especially dramatic. The League settled its membership issue quickly, with Cleveland taking the place of Detroit. It had overcome the financial problems of Indianapolis, and the Hoosiers were good to play at least one more season. From all published reports save the vindictive ones appearing in *The Sporting News*, Al Spalding and his tourists had achieved a host of successes booming America's national game abroad. Baseball's leaders had every reason to look forward to the new season.

It seems the reason things were relatively calm is that, even though the Brotherhood had made public comments regarding the National League's perfidy, the BPBP really did need its president, John Ward, to coordinate its response. That is why player objections to the Brush Plan had been individual ones rather than the Brotherhood making any complaint. Perhaps this gave the owners a false sense of security. When no coordinated response was forthcoming from the BPBP, they might have concluded that the Brush Plan was a success and that the organization was not as strong as rumors claimed. The apparent acquiescence of the players in the Brush Plan by the spring of 1889 contributed to this perceived feeling of success.

They had overlooked one thing, however. On March 14, newspapers in the U.S. revealed that one player on Spalding's tour planned to end his odyssey early: "Capt. John M. Ward's intention of leaving the Spalding base-ball party and sailing for New York tomorrow has been no secret among the members of the two teams or to Mr. Spalding for some days." Like the rest of the tourists, Ward had had no inkling of what was going on in the U.S. since leaving San Francisco the prior November. Upon arrival in Italy, however, he finally received mail, and Ward decided to alter his plans immediately. When asked why Ward planned to steam home early, one member of the All-America team simply said, "Johnny Ward knows that the Brotherhood of American Ball-Players wants him at home and he is going there; that is all there is to the matter."[46]

---

[46] "Mr. Ward's Return Home," *Chicago Daily Tribune*, March 14, 1889, 2.

Chapter 12

The Beginning of the End of the American Association I

IN THE PREVIOUS CHAPTER, I WROTE THAT THE BRUSH PLAN created a general conflagration in baseball, one whose immediate consequences took at least two years to play out fully. However, before finishing our story with how this drew the BPBP into its final showdown with the National League, we need to take some time to see how this also contributed to the demise of the National League's rival, the American Association.

Most histories of the Players League of 1890 note that after the Players League failed to establish itself beyond 1890, the National League's other rival, the American Association, also fell apart, playing its last season in 1891. The general storyline is that, with the Players League out of the way, the National League was free to deal with a weakened American Association and finish off its rival. While partially true, this view is incomplete and badly simplified. It does not do justice to the maneuvers bringing this denouement about. It is time to set the matter right and give the Association's demise the full explanation it deserves. We can trace the initial reasons for the American Association's destruction back to the seasons of 1887 and 1888 and their aftermath.

All through the 1880s, baseball writers observed that of the two major leagues, the National League seemed to have the more effective and harmonious leadership. Al Spalding led the way, certainly, but in addition, John Day of New York and John Rogers in Philadelphia, just to name two, were some of the most powerful and influential men in the game. As a result, the League successfully outmaneuvered the Association at several critical times, like when it lured Pittsburgh away from the Association to fill one of its vacancies in the place of Kansas City and the St. Louis Maroons in 1887. As one sportswriter put it,

> The business of the League is kept from the public, while the Association 'circle' has no secrets. . . . The Association grinds more axes in public in one year than the League will in a dozen. The Association magnates are always quarreling among themselves and talking of dirty ball, etc., while the League people have their little spats in some quiet nook, and the public is none the wiser.[1]

While true, the Association always seemed to muddle through. Up through the 1887 season, that is. In 1888, however, things changed. The issue that initiated the eventual demise of the American Association was, perhaps not surprisingly, the interlocked questions regarding player salaries and ticket prices.

Even by 1887, cracks started showing in the Association's armor. In St. Louis, Chris Von der Ahe was a wild card. No one knew what he might do next, and his moods swung wildly along with the fortunes of his beloved Browns. However, because he had the best team in the Association and its best drawing card, other

---

[1] Joe Pritchard, "St. Louis Siftings," *The Sporting Life*, August 8, 1888, 6.

owners had to humor him, and Von der Ahe often persuaded them to go along with his ideas, regardless of the consequences. The problem was that the other owner with the greatest clout in the Association, Charles Byrne in Brooklyn, often opposed Von der Ahe. Because Byrne also had a top team and resided in the second largest market the Association had left after 1887 when the Metropolitans retired from New York, his word counted for a great deal as well.[2]

Besides his clashes with Von der Ahe, which became increasingly frequent in 1888, Byrne was also partly responsible for another Association mistake in 1887. At a late-season meeting, he combined with Billy Barnie of Baltimore to convince his fellow owners to exclude O. P. Caylor from the meeting. Caylor was the manager of the New York Metropolitans and had every right to be there, but Barnie and Byrne convinced their brethren that Caylor was, first and foremost, a newspaper writer (he wrote a weekly column for *The Sporting Life*, as anyone who has read the footnotes of this book knows well by this point) and thus had no place in their councils.

Perhaps now would be the proper time for a few words concerning Caylor. Oliver Perry Caylor wore many hats and was involved with baseball in many different guises throughout the 1880s. When he kept his sarcasm within bounds, he was among the most entertaining baseball writers of the day, and one of the most courageous. He even participated in the launch of a daily paper discussing nothing but baseball, the *Daily Baseball Gazette*, although the paper put out only a few issues before going under.

More important to our story is Caylor's historic relationship with the American Association. He had been part of the organization from its birth. Caylor, along with Horace Phillips, late of Pittsburgh,

---

[2] Because the American Association split the Philadelphia market with the National League, one could even make a case that Brooklyn was the largest market remaining to the Association.

was among the men most prominent in starting the league over the winter of 1881-1882. He had also managed two clubs, Cincinnati and New York, so he was deep in the councils of the Association and knew most of its dirty secrets. When Association owners ostracized him at that fateful 1887 meeting, he turned against them, and some of those secrets came into the light.[3] Caylor knew enough about baseball that when the Brotherhood War began in 1890 and Al Spalding purchased a New York paper called *The Sporting Times* as his organ to combat the players, Spalding tabbed Caylor, along with Harry Palmer, as the editors. His acid wit and biting prose helped undermine the position of the Brotherhood as the 1890 season unfolded.[4]

Caylor, however potent his pen, had no formal role in the American Association after 1887. The men who did, however, often made decisions that left the group careening from one near-disaster to the next. The National League charged fifty cents for its cheapest tickets and seventy-five for the better seats in the grandstand. Before 1888, Association teams charged twenty-five cents for the bleaching boards and fifty for the grandstand. That year, however, the Association decided to operate on the same financial level as the League and increased its ticket prices to the League standard. The Association believed its baseball equal to that played in the League, which was true for the most part, and that because salaries had risen in the past five years, it needed to jump its ticket prices to League levels to compete for talent.

By midseason, however, many regretted the change. Baseball observers believed that Brooklyn was doing well and Cincinnati reasonably so under the new rate. Cincinnati owner Aaron Stern told sportswriter Ren Mulford, Jr., "The season, outside of Cincinnati

---

[3] Phillips' story has a rather sad ending. Midway through the 1889 season, he developed a mental illness diagnosed as acute paresis and ended up in an asylum in New Jersey. He eventually recovered his wits, however. "Phillips' Misfortune," *The Sporting Life*, August 14, 1889, 1.

[4] Lamster, *Spalding's World Tour*, 257-258.

and Brooklyn, has been a financial disappointment. We have been credited with making money. A few thousand dollars signifies what our profits have been, and if any man wants to buy out the Cincinnati Club I am willing to treat with him." Cleveland seemed to be in decent shape as well, but other Association cities were kicking hard against the fifty-cent minimum ticket plan.[5]

As we will see, it is not a coincidence that by 1890, all three of these clubs—Brooklyn, Cincinnati, and Cleveland—were in the National League, replacing Detroit, Indianapolis, and Washington. Mulford wrote, "The Association prospects are not cheering—that is certain. St. Louis is a dead rabbit town, and the club that is such a magnet away from home cannot draw more than mosquitoes and Joe Pritchard in its own bailiwick. The high tariff has crippled Baltimore, and would have killed Philadelphia. Louisville is struggling along, thinking much and saying little, while Cleveland is nearer a paying basis." Rumors that Cincinnati and Brooklyn planned to jilt the Association and join the League had been in the air for nearly a year already, and the rumors only increased while the American Association debated what to do.[6]

The experiment lasted only into July. Surprisingly, however, a National League team caved first. That the team was the Philadelphia Quakers is not a surprise because the combination of owner Rogers' loyalty to quarter admissions, the death of top pitcher Charlie Ferguson, a rainy spring, a disappointing 26-24 record at the end of June, and the resulting weak patronage of the club made Rogers decide to return to his comfort zone and resume offering twenty-five cent tickets.[7] The Association's Philadelphia Athletics had the right to drop their prices should this occur. They did so, but when the Association met in early summer to discuss retrograde

---

[5] Ren Mulford, Jr., "Cincinnati Chips," *The Sporting Life*, August 1, 1888, 7.
[6] Ibid. Recall that Joe Pritchard was Mulford's St. Louis counterpart writer for *The Sporting Life*. A dead rabbit town was one with little action taking place.
[7] Francis Richter, "A Break in the Association High Tariff Line," *The Sporting Life*, July 4, 1888, 1.

action on the part of the entire Association, it elected to stay with fifty-cent admissions, Philadelphia excepted. Cleveland, Brooklyn, and Cincinnati wanted to keep the current tariff, while St. Louis, Baltimore, Louisville, and Philadelphia did not, and Kansas City abstained. Needing a two-thirds vote to change their collective minds, the fifty-cent policy stood for the time being.[8]

This is not to say that, by its close, 1888 was a financial failure for all Association teams. In addition to Cincinnati and Brooklyn, Philadelphia did just fine according to its treasurer, in part because of the return to quarter tickets and in part because of a late-season surge in the standings that had some observers believing the team might overtake the mighty St. Louis Browns. The team claimed, "Financially the season has been very pleasant to us. We will close with quite a large profit. We are in favor of using all our profits and more besides to improve the surroundings of the team for next season. We are now considering the question of a new ground, and it is about decided that we will have new quarters next year."[9]

For the clubs struggling to draw patrons, however, most believed that keeping the fifty-cent minimum ticket price was an albatross. As a result, some tried to find loopholes. In Baltimore, manager Billy Barnie announced that while tickets sold at the team's box office remained fifty cents, patrons could purchase their tickets at the old price at certain business establishments in the Monumental City.[10] This was against policy, but O. P. Caylor asked, "What are the other magnates going to do about it? Louisville will do the same thing when she gets back. Von der Ahe will stand by Barnie and the Athletics will not vote against him. There you have it. That's what the Association constitution is worth."[11] As a result, the American

---

[8] "The Fifty Cent Rate," *The Sporting News*, July 7, 1888, 1.
[9] H. W. L., "In the Quaker City," *The Sporting News*, October 20, 1888, 5.
[10] T. T. T., "Baltimore Bulletin," *The Sporting Life*, August 1, 1888, 3.
[11] O. P. Caylor, "Caylor's Comment," *The Sporting Life*, August 8, 1888, 7.

Association called an emergency meeting for August 7, 1888, to try once again to work out a plan regarding admission prices.[12]

The executives met in Parlor C of the Continental Hotel in Philadelphia. Surprisingly, they did reach agreement. Unexpectedly, Byrne sided with the quarter-admissions faction, giving it five votes out of six (Cleveland and Cincinnati were not present to vote) when Kansas City announced its willingness to side with the majority. Considerable politicking accompanied the decision, however. The Kansas City management hoped to get on the good side of the rest of the Association because their franchise was a conditional one. The other owners retained the right to vote them out of the league after the season (itself another indication of the Association's questionable decision-making), so naturally, Cowboys management sought to make as many friends as possible.[13]

In exchange for his vote, Brooklyn's Byrne extorted concessions in return. The Association must return to a guarantee plan for distributing revenue to the visiting clubs, meaning that the visitors got a lump sum of money regardless of what the game's attendance was, and abandon giving the visitors a percentage of the gate. This would materially improve Brooklyn's finances because it was the most patronized team in the Association. In just thirteen Sunday games, it drew 59,841 spectators to Ridgewood Park, including over 10,000 on June 3.[14] Now Brooklyn could keep more of that money and no longer had to give a percentage of its gate to the rest of the league. Some teams made side deals around this issue, however, such as the St. Louis Browns agreeing to continue paying Louisville the percentage whenever the Colonels came to town. Still, even with the occasional exception, this was a steep price to pay, but the other members of the Association were desperate, so they agreed. It is also conceivable that Byrne extorted a player from Baltimore in return

---

[12] "Will Meet at Last," *The Sporting News*, August 4, 1888, 1.
[13] "Indiscreet Mr. Byrne," *The Sporting News*, August 11, 1888, 1.
[14] Henry Chadwick, "Chadwick's Chat," *The Sporting Life*, August 22, 1888, 4.

for his vote. Coincidence or not, within a few days, Baltimore's Tom "Oyster" Burns was a member of Byrne's nine in Brooklyn.[15]

Everyone seemed happy at that point. Except for Cleveland. The Blues had done reasonably well with fifty-cent tickets, and given the rising expenses of fielding a nine, its management believed it should keep ticket prices at a half-dollar. This led Cleveland's president to state, "This is a good fifty-cent ball town, and a League club would draw better here than in any other city in the country except Chicago, New York, and Boston. The Association has struck us a foul and cowardly blow and I am in favor of quitting." The new agreement did allow Cleveland to keep its fifty-cent ticket rate intact, which it did.[16] By the end of the season, the team ran a modest $3,000 in the red and believed that in 1889, once ensconced in the National League, the team could draw fans with new faces to compete against and would have a much better season.[17]

Some wondered how Cleveland could scheme to enter the National League when the League had no vacancies. Others knew better than to believe such an inconvenient truth would hamper National League owners. There had been no vacancy in the League before 1887, either, yet that had not stopped Spalding and company from booting Kansas City and replacing the Cowboys with Pittsburgh when opportunity favored such a course. If Cleveland wanted to come in and the League's owners wanted Cleveland in their ranks, they would find a way.

Cleveland's anger came back to haunt the Association before long. In October, even as the New York-St. Louis World Series was still in progress, the Detroit Wolverines decided to pack it in and drop out of the National League. Cleveland jumped on the opportunity to buy the Detroit franchise and switched leagues

---

[15] "The Association," *The Sporting Life*, August 15, 1888, 1; O. P. Caylor, "Caylor's Comment," *The Sporting Life*, August 22, 1888, 2; F. H. Brunell, "Brunell's Budget," *The Sporting Life*, November 21, 1888, 3.
[16] J. R. R., "Is It Only a Bluff?" *The Sporting News*, August 11, 1888, 1.
[17] F. H. Brunell, "Brunell's Budget," *The Sporting Life*, December 12, 1888, 5.

without hesitation. In place of Cleveland, with its respectable reputation as a baseball town and its population of 261,000 people (1890 census) the Association fell back on Columbus, Ohio, a city with roughly one-third of Cleveland's population (with about 88,000 souls, it ranked thirtieth in the nation in population) and a largely unsuccessful previous history of just two years in major league baseball.

Still, things could have been worse. In November, Baltimore's chief owner, Harry Vonderhorst, reassured Oriole fans that their city would continue fielding a team despite rumors that Baltimore was on the brink of dissolution after a lousy season financially. Some even believed that attendance had dropped into the double-digits at times in 1888. Although management had to admit, "next season the Baltimore management will have the balance on the right side of the book, a little thing that did not occur last season,"[18] Vonderhorst said, "We will show people a team next season as strong as any in the Association. It will be a decided improvement on that of last season." Vonderhorst was a man of his word in this case. The Orioles bounced back from 1888's 57-80 disaster to go a respectable 70-65 in 1889, largely thanks to pitcher Matt Kilroy.[19] Vonderhorst did not get to experience the comeback in person, however, because he sold most of his interest to Baltimore oyster packers B. F. Farren and Fred Booth in January 1889.[20]

At the same time, Brooklyn reaffirmed its loyalty, for 1889 at least, which meant that Cincinnati would remain in the fold as well. The primary reason for Brooklyn's return, besides Byrne's pledge not to leave without a championship in his possession, was that moving to the League would mean the end of Sunday baseball in the City of Churches, a step that Byrne was not yet prepared to take even for the fifty-cent general admissions charge in the League.[21]

---

[18] Job Lots, "Baltimore News," *The Sporting News*, November 24, 1888, 1.
[19] "They Will All Stick," *The Sporting News*, November 17, 1888, 1.
[20] "A Baltimore Deal," *The Sporting Life*, January 9, 1889, 1.
[21] "Brooklyn Aims True," *The Sporting News*, November 17, 1888, 1.

The Beginning of the End of the American Association I

The possibility also existed that, if Brooklyn did apply to the National League, the New York Giants might object to a competitor so near their home territory. The Giants would need two other franchises to vote with them to block a Brooklyn application (the National League requiring a two-thirds vote to change its membership) and if Cincinnati tied its fate to Brooklyn's, two existing National League franchises would get the boot. These two franchises, typically rumored to be Washington and Indianapolis, could then combine their votes with that of the Giants to block Brooklyn's admission, which would also stymie Cincinnati and prevent their own dismissal. Given that New York Giants owner John Day publicly expressed his opposition to seeing Brooklyn in the League, stating, "We want no gamblers in our organization, and Byrne will never get in with his club as long as I am in it," this was a serious roadblock.[22]

Even with this temporary affirmation, however, Brooklyn offered no guarantees beyond 1889. That is one reason why other Association teams grew extremely concerned when the Bridegrooms stockpiled talent as the 1888 season wound down. Not only did this contribute to general salary inflation throughout baseball, it also made it more likely that Brooklyn would prevail and win the 1889 championship (which it did), which made it more likely Brooklyn would leave the Association for the League (which it did), and if that happened, it would take all its star players to the League, leaving the Association that much poorer in terms of the drawing power of its players and minus another large market, as well.

Another of the Association's great mistakes was not replacing the New York Metropolitans with another New York franchise after Byrne bought the existing players before the 1888 season. Rather than replace the Metropolitans with another New York team, the

---

[22] Gotham, "Day Speaks of Byrne," *The Sporting News*, September 21, 1889, 1. Byrne was the owner of some gambling operations, thus Day's reference.

Association went through the farce of claiming that the New York franchise still existed even though no team played in New York. Only when it was obvious that no grounds acceptable for playing games were available did the Association end its charade. One consequence is obvious; there was no Association team playing in the nation's largest market, with the negative financial consequences one would expect.

Instead of New York, the Association put a team in Kansas City. This harmed it in multiple ways. Kansas City, despite rapid growth, boasted a population that was about nine percent of what New York offered. The move also unbalanced the Association geographically, leaving it with five western teams, Kansas City, Cleveland, St. Louis, Louisville, and Cincinnati, and only three eastern ones, Brooklyn, Baltimore, and Philadelphia. This necessitated classing Cleveland with the eastern teams for scheduling purposes, adding to that club's travel mileage and expenses, while also increasing everyone's expenses in time and money for the long train ride to Kansas City. While this probably played a modest role in Cleveland's decision to jump to the National League after the season, it could not have helped retain the Forest City club's loyalty, either.

The other obvious problem the loss of the Metropolitans created was the resultant speculation over how to put another team in New York at some point. Many advanced the idea of relocating the best team in the Association, the St. Louis Browns, who despite their enormous success in the standings were not drawing great crowds in the Mound City. Supporters believed that a team of the Browns' quality, with the New York market to support it, would rake in the cash. There were problems with such an idea, however, not least of which was that Brooklyn's Charles Byrne and St. Louis's Chris Von der Ahe did not see eye to eye very often. While never friends to begin with, things grew much worse between them in 1888 when Von der Ahe accused Byrne of tampering with one of his outfielders, Tip O'Neill, believing Byrne had encouraged O'Neill to play poorly, so the Browns would let him go. Byrne countered that he had simply stated his desire to acquire the prodigious hitter and had done nothing underhanded.[23]

Consequently, the Association did nothing to replace New York after 1888, to its collective detriment. The decision to grant a conditional franchise to Kansas City, meanwhile, created a new problem that festered. In some respects, the situation became that of a dog chasing its own tail. Kansas City's management was willing to spend money to bolster its ranks but only if granted permanent status. Association owners wanted to make sure the Cowboys had a better ballpark and team before granting that status. The team countered that it was afraid of the large expense necessary to secure better grounds if the Association did not guarantee a place in its ranks the following season. And so it went, round and round.[24]

This indecision resulted in other cities considering throwing their hats into the ring for Kansas City's spot after 1888, which could not have inspired the players, fans, or owners in Kansas City with much confidence in the team's future. Now that ticket prices were back to a quarter, Milwaukee and Buffalo had interest. Even Omaha, approximately equal to Kansas City in population and billing itself as the best baseball city west of St. Louis, considered making a move, although the team's manager, Frank Selee, later denied such intent. He admitted he spoke with some of the Association's leading men but claimed that the conversations were just discussions, not negotiations.[25]

A late-September meeting resolved the quandary at last. Kansas City finally persuaded the rest of the Association to grant it permanent status. A businessperson from the Cowboy City interested in cable railways, Mr. Holmes, stepped forward to resolve the difficulties. He owned the controlling interest in Kansas City's

---

[23] "The American Association," *The Sporting Life*, August 8, 1888, 1.
[24] "The Eighth Association Club," *The Sporting Life*, August 22, 1888, 1.
[25] Ibid.; "Omaha Not Overly Anxious," *The Sporting Life*, August 29, 1888, 5.

Western Association franchise, which had far better grounds than did the American Association team. Holmes proposed to merge the two teams, giving the Association Cowboys about thirty players from which to form a competitive team, plus the best ballpark in the city, as well as end the costly financial competition between the rival Kansas City clubs. With this promise, the Association voted Kansas City a permanent franchise.[26]

Things were looking up in Kansas City finally, but as 1888 turned to 1889, the Association's future remained muddled. Its winter meeting in December "was chiefly remarkable from the fact that for almost the first time in the history of the organization no glaring blunder was perpetrated." On the down side, however, "the prospect is not of the brightest, with no limit to salaries and expenses, probably reduced income, an awkward circuit and a lopsided contest in view."[27]

Furthermore, while the organization made no significant blunders, it was a close call. A dispute arose when Zach Phelps, former majority shareholder of Louisville, tried to marshal his former friends and have himself elected president of the Association, replacing Wheeler Wikoff. President Wikoff may not have been a perfect leader, but contemporaries described him as one who, "if not a brilliant man, had for years shown himself to be a safe, honest, correct, and every way deserving official."[28]

When Phelps made his move, four clubs stood with him, Philadelphia, Baltimore, Louisville, and Kansas City, while St. Louis, Cincinnati, and Brooklyn stood opposed. The Association had not yet admitted Columbus, but that city had pledged to support Wikoff, so the Phelps faction attempted to delay the admission of Columbus until it could convince one other team to switch votes. This nearly produced a rift because Columbus protested being a

---

[26] L. J. K., "Results of the Association Special Meeting," *The Sporting Life*, October 3, 1888, 1.
[27] "The Association Meeting," *The Sporting Life*, December 12, 1888, 2.
[28] "Association Presidency," *The Sporting Life*, December 19, 1888, 6.

hostage for the sake of one man's ambitions and threatened to withdraw its application for membership. This made things very dicey because the league could not function with seven members. Only some adroit maneuvering by the Wikoff faction managed to gain its point and admit Columbus to the Association's ranks before taking a vote on a new president, and the Phelps group then saw that it had lost its battle and relented. The harsh feelings generated, however, did nothing to foster greater brotherhood and cooperation in the Association's ranks.[29]

This is not to say that Phelps' defeat was necessarily a good thing. Wikoff, while honest and safe, possessed the saving traits of having pedestrian talent and an ability to do paperwork. Baltimore's Albert Mott wrote, "There are men in the Association who prefer mediocrity to brilliancy in order to give their own talents for leadership full swing. They might be arrested in their career of selfishness by abler minds, and that is a result strenuously fought against. All that is desired by them is an honest, faithful clerk, and Mr. Wikoff fills that bill." Mott compared this to Phelps, writing, "Mr. Phelps gave promise of being an able and honest president, fearless, firm and equitable; but that, of course, would never do for those who wish by their talents to gain advantage over weaker vessels. . . . The title of president in the Association is merely ornamental, and analogous to a clerk of a corporation." Mott preferred that his league find a man "who could also be a wise counselor, a firm upholder of the weak and the right, a peacemaker, a diplomat, a master of syntax and definition, but that would be an Association millennium."[30] The difference in quality between Wikoff and National League leaders was vast, and men like Mott knew it. They realized that the Association suffered thereby because men afraid of quality leadership were unlikely to work together effectively.

---

[29] Ibid.
[30] T. T. T., "Baltimore Bulletin," *The Sporting Life*, December 26, 1888, 5.

Outside the Lines of Gilded Age Baseball

The American Association allowed yet another poisonous practice to seep into its veins during the 1887 campaign, and it became even more pronounced in 1888. In an effort to make more money, some of the weaker teams with light attendance began transferring home games from their own grounds to cities with better patronage. The following tables, with the teams listed in their order of finish for each season, tell the selfish tale. Not all teams have the same number of games due to rainouts, ties because of darkness, etc. The Association schedule called for 140 championship season games, so each team would have 70 games at home and on the road if everything went perfectly. Any total greater than 70, therefore, indicates a team playing more games than it should have.

Table 1 American Association Home and Away Games in 1887

Team	Home	Away
St. Louis Browns	73	62
Cincinnati Red Stockings	73	62
Baltimore Orioles	63	72
Louisville Colonels	68	68
Philadelphia Athletics	69	64
Brooklyn Grays	73	61
New York Metropolitans	59	74
Cleveland Blues	58	73

The Beginning of the End of the American Association I

Table 2 American Association Home and Away Games in 1888

Team	Home	Away
St. Louis Browns	81	54
Brooklyn Bridegrooms	73	67
Philadelphia Athletics	75	58
Cincinnati Red Stockings	81	53
Baltimore Orioles	56	81
Cleveland Blues	60	72
Louisville Colonels	56	79
Kansas City Cowboys	57	75

The consequences were predictable. The better teams drew more fans because they won more often. Home teams won more often than road teams; therefore, the teams already doing well did even better, and the ones doing poorly, even worse. This might have paid short-term financial dividends in 1887 and 1888 but surely hurt the league for 1889 and beyond because fans of the teams at the bottom of the standings were less likely to attend games in the years to come, knowing that their home club was unlikely to succeed and might even turn home games that fans planned to attend into road games. Realizing this, the Association officially banned the practice at its next winter meeting in 1889, but the so-called ban did not hold up when Louisville transferred scheduled home games to Cincinnati early in the 1889 season.

When one writer asked Cincinnati owner Aaron Stern about the wisdom of this practice, seeing that such an imbalance affected the integrity of the pennant race, Stern demonstrated that such things as the integrity of the game, or the integrity of the American Association, were secondary to the bottom line. When the writer, Joe Pritchard, asked, "Do you think that this thing of transferring so many games to Cincinnati, is the proper thing to do?" Stern answered, "Why not? The Cincinnati Club has given these clubs large guarantees to come to Cincinnati, and we have done this because we know we will make money by the operation." Pritchard countered, "The American Association ought not to allow anything of the kind, especially at this stage of the game, when the race is so close." Stern finished by responding, "I don't think that the Association would meddle with anything that is none of its business. If two clubs agree mutually to change games whose business is it? And as for the Association, I don't know as I will be in the Association next year, and I am not certain that I will be in the base ball business at all in 1889."[31]

When faced with such selfishness and short-sightedness, people like Pritchard could only shake their heads and hope for wiser minds to prevail and put a stop to such practices. Although most teams stopped transferring games in 1889, the damage, in terms of lopsided competition, remained. Brooklyn and St. Louis battled for the pennant in 1889, but no other team finished within sixteen games of first place.

While the Association managed to patch one problem for 1889, as it turned out, its hull sprang many more leaks. So many, in fact, that 1889 proved the American Association's last year as an organization offering stable membership and major-league quality baseball.

---

[31] Joe Pritchard, "St. Louis Siftings," *The Sporting Life*, August 29, 1888, 7.

Chapter 13

The Beginning of the End of the American Association II

THE MOST ASTONISHING THING about the demise of the American Association is that so many of its wounds were self-inflicted. Unlike the National League, it had no Brotherhood to disturb its councils or complicate its decisions. The Association's leaders simply shot themselves in the foot again and again. For supposedly experienced businessmen, one wonders how they ever could have made money if they ran their main businesses the way they ran their baseball teams. Their behavior often demonstrates that baseball's owners had no business calling the intelligence of their players into question by lauding their own superiority.

Their personal greed was, unsurprisingly, their biggest stumbling block. Too often, baseball's owners behaved as if they were not a member of a league or association attempting to promote its mutual success; rather, they behaved as if their choices happened in a vacuum and did not affect any other team. This happened often enough in the National League, but by 1888 and 1889, American

Association owners took things to such extremes that they tore their league apart within three years. The Association made many mistakes in 1887 and 1888, as we saw in the preceding chapter. One of the most blatant of these poor decisions was when the Association allowed teams to transfer their home game to other venues, with the ruinous results that had for competition. In 1889, the AA compounded these mistakes with a host of others.

The worst thing to happen to the Association in the winter of 1888-1889 was Mordecai Davidson's purchase of Louisville from Zach Phelps near the end of the 1888 season. Davidson was very active in day-to-day operations, unfortunately for the Colonels. The result was that a team that had always been respectable became, over just one off-season, the first team in history to lose 100 games. They were so poor they also became the first team in history to lose *110* games, stumbling to a 27-111 record. True, Davidson had to depend on two players who were utterly undependable, Pete Browning and Tom Ramsey, but his constant, short-sighted, and poor personnel moves simply ran Louisville into the ground. This weakened the Association because when Louisville went an entire month (May 22 to June 22, 25 straight losses) without winning a single game, they simply could not draw spectators to Eclipse Park. This meant the Association ended the 1889 season with two of its best clubs leaving the circuit, Cincinnati and Brooklyn, and another in tenuous financial shape tottering on the verge of dissolution.

Davidson's knowledge of baseball was weak, and his story demonstrates the importance of finding qualified men to run an operation if that operation is going to succeed. The team Davidson bought had been respectable for most of the 1880s, although short of championship caliber. After six months of his management, however, one Falls City writer described the state of the team by proclaiming, "The Louisville nine now has few stars in it. There are only one or two men whom another club would desire to possess." The team's greatest weakness was its infield, especially defensively. In comparison to the Chicago White Stockings, with their stout "stone wall" infield, "our infield at the close of last season was denominated the 'rail fence' infield, and it certainly deserves the title."[1]

Davidson pretended that a team could win games without paying for quality players. As April of 1889 neared its end, he kept up the fiction that hard work and individual initiative could take the place of spending money to acquire talent, saying, "I have fifteen men under contract, and I am better satisfied with them every day. My plans are working out well in every respect, and while I shall make no brags, I want to repeat that we will make a showing that will astonish some people. I am running my team on business principles this season. The men are being worked harder than they ever were before, both in the games and at practice exercises."[2]

Perhaps it is too easy to put down Davidson when other owners did similarly unwise things, but he merits mention for doing unwise things consistently and for believing what he wanted to be true rather than what really was true. After the 1889 season opened, he continued to do silly things. Even before the first road trip was complete, Davidson decided to release his captain, Dude Esterbrook, for being unpopular: "Esterbrook has made some enemies among certain members of the club who are inclined to shirk, by requiring them to play ball and take all chances. These, in revenge have in divers ways incited the bleaching boards and some of the know-all dudes that occupy the grandstand to jeer and guy Esterbrook on every occasion that there was a possible chance." Not only did releasing Esterbrook call Davidson's judgment into question because he appointed the Dude captain in the first place, but in addition, he dismissed Esterbrook for demanding the team do the very things that Davidson had just said he wanted his team to do.[3]

---

[1] J. A., "Louisville Laconics," *The Sporting Life*, January 23, 1889, 5.
[2] R. W. L., "Davidson of Louisville," *The Sporting News*, April 20, 1889, 1.
[3] "A Rumor That Louisville Will Release Esterbrook," *The Sporting News*, April 27, 1889, 1.

Furthermore, when Davidson cut the Dude loose, he attempted to shift the blame for the team's poor start to Esterbrook as well, one writer stating, "The main cause, in fact, of Esterbrook's decapitation was the poor showing of the team." Given no resources and unable to pull a rabbit out of a hat, Esterbrook became the first fall guy for Davidson's ineptitude. Esterbrook may not have been the perfect captain; for one thing, he tended to scold his men on the field for their shortcomings. He kept up the same behavior when the London, Ontario, team tabbed him for their captaincy after his release from Louisville: "In the last games here with Detroit, Esterbrook gave such an exhibition of bad temper and tyranny on the field that the sympathies of the audience were turned to the visitors, and most of the spectators showed their aversion to Esterbrook's methods very plainly."[4] This begs the question, however, of why Davidson made him captain in the first place. Esterbrook first appeared in the major leagues all the way back in 1880, so it was not as if no one knew what his personality was like.[5]

The nightmare of Davidson's ownership was, mercifully, over before the midway point of 1889, but by then it was far too late to do anything that year. To finish the story of Davidson's follies, consider his choices in early May. Tiring of Phil Tomney's performance at shortstop, he released Tomney (then changed his mind and signed him back within a week) and moved right fielder Chicken Wolf to shortstop. Wolf, who often received negative press for his healthy paunch and lack of physical conditioning, made eight errors in ten games. Just to cite two references to Wolf's gastronomical prowess, in 1889 we read, "The Louisville team has a leader in at least one particular. Jimmie Wolf has the reputation of being the biggest eater in the profession."[6] Similarly, in 1887, teammates said of Wolf, "When the fat boy is hungry he will often

---

[4] "Esterbrook's Ebullitions," *The Sporting Life*, June 26, 1889, 6.
[5] "The Dude Dethroned," *The Sporting News*, May 4, 1889, 1.
[6] "Notes and Comments," *The Sporting Life*, September 11, 1889, 4.

enter a restaurant and eat as many as four chickens."[7] Wolf's transfer to shortstop meant that Red Ehret, a pitcher, ended up in the Louisville outfield where he made an error on every fourth ball hit to him. With Louisville's ship taking on water at an alarming rate, Davidson next announced his intention to sell his controlling interest, further threatening that if a buyer did not step forward within a few days he would disband the team, sell the players individually, and leave the American Association with just seven teams less than one month into the season.[8]

Davidson's putrid career in Louisville is an example of pure greed. He bought a controlling interest in the team in late 1888 and immediately sold two of his better players, infielder Hub Collins and pitcher Elton Chamberlain, for cash to realize a profit. Making no move to sign any player of value before the next season, Davidson pretended that hard work and rigid discipline would win games. The team just happened to perform respectably in preseason exhibitions, allowing Davidson to feign disappointment with his players once the championship season began and the team's lack of talent showed through. He then shifted the blame to the players rather than putting it squarely on his own shoulders where it belonged. In mid-May, Davidson then held an entire city hostage while demanding someone take his lousy team off his hands.

At least the American Association had countermeasures for such a contingency. If Davidson tried to disband the team, the Association's constitution stated that the league could step in and run the team jointly until a new purchaser appeared. Milwaukee might be ready to come aboard, should things go that far, with Worcester also in the field.[9] After a week, however, the story became even more surreal when Davidson declared the franchise off the market. When no one met his inflated price, he decided to keep

---

[7] X. X., "From the Falls City," *The Sporting Life*, September 7, 1887, 4.
[8] "Who Wants to Buy?" *The Sporting News*, May 11, 1889, 1.
[9] "Mr. Von der Ahe on Louisville," *The Sporting News*, May 11, 1889, 1; "The Milwaukee's Position," *The Sporting News*, May 11, 1889, 1.

possession himself. In a feeble attempt to keep up attendance and the waning enthusiasm in the Colonels, he said, "I might as well lose money one way as another so I will hold on for a while, at least. I will make a change or two that I think will put the club in pretty good shape."[10]

When that failed to help, in June Davidson revived the sordid practice of having Louisville transfer home games with the Red Stockings from Louisville to Cincinnati, transforming the Colonels into sacrificial lambs to mitigate his financial losses. Soon, he made similar arrangements with other ball clubs.[11] This led *The Sporting Life* to editorialize:

> It also means more than the death of the Louisville Club; in plain words, it threatens the integrity of the game. To permit clubs to change their scheduled dates at will and to move about from city to city in search of gate receipts, like tramps, is positively insulting to the city which the peregrinating club is supposed to represent, and absolutely unfair to the leading clubs in the race, as some of them must reap undue advantage from such transfers. In short, such transferring is nothing more or less than hippodroming, and the quicker the practice which was started last fall by Baltimore, and is already cropping out this year with the season so young, is stamped out the better for the game and the good repute of the Association.[12]

With the situation growing worse daily, one writer described the state of local enthusiasm by comparing 1889 to previous seasons, writing,

---

[10] "Louisville Not to be Sold," *The Sporting Life*, May 22, 1889, 1.
[11] "Notes and Comments," *The Sporting Life*, May 29, 1889, 4.
[12] "A Dangerous Innovation," *The Sporting Life*, June 12, 1889, 4.

Then when the club was away from home, crowds were around the bulletin boards to watch the score as it came in by innings, and if Louisville won there was a cheer of triumph, if she lost, everybody was blue; now nobody goes to any bulletin board. There isn't any bulletin board to go to. They were discontinued because nobody ever looked at the score. Even the saloons don't have them any longer.[13]

This was an ill omen for a league trying to withstand many such omens by 1889.

In addition to depriving Louisville audiences of the chance of even seeing their team play, Davidson also destroyed any semblance of cooperation with his players. Following Esterbrook's dismissal, Chicken Wolf became team captain but immediately began berating his men in much the same manner as Esterbrook. By mid-June, with the team mired in a catastrophic losing streak that now stood at twenty-three straight games, Davidson decided to begin fining his men for poor play. Failing to provide the team with quality players, he chose to mulct mediocre ones when they played down to their limited potential, hoping to get some of his money returned to him through this devious route: "Manager Davidson, enraged at the team's ill success, yesterday imposed a twenty-five-dollar fine on Second Baseman Shannon for fielding errors, and on Catcher Cook for stupid base running." The Louisville players, knowing it was only a matter of time before the rest of them saw the same treatment, revolted: "At this all the men protested by signing a round robin saying they would not play to-day unless this wrong was righted."[14]

Captain Wolf tried to talk Davidson out of this ill-considered course, but Davidson instead decided to leave Louisville and travel to New York. Before he left, however, he told his players that if the

---

[13] J. A., "Disgusted Louisville," *The Sporting Life*, June 12, 1889, 1.
[14] "Ball Players on Strike," *New York Times*, June 15, 1889, 3; T. T. T., "The Louisville Strike," *The Sporting Life*, June 19, 1889, 1.

team did not play as scheduled, "He would fine every man $100, and that in case they did play and lost he would impose $25 on each man." After considering the best way to make their point, six Colonels decided to lay down their tools and strike while the other six took the field against Baltimore, along with three local semi-professional players to fill out their lineup. They played just one inning, however, before a heavy rain fell and the umpire called the game.[15]

The same six men, Chicken Wolf, Farmer Weaver, Scott Stratton, Bill Gleason, Farmer Vaughn, and Tom Ramsey, attempted to play with the help of the semi-pros against the Orioles in a doubleheader (to make up the rainout) the next day. The rest of the team, Guy Hecker, Dan Shannon, Pete Browning, Harry Raymond, Paul Cook, and Red Ehret, stayed firm in their purpose to play no more games until Davidson remitted the fines, which he absolutely refused to do.[16] A resolution came only when both parties agreed to state their case to the directors of the American Association and abide by whatever decision that body made. In the meantime, "A kind of truce was patched up between the players and their erratic manager, and the men did the best they could to win under the disheartening circumstances of an uncertain future and the dead weight of the management."[17]

Those players who sat out the first game of the Baltimore series got their pay returned to them, but those who boycotted the second game in disregard of instructions from Association President Wheeler Wikoff saw their additional $100 fines from that game upheld.[18] Davidson finally ended the nightmare by selling his controlling interest to a collection of Louisville capitalists in early July. By then, of course, the team had few quality players and no

---

[15] "Ball Players on Strike," *New York Times*, June 15, 1889, 3; T. T. T., "The Louisville Strike," *The Sporting Life*, June 19, 1889, 1.
[16] T. T. T., "The Strikers Firm," *The Sporting Life*, June 19, 1889, 1.
[17] T. T. T., "Baltimore Bulletin," *The Sporting Life*, June 26, 1889, 6.
[18] "General Base-Ball News," *Chicago Daily Tribune*, July 6, 1889, 3.

shot at anything better than eighth place in 1889, but at least Louisville's supporters could look to the future and envision better days.

Once Davidson was out of the picture and they were no longer at risk of further fines, Louisville's players unburdened themselves to the press about how tyrannically their former owner had treated them. Second baseman Dan Shannon said Davidson fined him an entire month's pay in May, and when he asked how he was going to pay for food, Davidson replied that was not his concern. In a similar vein, pitcher John Ewing was going to accompany the team on a road trip, but Davidson instructed him to stay in Louisville because he felt the team did not need Ewing and wanted to save on travel expenses. Ewing did so, only to find that Davidson lied to the press, claiming Ewing had an injury. Davidson then changed Ewing's status to a suspension without pay and did not intend to pay him for any of the twenty days the team spent on the road.

Davidson hit his captain, Chicken Wolf, with a $25 fine just for trying to get Pete Browning to play harder. When Wolf told Browning, "I'll smash your face if you don't brace up and play ball," it cost him the fine. Not that Browning escaped censure, either. He said, regarding his own fines, "He has fined me $335 and I find that after playing for the club for two months I am indebted to it $225. At this rate I will soon owe the Louisville Club more money than I can pay back in a lifetime." When shortstop Phil Tomney made a throw that first baseman Guy Hecker dropped, Davidson demanded $25 from Hecker. Thinking he was on decent terms with the owner considering his quality play of late, Tomney tried to take responsibility by claiming it was his fault for a poor throw, and then Davidson soaked him the same amount. Hecker's salary for the month of May, after deductions for fines, amounted to two dollars. In all, only three players on the team escaped fines during June.[19] Louisville's loss of team morale and poor performance on the field,

---

[19] "Very Funny Stories," *The Sporting News*, June 29, 1889, 1.

without question, reflected this disastrous policy emanating from Davidson.

That was not all. By this time, some players, such as Browning, had seen no pay at all for three consecutive paydays (players received their pay twice per month). When the team set out on one of its road trips, one player related, "We had no money on all the trip, and Manager McKinney had received orders from Mr. Davidson to not even give us money with which to have our uniforms washed. Nearly all of the players were compelled to borrow money from the Kansas City and St. Louis players, and several of the boys had to pawn their jewelry to pay their laundry bills."[20]

The new manager this player described, Buck McKinney, was a curious hire to say the least. His main qualification appears to have been his muscular stature. He reportedly stood six-foot, weighed 225 pounds, and was "a great big double-fisted fellow" who had spent the past twenty-five years as a "doorkeeper" (read: bouncer) at Louisville theaters and at Eclipse Park. He was, undoubtedly, a great fan of baseball and apparently was on good terms with the players, but given his utter lack of baseball experience, one writer charitably described the situation by stating, "but whether or not he will be a good base ball manager, of course, no one can venture a safe prediction."[21] The reason for his hire, ultimately, was to protect Davidson from his own players: "The players hold the bitterest feelings against him, and he is constantly apprehending bodily harm from them. This is the reason he didn't accompany the team on its last trip. He had to look around for some time before he could induce any one to go in charge of the men."[22]

While Davidson's behavior was reprehensible when it came to assessing fines for poor play, other Association teams did so as well,

---

[20] J. A., "Davidson Out," *The Sporting Life*, July 10, 1889, 3.
[21] J. A., "The Louisville Muddle," *The Sporting Life*, July 3, 1889, 3.
[22] J. A., "Davidson Out," *The Sporting Life*, July 10, 1889, 3.

with the expected results for team morale. St. Louis president Von der Ahe fined players whenever his Browns hit the skids for more than a game or two. The Association's newest member in 1889, Columbus, also took up this sordid practice with relish. It released one of its players, catcher Jimmie Peoples, on July 26, and at the same time announced its intention to light a fire under the remaining players with threats: "This is supposed to mean that those who continue to play poor ball will be suspended without pay."[23]

As usual, the main cause of the poor play was drinking. The club hired a detective to watch over its players, and in August this detective reported, "that the first night had resulted in finding several of the men were filling up on beer, and one, especially, was reported as having drunk twenty-four glasses of the foaming amber. Upon being brought up to a strict account he ... confessed to having surrounded twelve glasses of beer, but held up his hands in holy horror at the balance of the two dozen."[24] Regardless of the cause, when it came time for the players to receive their pay, "Columbus offers big salaries, but on pay days the men find a shortage, which amounts have been deducted in the shape of fines."[25]

As if these various examples of poor management were not enough on their own, fate, volcanic personalities, and pretensions to public morality also damaged the American Association in 1889. The most prominent example of how public morality hurt the Association's cause was when the Cincinnati, one of the Association's most profitable clubs, had to face a new Ohio law preventing baseball on Sunday. Team owner Aaron Stern tried many strategies to evade the law, but all proved unsuccessful. This severed the main tie holding Cincinnati in the Association. Stern believed in playing Sunday baseball because large numbers of working-class Porkopolitans attended on the Sabbath, being unable to make it any

---

[23] "Jimmie Peoples Released," *The Sporting News*, July 27, 1889, 1.
[24] F. W. Arnold, "Columbus Chatter," *The Sporting Life*, August 7, 1889, 5.
[25] "Salaries in Columbus," *The Sporting News*, August 24, 1889, 1.

other day of the week because they had to work. This helped the Red Stockings profit even though, with a minimum ticket price of twenty-five cents, they received less money per patron than they would in the National League.[26]

If Ohio insisted on banning Sunday games, however, odds were that Stern would try to transfer Cincinnati's allegiance to the National League where the Red Stockings could increase their take from selling tickets. The temptation proved too great to resist.[27] Immediately after he received the final verdict regarding Sunday baseball, reporters asked Stern what he planned to do. He replied revealingly, "I can not say as yet. We have as yet received no word from the league. If they offer us a place, and we think we can better ourselves, we will jump."[28] O. P. Caylor, ruminating on the same question, was blunter. Regarding it as a near certainty, he wrote, "Will the Cincinnati Club go into the League? Will Pete Browning take a drink if you ask him?"[29]

Things in the Association grew tenser in September due to the conflicting personalities of Charles Byrne in Brooklyn and Chris Von der Ahe in St. Louis. With their teams locked in mortal combat for the Association pennant, things took a surreal twist when, feeling wronged in the first game of a scheduled three-game series in Brooklyn, Von der Ahe became so enraged he ordered his nine not to take the field for the remaining two games. He accused Byrne of, first, trying to bribe umpire John Kerins with both cash and a chance to earn more money umpiring in the World Series; second, of controlling all the umpires of the Association; and third, of trying to control the Association itself. These accusations constitute just part

---

[26] "No Sunday Games in Cincinnati," *The Sporting News*, August 17, 1889, 1.
[27] Ibid.
[28] "Cincinnati and the League," *The Sporting News*, August 17, 1889, 1.
[29] O. P. Caylor, "Caylor's Comment," *The Sporting Life*, August 21, 1889, 3. For more on Pete Browning's career-long battle with alcohol, see chapters one and two of Rob Bauer, *Outside the Lines of Gilded Age Baseball: Alcohol, Fitness, and Cheating in 1880s Baseball*.

of Von der Ahe's rant. His refusal to play meant that the Browns would forfeit two critical games in the heat of a fierce pennant race and face a $3,000 fine besides just to appease the anger of their mercurial and borderline unstable owner. Furthermore, St. Louis would not receive any money from gate receipts at other games on its road trip until it paid up.[30]

The circumstances of the controversial first game demonstrate much of what was wrong with baseball on the field in this era. Brooklyn led the game at Washington Park, 2-0, in the early innings. The Browns initiated stalling tactics, hoping to stall so long that darkness might cancel the game and save them from defeat if it became too dark to play before finishing five innings. The Browns, fully aware of umpire Fred Goldsmith's indecisive tendencies, frequently stopped play for several minutes at a time, doing things as extreme as calling in the left fielder for a conference at first base. However, when the Browns took the lead in the middle innings, then they stalled even worse, but for the opposite reason. Now, they hoped to delay the game so long that it would be impossible to play nine innings, looking for a darkness-assisted victory. They employed all the same tactics, repeating them after almost every pitch.[31]

By the seventh inning, with a 4-2 lead, the Browns demanded the game cease due to darkness. They purchased candles, arraying them about their bench and on the field, and then lighting them to emphasize the point. In the process, a fire almost started in the grandstand when disgusted spectators began hurling paper debris at the St. Louis bench, and finally, when Goldsmith still refused to call the game in the ninth inning when one Brooklyn player reached base, team captain Charlie Comiskey simply ordered his men off the field. On their way off the diamond, one Brown, Tommy McCarthy,

---

[30] J. F. Donnolly, "The Row of the Season," *The Sporting Life*, September 18, 1889, 5.
[31] Ibid.

tussled with a spectator, starting a fight numerous law enforcement officers blamed on McCarthy. This minor spat became Von der Ahe's stated reason for declining to play the next day as he feigned concern for his players' safety. In the meantime, Umpire Goldsmith had not declared the game over. Therefore, he awarded Brooklyn the game by forfeit.[32]

Writers outside of St. Louis lost no time upbraiding the Browns for their childish tantrums. Ren Mulford, Jr., described their boycott by writing, "The minority who wished St. Louis luck because they were partisan enough to want the pennant to remain in the West have sunk that desire in the later hope of seeing St. Louis' blindness, its foolhardiness, its asininity, its criminal disregard for existing regulations, rebuked as they deserve."[33] Even those of a more charitable mind still believed that the Association must "curb Mr. Von der Ahe's tendency to make wild and unjustifiable charges against managers, umpires and players."[34] Gentlemanly Henry Chadwick, who only rarely had a harsh word for contemporaries, wrote, "Evidently the Heathen deities have got hold of Chris Von der Ahe, and have him on the slate for destruction."[35]

By the time everyone involved finished appealing everything, the Association awarded St. Louis victory in the first game, upheld the forfeit to Brooklyn of the second, and fired Umpire Goldsmith for not showing more resolve and better judgment. The Association replaced Goldsmith with Guy Hecker, only recently released from the purgatory of playing ball in Louisville. It also voided the fine St. Louis earned by its refusal to finish on Saturday, although the fine for declining to play on Sunday stood.[36] Byrne was apoplectic at the

---

[32] Ibid.
[33] Ren Mulford, Jr., "Cincinnati Chips," *The Sporting Life*, September 18, 1889, 2.
[34] W. I. Harris, "New York News," *The Sporting Life*, September 18, 1889, 2.
[35] Henry Chadwick, "Chadwick's Chat," *The Sporting Life*, September 18, 1889, 3.
[36] "The St. Louis-Brooklyn Dispute," *Chicago Daily Inter Ocean*, September 24, 1889, 2.

decision to overrule Goldsmith's authority: "Had the cases been considered on the weight of the evidence, we would have found no fault, but the whole thing was cut and dried, and it would have made no difference if we had had ten times as strong a case. The result would have been the same."[37]

The National Agreement stated that the umpire had sole discretion over whether conditions permitted play to continue. The fact that the Association did not sustain Goldsmith in his judgment, however poor that judgment might have been, was a breach of the rules by which all teams played. *The Sporting Life* easily saw through the charade, declaring, "It became a question of petty base ball politics and resulted in a weak and contemptible compromise, which reflects nothing but discredit upon the men who had a chance to show that laws are made to be respected and upheld, not violated with impunity." The paper also placed some blame before the vacillating president of the Association, Wheeler Wikoff, stating, "It was painfully apparent throughout the proceedings that the Association needs a competent head. A competent man in the chair would have doubtless brought the members of the Board to a realizing sense of their responsibilities."[38] Likewise, grizzled Henry Chadwick wrote that if the Association's owners "had intended to give a severe blow to the future welfare of the Association and the national game, they could not have succeeded better than they have done in the decision they have rendered in the case of the disputed game at Washington Park between the St. Louis and Brooklyn clubs."[39]

---

[37] "President Byrne Much Aggrieved," *Chicago Daily Tribune*, September 27, 1889, 6.
[38] "The Association," *The Sporting Life*, October 2, 1889, 2.
[39] Henry Chadwick, "Chadwick's Chat," *The Sporting Life*, October 2, 1889, 6. Chadwick, a longtime resident of Brooklyn and a frequent attendee of Brooklyn's games, often commented upon things concerning the Bridegrooms, although he was free to write upon any subject he chose.

The Brooklyn-St. Louis rivalry did not end there. As fate would have it, they fought to the season's final week for the pennant. On the last day of the season, October 14, Brooklyn's record stood at 93-44, St. Louis's at 89-44, making Brooklyn the clear winner. Not ready to concede after such a bitter campaign, however, St. Louis engaged in a series of dubious maneuvers. Even though the season was over, St. Louis arranged to play games cancelled by rain earlier in the season with both Cincinnati and Philadelphia in hopes of winning all the games, raising its winning percentage (baseball awarded pennants based on winning percentage, rather than number of wins) and thus stealing the pennant away from Brooklyn by playing extra games. The Browns made plans to make up five games in this fashion—just enough that they would edge out Brooklyn if they won all five. To tempt the Red Stockings and Athletics into such perfidy, Chris Von der Ahe offered them all the gate receipts from the bonus games rather than taking the customary share paid to the visitors. With this extra boodle dangled as bait, both franchises accepted.[40]

This was clearly outside the rules, but the rules did not always matter in the American Association. Therefore, on October 15, the Red Stockings and Browns played a doubleheader. Hoping to thwart St. Louis's attempt at sabotage, Brooklyn took measures that, while not exactly illegal, were shady, although less shady than what St. Louis was trying to do. Prior to the first game in the Queen City, Brooklyn catcher Doc Bushong arrived at the grounds. As soon as he learned that the Red Stockings planned to use pitcher Jesse Duryea and catcher Jim Keenan as their battery, Bushong offered both men a $100 bonus, courtesy if his owner, if they would be so kind as to defeat St. Louis that day. They did, and the men got their money while St. Louis screamed theft and bribery. The rest of the Cincinnati nine received fur overcoats and cigars courtesy of the

---

[40] Henry Chadwick, "Chadwick's Chat," *The Sporting Life*, October 23, 1889, 3.

good doctor and Charles Byrne.[41] (We should note that the same thing happened in the National League's 1889 pennant race. Boston manager Jim Hart and pitcher John Clarkson offered the round sum of $1,000 to Cleveland if they beat the New York Giants in the season's final series [they did not] while New York's manager, Jim Mutrie, offered undisclosed presents to Pittsburgh's players if they did the same to Boston. The Alleghenys did defeat Boston once.[42])

The Browns also accused the Association's umpiring staff of being on Brooklyn's payroll, pointing out that they had both out-hit and out-pitched Brooklyn all year. Furthermore, the Browns raised suspicions that a few members of the Columbus Solons might have received some boodle of their own for losing to Brooklyn on October 14, citing four errors by Solon third baseman Lefty Marr to make their case. Last, because Bushong was an old teammate who still had several friends in the Mound City, the Browns claimed he had treated their second baseman, Yank Robinson, to drinks all night to be sure that Robinson arrived at the grounds hung over and unable to play his best ball.[43] Robinson failed to get a hit in either game, although he did draw some walks.

This series of incidents between Brooklyn and St. Louis had serious blowback for the entire Association. While it would be absurd to say these controversies alone prompted Brooklyn to leave the Association for the National League for 1890, it certainly did not give Brooklyn cause for greater loyalty to the Association. As one Brooklynite declared, after the Association failed to uphold Umpire Goldsmith, "I have to add that this rank act of imposition has put a keen edge on the desire for jumping out of the American Association and given a new zest to the discussion of the possibility of Brooklyn

---

[41] "Bushong Distributing Boodle," *The Sporting News*, October 19, 1889, 3; "Silent Influence," *The Sporting Life*, October 23, 1889, 1.
[42] W. I. Harris, "New York News," *The Sporting Life*, October 23, 1889, 4.
[43] "Wolves!" *The Sporting News*, October 19, 1889, 3.

entering the League."⁴⁴ Even if Brooklyn had gotten everything its way in the controversy, the prospects of dealing with such an unstable personality as Von der Ahe, after everything that happened in the waning days of 1889, cannot have appealed to the Bridegrooms or their cranks. When piled atop all the other things discussed in the last chapter and in this one, the evidence presents many reasons why Brooklyn desired a change of scenery.

Following the end of the 1889 season, it did not take long for the Association to fall apart, albeit temporarily. When the Brotherhood announced its independence from the National League in early November and the League debated how to respond at its meeting a week later, the American Association held its conference in New York at the same time. One thing the National League *had* decided on was that this was its opportunity to snare Brooklyn and Cincinnati. While the Association haggled over replacing its president, Wheeler Wikoff, a League spy informed the National League delegates of the proceedings and those delegates lost no time in offering spots to the discontented owners of Cincinnati and Brooklyn. Further motivated by the actual (Cincinnati) or impending (Brooklyn) loss of Sunday baseball in both cities and the fact that they had already signed some key players and were in a strong position to compete in the National League in 1890, both Aaron Stern and Charles Byrne accepted the offer. The next day Kansas City defected back to the Western League, and before November was over, Baltimore threw in the towel as well and joined the Atlantic Association.⁴⁵

Even though the American Association still had two more years of life remaining, this was the end of that body as a major league-

---

⁴⁴ J. F. Donnolly, "Brooklyn Boiling Over," *The Sporting Life*, October 2, 1889, 3.
⁴⁵ Nemec, *The Beer and Whiskey League*, 186-187. The calculations of Brooklyn and Cincinnati that they could compete in the weakened National League proved correct; Brooklyn won the pennant with an 86-43 record while Cincinnati posted a quite respectable 77-55 mark.

caliber organization. With the situation rapidly deteriorating, on December 6 the Association was desperate enough to send out feelers regarding a merger with the Brotherhood. With the BPBP fully confident of ultimate success, it declined.[46] Meeting with failure on that front, the Association instead replaced the departed teams with Syracuse, Toledo, Rochester, and a new Brooklyn team. This new Brooklyn aggregation did not even complete the season, folding on August 26, and Baltimore jumped back from the Atlantic Association to replace it for the last thirty-four games on the schedule. In place of Brooklyn, Baltimore, Cincinnati, and Kansas City, cities ranking fourth, seventh, ninth, and twenty-fourth in population in the 1890 census, the Association ended up with Rochester (twenty-second), Syracuse (thirty-first), Toledo (thirty-fourth) and the Brooklyn-Baltimore hybrid.[47]

Of course, it did not help matters when the Brotherhood began taking Association players into its ranks before the 1890 season. With drastically reduced markets and drastically reduced talent, the American Association was in poor condition even before 1890 began. How drastic was its decline? Louisville, which posted a 27-111 record and finished a titanic 66.5 games back of first place in 1889, vaulted to an 88-44 record in 1890, fully ten games better than any other team in the Association. This increase in winning percentage, from .196 to .667, has no equal as a one-season turnaround in major league baseball history for a team playing a schedule of modern length.

It is important to stress, however, that the decline of the American Association was not primarily due to the Players League. The coincidence of the timing makes this conclusion a very tempting one, and the Brotherhood had something to do with the loss of the Association's prestige when the BPBP lured away some of its players. However, so much evidence exists here predating these

---

[46] Alexander, *Turbulent Seasons*, 17.
[47] Nemec, *The Beer and Whiskey League*, 188, 197.

events that it would be simplistic at best and inaccurate at worst to say the creation and failure of the Players League caused the failure of the American Association. The Brotherhood had nothing to do with the three key reasons why Brooklyn and Cincinnati left the Association after the 1889 season, followed by the defection of Baltimore and Kansas City. The end or probable end of Sunday baseball in Brooklyn and Cincinnati, the desire of the National League to replace weak franchises in Indianapolis and Washington with two stronger ones, and the erratic behavior of Chris Von der Ahe and his conflict with Charles Byrne each would have happened even had the Brotherhood never existed. The same holds true of Mordecai Davidson's decision to dismantle the Louisville team.

These events demonstrate that even though the American Association continued play until 1891, by the end of 1889, it was in rapid decline with little hope of rejuvenation. The foibles described in this chapter are the greatest reasons why. There were still maneuvers to come, and tactics employed to keep the Association going, but one did not need a crystal ball to figure out what probably lay in store by the end of the 1889 season.

Chapter 14

The Storm Gathers

WHEN JOHN WARD ANNOUNCED HIS DECISION to leave the Spalding Tour early, it was a sign that trouble lay ahead for the National League. While Ward's ship plowed the waves of the Atlantic, the baseball press speculated on what would happen when he reached New York. The Brotherhood's Secretary-Treasurer, Tim Keefe, issued a call for a meeting of the Brotherhood's officers and team representatives upon Ward's arrival, although given that the organization had a meeting scheduled for the spring anyway, little difference existed between a special meeting and the regular one. The question was what course the organization would take. Most of its men had signed contracts for 1889. A few had not. As March neared its end, the BPBP lacked time to raise grievances or to try to negotiate. The more ominous question was whether the Brotherhood might consider more drastic measures, perhaps even a strike.

Some papers feared the worst. The *Chicago Daily Tribune* offered, "Tim Keefe has sent out a call for a meeting of that organization to be held in New York next Tuesday. There is little doubt but this means a fight, and it looks as if the players would have all the best of it if they stick for a short time. The classification clause in the contract looks weaker as its defects are coming to light."[1] New York's George Stackhouse wrote, "That the Brotherhood players, as a body, are decidedly opposed to the classification rule recently passed by the club owners of the League, is assured." Stackhouse quoted Tim Keefe on the Brotherhood's current stance:

> I have read with considerable amusement about how all the troubles between players and managers had been settled. But that don't make it so by long odds. Only a few have reached an amicable settlement. Some of the misunderstandings have been heard little of, for the men have been reserved and have not stated their troubles through the newspapers. I am not at liberty to say just what will be done, although all that the players will ask will be simply justice.

Another, unnamed, League player told Stackhouse,

> I think that there will be some lively times in base ball before the season opens a few weeks from now. I don't think the Brotherhood will countenance that classification clause for several reasons. First, if it was an absolute necessity for the welfare of base ball that players should be classified and salaries reduced, the men would take their medicine calmly, and quietly submit. But there is no such necessity. That rule as originally drawn up and since enforced is a fraud, and it will not stand. It was made to protect one or two clubs, and the rule will only be enforced in one or two clubs. Why should the players of the New York, Boston and Chicago clubs have their salaries tampered with, simply because the

---

[1] T. H. Murnane, "Ball News from Boston," *Chicago Daily Tribune*, March 24, 1889, 6.

Indianapolis, Cleveland and Washington clubs may live. . . . When the Brotherhood had its hearing before the League, the League promised to make certain concessions. Those promises have not been kept.[2]

In the meantime, however, rumors flew. With Ward now back to head the Brotherhood's affairs, the organization could coordinate what information it wanted revealed and when to reveal it, and so prior to the meeting, the sporting press could only offer guesses. Ward and his Brothers played things close to the vest, and as a result, "just what will be done at this meeting can only be conjectured, as the members of the order are unusually secretive about their intentions."[3]

The Brotherhood embraced Ward the moment he stepped off the gangplank in New York Harbor, some even waiting there overnight just to meet him as quickly as they could. Reporters flocked to interview the BPBP's president to get the latest baseball scoop, so much so that the world-renowned pianist who was also aboard the steamer *Saale*, Hans von Bülow, all but escaped notice. He remarked, "What is the use of playing the piano in this country? I am too old to play ball, therefore I am nobody. I do not understand the game at all, but it must be something splendid, and I cannot complain if no one comes to my concerts."[4]

It took Ward some time to meet with other Brotherhood leaders and form a strategy. In fact, he moved so deliberately that some papers prophesied the early demise of the BPBP. While such a development certainly would have pleased National League owners, it was not to be. After some discussion with fellow New Yorkers, Ward next moved to Boston. Former Detroit Brotherhood representative Dan Brouthers now played there, in addition to all the

---

[2] George Stackhouse, "New York News," *The Sporting Life*, March 27, 1889, 3.
[3] Gotham, "John Ward's Nerve," *The Sporting News*, March 30, 1889, 1.
[4] Henry Chadwick, "Chadwick's Chat," *The Sporting Life*, April 3, 1889, 3.

Boston men already members of the Brotherhood, and they held discussions at the Park Avenue Hotel where "subjects of much importance were discussed." The one important decision they arrived at during this meeting was the idea of trying to negotiate with baseball's magnates during the upcoming season, rather than waiting until the winter of 1889-1890.[5]

If true, the Brotherhood's official May 19 meeting would be one of great significance. Despite the efforts of Ward and others to keep things quiet, rumors began to seep out that the BPBP might challenge the League on certain issues. Besides the Brush Plan, another issue rankling with some Brothers was the fate of the four Chicago players, Mark Baldwin, Tom Daly, Bob Pettit, and Marty Sullivan, who traveled around the world on the Spalding Tour only to receive their releases from Spalding when the tourists reached Chicago. Some members felt that if Spalding planned to release these men, he should have done so immediately upon reaching the U.S. so that the quartet would have had a better opportunity to catch on with another club. They also objected that Spalding continued to use these players in exhibition games in the U.S. in April, thus making money from their services, while all the time planning to dispense with them.[6] (Baldwin, by a stroke of luck, did well in this transaction, although his companions were not so fortunate. At Spalding's request, all other National League teams refused to sign Baldwin, so he escaped the clutches of the Brush Plan and signed in the American Association with the Columbus Solons for $3,500.[7])

Spalding put little stock in any of the rumors. He said, referring to the BPBP, "I should say that a battle with the League would be the last thing it would undertake." Regarding any challenge to the Brush Plan, he stated, "I do not think any members of the brotherhood possessed of influence enough to embroil that

---

[5] "Ball-Tossers in Conference," *New York Evening World*, April 26, 1889, 1.
[6] "Rumors of Trouble in the League," *Chicago Daily Tribune*, May 7, 1889, 3.
[7] "Columbus Gets Pitcher Baldwin," *The Sporting Life*, May 8, 1889, 1.

The Storm Gathers

organization in a difficulty with the league have suffered from it in the least." Furthermore, "In truth, the same dire rumor has been circulated before, but you see that both the league and the brotherhood continue to do business at the old stands." When his interviewer asked what the League might do if worst came to worst and the Brotherhood challenged the League with teams of its own, Spalding said, "That is the sheerest nonsense."[8]

The reason the BPBP wanted to make its requests during the 1889 season rather than waiting until afterward was no mystery. Any threat of action it might make, including a possible strike, was only effective in the summer. Such threats had no force behind them once the season was over. In addition, the playing season was the only time when each chapter of the Brotherhood could meet as a group. Once the season ended and players dispersed to their homes, it was exponentially more difficult to contact members, conduct business, and make decisions. Therefore, not caring to forfeit its bargaining power, the Brotherhood met in mid-May.

When the big day in New York came around, the initial news was less than earth-shattering. The group, represented by John Ward and Tim Keefe of New York, Dan Brouthers for Boston, Ned Hanlon for Pittsburgh, John Healy of Washington, George Myers of Indianapolis, Fred Pfeffer of Chicago, Ben Sanders of Philadelphia, and Larry Twitchell of Cleveland, nominated new officers. Many other Brotherhood members attended as well and discovered that the organization's treasury was in fine condition. They also learned that almost every player in the National League was a member because all players from the NL's newest team, Cleveland, applied for and received membership, and ten new players from Chicago did the same. The only immediate action the BPBP planned was to contest Indianapolis's act of fining Henry Boyle $100 late in the 1888 season. Boyle became very ill, and although the team refused to pay

---

[8] "Rumors of Trouble in the League," *Chicago Daily Tribune*, May 7, 1889, 3.

him during his illness, which was within its rights, it also fined him for getting sick, which was not.[9]

When it came to the big question, what to do regarding the Brush Classification Plan, the organization went on record as being against it, of course, but did not announce what else it planned to do. The Brothers ruled out any possibility of an immediate strike, deciding to try negotiating first.[10] The outline of their plan was that no player should sign a League contract before the League's next meeting, at which time the BPBP would present its grievances.[11]

Given such a moderate stance, the meeting produced little immediate drama. Even most League owners did not seem perturbed. The next day, New York Giants owner John Day gave an interview. Day, a relative supporter of player rights, saw no reason for alarm. He said, "All this talk of a strike is nonsense. . . . The Brotherhood is strong—strong enough not to fear the League, and the League does not fear the Brotherhood. If there is any cause for dissatisfaction among the players as against the League, the two bodies, having a common interest, certainly will meet and by discussion come to an agreement." Asked about the justice of the players' cause, Day said, "If the players demand what is unreasonable the public will not support them, and if the League refuses to grant a just request, the players will have all the backing they can want."[12]

Day then continued with some interesting statements concerning the current state of things. After reviewing how each side had resolved their differences in the past, he claimed, "This time the causes which are to lead to the alleged coming strike, seem to be the Salary Limit law [of 1886], the classification system and the sale of

---

[9] "The Base-Ball Brotherhood," *Chicago Daily Tribune*, May 20, 1889, 3; "Ball Players in Session," *New York Times*, May 20, 1889, 8.
[10] "The Baseball Brotherhood," *Los Angeles Daily Herald*, May 20, 1889, 4; "Baseball Brotherhood," *Pittsburgh Dispatch*, May 20, 1889, 6.
[11] "The Players," *The Sporting Life*, May 29, 1889, 1.
[12] "A Baseball Strike?" *New York Evening World*, May 21, 1889, 1.

players by one club to another." He added, "I, for one, am utterly opposed to all three. The first two laws are dead letters, and of no value whatever to any one." Regarding the 1886 salary limit, "The salary limit law was made for the benefit of the Louisville Club, and the wrecked condition of that organization shows of what little benefit the law has been." Furthermore, "The classification law was a wrong in the beginning, has been of no use whatever, and is now to all purposes dead. It has injured no one that I am aware of, but it has certainly benefited none." He then stated his opposition to selling players, noting the only time he had ever done so was when requested to by a player: "This sale of players is, I think, the thing which the Brotherhood will ask to have rectified, and I think the request would be a just one and would receive the support of all fair-minded people." (Day later corrected one part of this statement, clarifying that he called the classification plan a "dead rabbit," meaning a bad rule, rather than a "dead letter," meaning that others were not following the rule.)[13]

Other League magnates spoke soon after Day. In Philadelphia, Al Reach believed, "Whatever differences there may be between the players and the proprietors, will be amicably adjusted. The players who have grievances will be granted a respectful hearing and full justice done them. Both sides have a common interest." He stated optimistically, but also naively, "The number of dissatisfied players is exceedingly small and their grievance is more imaginary than real." Still, he believed the classification plan a good thing and pledged his franchise to stand by it, come what may.[14]

Arthur Soden in Boston felt about the same. Regarding perceived grievances, he stated, "I should favor giving them a hearing and think matters could be arranged satisfactorily. But as for anticipating that they would demand an abolishment of the classification or would think of striking, why, I think that is absurd."

---

[13] Ibid.; "League Views," *The Sporting Life*, May 29, 1889, 1.
[14] "League Views," *The Sporting Life*, May 29, 1889, 1.

Like Reach, Soden favored the classification scheme, citing his belief that only a few League teams appeared likely to make any money in 1889. The rest of the League's owners voiced similar thoughts. Pittsburgh, Cleveland, and Washington announced they considered the plan the only measure that would allow them to continue, while of course Indianapolis, primary author of the plan, remained in favor.[15]

While many downplayed the possibilities of what might happen, a few writers seem to have had their fingers on the pulse of the situation. One New Yorker, who possibly had some inside information considering that so many prominent Brotherhood members played in his city, stated, "What the players will demand will be an agreement on the part of the clubs to divide with the player the money received for his release and the abolition of the classification rule." Although he too believed that "all talk about a strike during the present base ball season is idle gossip," the writer's next statement hit the mark squarely: "The alternative the League will have to face will be the desertion of the entire Brotherhood, the formation of a new league, and the liveliest competition. The magnates will, of course, laugh heartily at this programme, but their hilarity will not last after an investigation of the means at the command of the players."[16]

Ward and the Brotherhood took a few measures to test the waters over the summer. In early June, Ward, Ned Hanlon, and Dan Brouthers sent a letter to Nick Young stating their grievances, most prominently the classification plan and the practice of selling players.[17] About a week later, John Ward gave an interview debunking some of the reasons given in support of the Brush Plan. He again pointed out that it was a breach of contract: "Of those classified the great majority have been held at a figure less than that

---

[15] Ibid.
[16] W. I. Harris, "New York News," *The Sporting Life*, May 22, 1889, 4.
[17] "League Vs. Players," *The Sporting Life*, June 5, 1889, 1.

The Storm Gathers

received last season, and the fact that two or three have been given an advance is a blind too transparent to deceive anyone as to the true character of the steal." To arguments that the smaller cities of the League, Washington and Indianapolis, needed the classification plan to compete, Ward responded, "If Indianapolis and Washington cannot afford the rate of salaries their associate clubs pay, then they are not entitled to the same class of ball. They are in too fast company, and they ought to get out." He illustrated further by stating, "Indianapolis has about as much right in the National League as Oshkosh. Yet if the League admitted the latter city, would it be fair to ask Denny, Myers, Boyle, Glasscock, etc., to play there at figures which would allow Oshkosh to clear expenses?"[18]

Ward believed that the real problem was not lack of profits but poor distribution of profits. If teams decided to group themselves together into a league and play games for profit, they should divide their revenue between themselves rather than some taking more just because they played in larger cities. In other words, if the National League really was an association or league of clubs, it should act like one, rather than acting like eight disaggregated individuals:

> It is a fact that cannot be gainsaid that taking all the clubs together there is a great deal of money made each year from base ball. The Boston, New York and Chicago clubs pay immense dividends. The low-salaried Philadelphia Club, notwithstanding the wails of its owners, pays largely. Pittsburg makes something, and Detroit, which was said to have lost last season, is now settling up its affairs and publicly chuckling over the division of $54,000 profit derived from somewhere. Now, if the National League wishes to carry several weak cities along, why did it not devise some scheme by which the deficiencies in those clubs

---

[18] "Ward 'Agin' It," *The Sporting Life*, June 12, 1889, 1.

would be made up out of this enormous profit, instead of taking it out of the pockets of the players in those clubs?[19]

The Sporting Life reinforced Ward's point in the article following his front-page interview. It provided a table showing that eighteen Boston home games saw 97,111 fans in attendance, while almost that many cranks, 90,532, had shown up for just twelve games in Brooklyn through early June, despite the uncertain weather of spring in those locales. The five clubs that had played in Boston "have taken away from Boston $12,000 in cold cash, and the triumvirs' net receipts for admission and grand stand have already reached $50,000. The three directors are sure to divide between them over $100,000 as the profit of the season."[20]

In response to Ward's letter, Nick Young disseminated the missive to other League owners, and they agreed to appoint a committee to study the matter. The membership of this committee was very important. John Day of New York, John Rogers of Philadelphia, and, of course, Al Spalding of Chicago composed the group. Of the three, Day appeared most favorably disposed toward compromise, Rogers least so, with Spalding in the middle. Spalding had been one of the owners willing to recognize the Brotherhood in 1887 and had worked with them to revise the contract at that time. Since then, however, he had declared himself strongly in favor of the Brush Plan, so anything was possible. The ownership committee had no power to act, but given the influence of its members, whatever the three men decided likely would become official policy.[21]

The meeting with Ward occurred on June 24, a private conference lasting two hours. Despite the lengthy discussions, the interview ended inconclusively: "President Ward is desirous of

---

[19] Ibid.
[20] "Great Ball Towns," *The Sporting Life*, June 12, 1889, 1.
[21] "The Brotherhood's Demands," *Pittsburgh Dispatch*, June 23, 1889, 14; A. G. Ovens, "Mr. Brush's Views," *Pittsburgh Dispatch*, June 23, 1889, 14.

arranging a meeting between the two committees at once, and President Spalding has not fully made up his mind that the questions at issue are of a sufficiently urgent nature to warrant such action." Ward stated simply that Spalding, as the chairman of the National League's commission, "Is now in possession of the brotherhood's views, and has been informed as to the questions we wish to discuss in joint meeting. . . . I anticipate hearing from him at an early day; thus the matter stands."[22] Temporarily, this calmed all the rumors circulating about a strike by the BPBP on Independence Day, or potential measures even more extreme.

Still, the announcement sent sportswriters scurrying to the presidents of their respective teams. Washington planned to stand firm. The Nationals wanted to keep the classification plan or replace it with something equally beneficial such as a guarantee of half the gate receipts at all games. Boston's reaction was interesting, given that Arthur Soden had joined John Day in opposing the classification plan in the first place. While he and the other Triumvirs still believed a strike highly unlikely, he pledged that if one happened, the Beaneaters would sign new players and move forward. Soden also said he did not oppose granting most of the things the Brotherhood asked because they were not an issue for Boston. This seemed scurrilous, given how many players Boston had purchased recently, but his reasoning was typically Soden-esque: "I am willing to do away with the sale of players; we have none to sell, and we do not want to buy any more."[23]

John Brush of Indianapolis, as the plan's author, of course supported keeping the current status quo, maintaining that the players had nothing significant about which to complain. John Day in New York wanted no part of any rule limiting what a club paid its players, essentially agreeing with Ward that if a team could not

---

[22] "The League Vs. the Brotherhood," *Chicago Daily Tribune*, June 25, 1889, 3.
[23] Larner, Mugwump, A. G. Ovens, Harris, Harry Palmer, Brunell, and Circle, "Sentiment of the Clubs," *The Sporting Life*, June 26, 1889, 1.

compete with what it could afford, then the team should relocate to a league where it could compete and still profit. Al Spalding was noncommittal beyond the comments above, reminding his interlocutor that the National League did not conduct its business through the newspapers. Cleveland signaled a willingness to stand by and await the outcome of negotiations between the Brotherhood and the League committee. Pittsburgh vowed to stand by Washington and Indianapolis, and Philadelphia did the same.[24]

Spalding got around to answering Ward about two weeks later. He informed Ward, Keefe, Hanlon, and the other Brothers,

> It is the unanimous opinion of this committee that it is inadvisable to hold a meeting with the Brotherhood committee at present for the reason that no material interests will suffer by postponing this meeting. . . . It is contrary to the past policy of the League to call a special meeting in mid-season except for some extraordinary emergency, and we fail to discover any necessity for immediate action.[25]

This confrontational response was a risky decision. The benefit was that with the players dispersed and gone home for the winter, collective action on the Brotherhood's part was less likely. The risk was that the players might decide to do something drastic before then and prove harder to placate whenever the meeting finally took place.

The Brothers were boiling mad at their rebuff and lost no time in accusing the League of hypocrisy on multiple fronts. Tim Keefe said, "Spalding says they can't call a meeting in summer. Why, didn't they hold one at Asbury Park last summer and consider a trifling matter? There is one thing certain, they won't classify as many men this fall as they think. Why, this talk about Nick Young

---

[24] Ibid.
[25] Harry Palmer, "In No Hurry," *The Sporting Life*, July 10, 1889, 1.

classifying the men is rot. The clubs send in the salaries and he puts them in classes to correspond."[26] In actuality, the meeting at Asbury Park took place in 1887, not 1888, but considering that the "emergency" was merely to decide the outcome of a protested game between New York and Detroit with no impact on the standings, Keefe's first point remained valid.

Other proof corroborates Keefe's second claim, that the teams, not the League, classified the players. Jay Faatz, first baseman and captain of the Cleveland Spiders, wrote a letter to Nick Young in the off-season, complaining that his classification was unjust. Young wrote back "to the effect that the clubs, not the President of the league, classed the players."[27]

Various members of the League also continued doing things to call their own integrity into question. Just a couple days later, when Washington sold second baseman Al Myers to Philadelphia, which needed a replacement for the injured Ed Delahanty, Washington paid Myers $600 out of the sale price to keep him happy and gain his willing acceptance of the transaction.[28] Considering that League policy was dead set against sharing any of the profits from sales with players, this raised a few eyebrows.

Ward was plainspoken when next interviewed: "They know that they have broken faith with their players and dared not face the issue." Spalding's reasons for refusal were "amusing and simply absurd." In answer to the question of the moment, what the Brotherhood would do next, Ward was more reserved: "On that question just at the present time I am neither able nor at liberty to say. There is one thing, however, of which you may be certain. The players have asked only what is right, and they will not rest until they get it. The men who are playing ball nowadays are not of the caliber to be hoodwinked or talked out of their rights."[29]

---

[26] "Brotherhood Sentiment," *The Sporting Life*, July 10, 1889, 1.
[27] "They've Struck the Slide," *Chicago Daily Tribune*, July 14, 1889, 12.
[28] R. M. Larner, "Washington Whispers," *The Sporting Life*, July 10, 1889, 2.
[29] "Great Joy in New York," *Chicago Daily Tribune*, July 14, 1889, 12.

Spalding, meanwhile, began hatching some plans of his own, with the intent of bringing all of baseball into one salary scheme and regularizing the relations between the major and minor leagues. In a letter to Nick Young, he laid out his plans. His scheme divided all minor leagues into four categories, A, B, C, and D. Class D was for the weakest minor leagues and called for a team salary cap of $600 per month, and an individual player cap of $60 per month. Minor league teams of superior classification could obtain players from Class D clubs for $250. Those leagues in Class C would have a team salary limit of $1,000 each month and an individual monthly limit of $100. Teams from a higher classification could obtain players from Class C teams for a $500 payment. Clubs in Class B had monthly salary limits of $1,500 for the team and $150 for individuals, and Class A and major league teams could acquire their players for a $1,000 payment. Finally, those minor leagues grouped in Class A had a monthly limit of $2,000 and an individual limit of $200 and would receive $1,500 in payment should a major league team want one of their men.

Spalding's plan also called for modifying the Brush Plan by ignoring it for players with exceptional personal habits and at least three years of service on their present team. Spalding favored some concessions to the Brotherhood on player sales, although his plan did not go as far as the Brotherhood wished. He believed that half of the sale price should go to the selling team, one quarter to the player, and the final quarter to the league of which the selling team was a member, presumably to give the weaker teams a bit more financial support. Finally, he wanted to see a so-called "Supreme Court" of baseball created that would rule on all matters in dispute that might arise between the major leagues, the minor leagues, individual teams, players, interpretations of the rules of play, and so forth. This court's membership would consist of the presidents of the National League and American Association, plus one man outside the game (probably he had former National League president A. G. Mills in mind) whom all parties recognized as interested in the good of the game.[30]

The primary merit of Spalding's plan was not that it had any chance of immediate adoption, but that it set in motion serious discussion of how to improve the general state of baseball. Boston manager Jim Hart, a longtime baseball man, published a plan of his own soon afterward. In fact, he had sent this plan to Spalding for comment, and thus the Chicago owner's work was in many respects derivative of Hart's, particularly in its call for a board to oversee all technical aspects of the game. Other noteworthy features of Hart's scheme were to give players an option if they wished to assent to player sales and to keep most of the features of the pre-Brush Plan contract between the League and the Brotherhood. He also called for grading cities in categories A through G, with set contract sizes, prices for attending games, and many other business details precisely worked out. The one other notable aspect of the plan, however, that virtually guaranteed a poor universal reception, was the transfer of Cincinnati and Brooklyn to the National League in exchange for Washington and Indianapolis, relegating the weakened American Association to a status below the National League.[31] Given that this is very nearly what happened within two years, however, perhaps Hart knew his business.

What all such plans had in common, however, was to consider the situation from the perspective of the owners and their quest for profit. This was natural enough, considering the plans' authorship. What that also meant, however, was that no matter how the owners tweaked these various plans of classification, each was unpalatable to the players and did little to resolve the coming dispute. Why bother with working out such schemes, then? Rest assured that when Al Spalding took public action, deeper motives were at work. Even though July 4 had come and gone with no strike, Spalding was doing

---

[30] A. G. Spalding, "A Draft System," *The Sporting Life*, July 17, 1889, 1.
[31] Jim Hart, "Another Scheme," *The Sporting Life*, July 31, 1889, 5.

his best to find out what the Brotherhood was up to. He sent detectives to shadow key members of the Brotherhood. Spalding knew, therefore, that the BPBP had held a meeting on July 14 (This was the meeting where it made the final decision to initiate plans for its own league.) but did not know exactly what decisions the organization had made. The fact that July 14 was also Bastille Day, however, did not escape his notice. This was the background behind his decision to lay out his new plan as a trial balloon.[32]

This is where the situation stood as the 1889 campaign wound through the dog days of August. The Brotherhood, still simmering after the League's rebuff, continued its work behind the scenes. The owners remained serene in their belief that their position was impregnable, that the players would not dare a dramatic move and challenge them directly, and that all they needed to do was continue refining a plan that would pad all their pockets more consistently.

Meanwhile, the pennant races of both the League and Association turned into great ones. Four teams, two in each league, battled down to the last week of the season to see which would end up in the World Series. We might forgive baseball observers, therefore, if the action on the field took up most of their attention. As September dwindled and turned to October, however, concrete and tangible things began replacing the rumors that observers had spent the summer sifting and evaluating. It was time for a final showdown.

---

[32] Stevens, *Baseball's Radical for All Seasons*, 87. Bastille Day marked the well-known event from the French Revolution where the people of Paris stormed the Bastille, a fortress in Paris that stood for the arbitrary rule of the Bourbon dynasty. The fact that the Brotherhood met on this day was purely coincidence, however. It was a Sunday, the only day of the week that the players had free from games when they could meet, and the schedule just happened to have most BPBP members near enough that they could attend a meeting on that day.

Chapter 15

The Storm Breaks

THE FIRST SOLID HINTS OF THE IMPENDING CRISIS leaked out in September of 1889. Various rumors had circulated all season long. However, with the games on the field distracting everyone's attention, the summer saw many rumors but few definitive events either proving or disproving them. At least, few definitive events reaching the press or the public.

Before describing what happened, however, we should take a moment and describe how the scheme for a Brotherhood League originated. According to Al Johnson, the original financier behind the plan, it was Ned Hanlon, rather than John Ward, who first approached him with the idea. Hanlon and Ward, along with Fred Pfeffer and Jim Fogarty, had been companions on the Spalding Tour. These four men, with nothing better to do on the long ocean voyage, worked up a plan to liberate the players. They believed that their fellow Brothers would support the plan, but the organization lacked the capital to attempt it without outside help.

That is why Hanlon approached Al Johnson. Johnson, based in Cleveland, was a big baseball fan and somewhat of an idealist who hated the lopsidedness of baseball contracts. He also, admittedly, visualized huge profits if he located a successful baseball park on the route of his streetcar lines. Johnson socialized with ballplayers often and became sympathetic to their cause. After meeting Hanlon, he then discussed possibilities with members of the hometown Cleveland Spiders. One by one, when other teams of the National League came through Cleveland, Johnson met their members: "So as each visiting club came we held meeting after meeting, until every league player had heard our views and had been given a chance to express himself and suggest whatever he thought would be for the best interests of such an organization." Johnson then described how completely these players backed the plan: "To show how they feel I will state what happened at one of our meetings. Every player of both New York and Cleveland had attended three evenings in succession, and our sessions were never less than three hours' duration."[1]

Johnson also took appropriate precautions to avoid anyone catching on to the true nature of what he and the Brotherhood contemplated, perhaps aware of the penchant of National League owners to spy on players with detectives. Not only did he station a burly employee in the hallway with instructions to bounce anyone who tried interrupting his meeting, but he also bribed the police who worked the beat outside the hotel to keep quiet, just to make sure that no one knew the identity of the men going in and out of his meetings.[2]

After these early-season sessions, the players asked for a meeting with the National League. This was the meeting mentioned in the preceding chapter that Spalding, Day, and Rogers refused to schedule. The chapters of the Brotherhood then voted on whether to hold a strike on July 4 or attempt a "reorganization," meaning their own league, after the season. The men voted in favor of

---

[1] "Albert Johnson Talks," *Chicago Daily Tribune*, October 30, 1889, 6.
[2] Seymour, *Baseball*, 226.

reorganization by a decisive margin. At that point, Johnson and some of the BPBP's leaders began contacting additional financial backers, finding grounds for play, and so forth. The fact that they did so without drawing any notice or leaking any of their plans until September, when those plans were nearly mature, was a phenomenal achievement.[3]

It was not quite a perfect achievement, however. A few stories appeared by September that presaged the cataclysm to come. The *Chicago Daily Tribune* interviewed an unnamed Indianapolis Brother and learned that the plan for an independent league remained alive and well. It was at this time that the public learned Johnson was the leader of the scheme on the financial side. This Chicago correspondent wrote, "When the various league clubs offer their players contracts for 1890 they will be rejected. The players signed by Johnson are to be apportioned among the present league towns, Pittsburg and Indianapolis. A new national league is to be formed." While the writer had a couple of the cities wrong, the rest of the statement was accurate.[4]

Even though the statement was true, in early September most did not believe such a thing would ever happen. Most continued to think it was a bluff, like the bluff (or was it really a bluff?) the Brotherhood had used in 1887 to gain concessions on the contract issue when Erastus Wiman was supposedly the money behind the plan. Even the Chicago interviewer did not really believe it. He admitted, "Johnson is well known in baseball circles. He is a businessman of a good many interests. There is little of the visionary about him. While he might be induced to handle the Cleveland corner of the trust if there was a promise of financial success, he certainly would not handle it nationally." The writer concluded, however, "The more the story is probed the more it assumes spectral hue." Rather, "The Johnson plan is the last device in the way of a

---

[3] "That Baseball Combine," *Chicago Daily Tribune*, September 10, 1889, 6.
[4] Ibid.

sledgehammer on this classification law. It will be used during the winter and may serve its purpose."[5]

Others were less certain. They noted that Al Johnson, under the cover of looking after his St. Louis street railway interests, had spent the past several weeks in New York City and other eastern National League cities, presumably in conference with John Ward and other Brotherhood members. One of Johnson's brothers, Will, was also good friends with Fred Dunlap, and speculation centered on the ability of the Johnson brothers (older brother Tom was also a wealthy businessman who dabbled in politics) to supply the baseball Brothers with ballparks in which to play if they challenged the League.[6] When asked about his intentions regarding baseball, Al was noncommittal, but shortly afterward reports spied him dining at the Continental Hotel with Brotherhood members Ned Hanlon of Pittsburgh and Jim Fogarty and George Wood of Philadelphia. He later met with Arthur Irwin of Washington as well.[7]

Leaks of more information dribbled out in mid-September. Soon, baseball fans learned of plans that, if put into practice, would materially transform the business of baseball. Profits would go to a pool, and each team would share in them equally to avoid the constant hobgoblin menacing competition in the League and Association, that of some teams being weaker financially than others and thus creating Brush Plans and other schemes to compensate for their weakness. Not only that, the players would share in the profits, splitting them equally with their financial backers to supplement their salaries, which would be smaller in up-front money. The new league would adopt prizes for finishing in the top of the standings

---

[5] Ibid. While the *Daily Tribune* did not print the authorship of individual articles on baseball at this time, the person supplying the information can be none other than A. G. Ovens, Indianapolis correspondent for both that paper and *The Sporting Life*.
[6] "The League Strike," *The Sporting News*, September 14, 1889, 1.
[7] "The Rumored Trust," *The Sporting Life*, September 18, 1889, 6.

and like the National League (at least officially), would eschew Sunday games and liquor sales at the ballpark.[8]

If anything major did happen, Al Spalding would be the point man for the League, whether in negotiations or war. For Spalding, one of the first signs that something serious was in the offing came when he tried to locate new grounds for his White Stockings. He allowed the lease on his old grounds on the corner of Congress and Loomis streets to lapse and purchased a new site where he planned a ballpark modeled on the Victorian Grounds in Melbourne, Australia, that he and his tourists visited the previous winter. However, when the construction plans bogged down and Spalding learned the site would not be ready for the next season, he attempted to renew his option on the old site, just in case. It was almost too late because someone else, an agent for the backers of the Brotherhood, tried preempting Spalding by purchasing an option on the grounds.[9]

Nor was Chicago the only place where Brotherhood backers were trying to outmaneuver the League bosses. On September 20, Al Johnson told an interviewer that backers had also acquired leases on the old Polo Grounds site in New York and one of Brooklyn's parks (although it was not either of the Bridegrooms' two parks, Washington or Ridgewood. Brooklyn played in two parks to help dodge the always-thorny issue of Sunday baseball in Brooklyn, Ridgewood being the designated Sunday site.), as well as two other locations. In securing the Polo Grounds, the Brotherhood had the help of James Coogan, a prominent New York baseball figure. Johnson also disclosed the lineup of cities for the new league, those being New York, Boston, Brooklyn, and Philadelphia in the East and Chicago, Cleveland, Pittsburgh, and Buffalo in the West. Securing grounds in Buffalo was simple because Jack Rowe was both a Brother and the part owner of the existing Buffalo franchise

---

[8] "The Baseball Business to be Reorganized," *Los Angeles Daily Herald*, September 15, 1889, 7.
[9] "Revolutionizing Ball Playing," *Milwaukee Sentinel*, September 15, 1889, 4.

of the International League (see the Rowe-White controversy in chapter ten for more). Finally, Johnson stated that every single National League player, with Cap Anson of Chicago the singular exception, was on board with the Brotherhood.[10]

Spalding's concern no doubt deepened when the press reported that one of his own men, stalwart second baseman Fred Pfeffer, was the likely manager of a rival Chicago team. Pfeffer, who not only authored a book about baseball but frequently cornered the concession for printing scorecards at Chicago games as well, had saved a tidy sum from his combination of ball playing and entrepreneurial activities.[11] Ward, meanwhile, while not giving out what the Brotherhood ultimately planned to do, did say, "The Brotherhood will show the League that it means business. We have temporized enough. We shall be put off no longer. The League has got to consider our complaints and rectify them." When asked if that was a declaration of a new league and war, Ward did not commit, simply adding, "That is a question that will come afterwards. I do not care to say what steps we will take."[12]

It was not long before the public discovered what those steps were. Within a week, the *Chicago Daily Tribune* and other papers reported the revolutionary financial plan agreed on by the Brotherhood and its backers. Player contracts would change little from what each man earned in 1889. However, out of whatever profits the league made, the first $10,000 went to the teams finishing first through fourth, in a distribution scheme of $5,000-$2,500-$1,500-$1,000. The next $80,000 of profit went to the backers, divided evenly among the eight clubs. Additional profits up to the next $80,000 went to the players in the same distribution arrangement. After that, the players and backers split any further

---

[10] "The Brotherhood," *The Sporting News*, September 21, 1889, 1; "A Baseball Scheme," *Pittsburg Dispatch*, September 21, 1889, 7.
[11] "Revolutionizing Ball Playing," *Milwaukee Sentinel*, September 15, 1889, 4.
[12] W. I. Harris, "New York News," *The Sporting Life*, September 18, 1889, 2.

profits fifty-fifty.[13] The plan underwent modifications in time, but such a profit-sharing scheme was radical for Gilded Age America no matter what the details eventually became.

That plan, while revolutionary enough, was not nearly all. Team management was also a joint venture between the players and owners. Each ball club had a board of eight men, four players and four backers, while the league featured a senate of sixteen members, two from each team, one player and one backer.[14] The plan even addressed the vexing umpire question, deciding on the long-desired double umpire system, and tried to get together a staff including the most prestigious officials in the game, including John Gaffney, Bob Ferguson, John McQuaid, and John Kelly.[15]

With the scheme now out in the open, reporters rushed to Al Spalding first to get his take. Like Spalding had done so many times previously, he immediately worked the propaganda angle by portraying the League as the responsible father to the unruly and ungrateful children of the Brotherhood: "The league has existed for fifteen years. It wiped out the gambling element in baseball and cleared it of crooked playing. . . . Now that the game is clean and on a healthy basis all the purifying work is forgotten by the players, and 'long chance' capitalists are ready to step in and assume the possible profits that may come through the game." Furthermore, the BPBP was suddenly "an oathbound, secret organization of strikers which has plotted against the life of the league, through the care of which it became a possibility."[16]

Spalding finished the interview with both a carrot and a stick. While some League teams might struggle against this challenge, others would fight on, to the death if necessary. However, despite a

---

[13] "A Great Baseball Trust," *Chicago Daily Tribune*, September 22, 1889, 9.
[14] Ibid. While sportswriters for the *Daily Tribune* did not sign their articles, the author was Frank Brunell, who had recently moved from Cleveland to Chicago and joined the staff of the *Daily Tribune*.
[15] "The Ball Players' Revolt," *New York Times*, September 23, 1889, 2.
[16] "League Men Will Fight," *Chicago Daily Tribune*, September 23, 1889, 3.

general feeling that conciliation might be too late, he intended to try that route first: "New York, Boston, Chicago, Philadelphia, and Pittsburg will fight hard and go on with teams made up of the best players they can secure. It is a tremendous plot, and I hope for the good of the game that all the differences between the league and its players may be overcome and the threatened break averted."[17]

Spalding's next move was reconnaissance. Accordingly, on September 28, he sent a public letter to Ward (his earlier statements about not doing business through the newspapers notwithstanding) asking the Brotherhood's president to name a date following the season to hold the conference he had denied Ward during the summer. Ward's response, while not proclaiming a definitive break, was not conciliatory, either. Referring to the BPBP's negotiating committee, Ward wrote, "The committee was, however, unable to obtain a hearing from the league and it so reported at a subsequent meeting of the brotherhood held July 14, and was accordingly discharged. It was not a standing committee. I will refer your communication, therefore, to the entire brotherhood." In theory, this meant the BPBP might still treat with the League. Given the reports from various newspapers, however, in which the Brotherhood had chosen reorganization (its own league) over a July 4 strike as its preferred method of retaliation for Spalding, Day, and Rogers standing them up, this gave Spalding a good idea of where the situation might go.[18]

The same day, the New York members of the Brotherhood's financial support purchased land adjoining John Day's new Polo Grounds to construct a Brotherhood ballpark. Included in the group was James Coogan, owner of both properties, and Erastus Wiman, former New York Metropolitans owner. The syndicate also

---

[17] Ibid.
[18] "The Brotherhood's Position," *Chicago Daily Tribune*, September 29, 1889, 14.

purchased the lease on Day's existing Polo Grounds after Day's current lease expired, which would be following the 1891 season.[19]

Another issue was the 1887 Brotherhood contract, specifically as it related to the reserve rule. Recall that in this contract, the Brotherhood explicitly recognized the reserve rule because it wanted the full obligations of both parties written into the contract. Section eighteen of the contract said that the player agreed to give his club the right to reserve his services for the following season. Some concluded, therefore, that the Brotherhood would be guilty of contract-breaking should the players refuse to sign with their League team for 1890 because the courts would consider this a binding agreement. Others believed that this argument did not hold, however, because the reserve rule merely gave teams the option to renew the contract of the previous season. It did not obligate the player to sign the contract, although it did bar the player from playing on or against any team party to the National Agreement if they chose not to.

An additional consideration from the National League's view was that if the League did end up in court trying to enforce this contract, it might create the opportunity for the players to challenge the reserve rule's legality. Many lawyers considered it questionable at best, so this was a possibility that the League wanted to avoid. John Ward pointed out another weakness in the argument, stating, "If they had any such right why haven't they prevented men playing outside the League before to-day, as there have been several instances where men have broken contracts and gone to California and other outside places. This whole question hinges on the meaning of that one little word, 'reserve.' It is all one-sided and could not hold a player who wanted to go outside."[20] Furthermore, Ward said, "The League can reserve players from year to year, within League

---

[19] "The New League at Work," *Chicago Daily Tribune*, September 29, 1889, 14; "New Syndicate's Grounds," *Los Angeles Daily Herald*, September 29, 1889, 8.
[20] John Ward, "Ward's Reply," *Pittsburgh Dispatch*, October 24, 1889, 6.

limits, but they can no more prevent a player from playing with another organization than they can prevent him from earning a living by keeping a hotel or driving a dray. The Brotherhood is, of course, interested in protecting the players. That is its sole and only object."[21]

Because the proposed new league did not recognize the reserve rule and was not a party to the National Agreement, this would only matter if the courts decided in the League's favor. They did not. National League clubs brought injunctions against both John Ward and Buck Ewing. In Ewing's case, Judge William Wallace denied the injunction, writing, "In a legal sense it [the baseball contract] is merely a contract to make a contract if the parties agree."[22]

More relevant was Section 2(a) of the National Agreement, which stated that no player could sign a contract for longer than seven months, that contracts expired, at the latest, on October 31, and that negotiations for new contracts could not occur prior to October 20 without the club's permission. If the men in the Brotherhood had already signed an agreement to play for a new Brotherhood team during the month of September, they were in violation of this last provision. If true, it was pointless to negotiate because no compromise was possible at that point, not to mention that if any player went back on his Brotherhood contract to sign another agreement with the League, the Brotherhood could prevent this through court action. Thus, informed observers concluded that the Brotherhood was in earnest, and that both sides must prepare for battle. Later events proved that both players and clubs would ignore such legal niceties in the heat of combat, but in late September, such arguments helped clarify the position of the players and the League.[23]

---

[21] "The Players to Meet," *The Sporting Life*, October 30, 1889, 5.
[22] Thorn, *Baseball in the Garden of Eden*, 240-241.
[23] "The Latest Development," *The Sporting Life*, October 2, 1889, 5.

The Storm Breaks

Various reasons explain why the Brotherhood succeeded in attracting capital from interested parties. Many investors thought that they could profit from baseball, if only people agreed to an even distribution of money so that financial success did not largely depend on where one's team played. Others had personal motives. According to Tim Murnane, several Boston capitalists wanted to back the new league because when they were stockholders in the Boston Beaneaters, the Triumvirs' heavy-handed financial manipulations had deprived them of their stock and frozen them out of the organization. These investors wanted revenge on the haughty trio.[24]

Besides recruiting backers from outside the present group of owners, several players and ex-players of means joined the rebellion. In addition to Fred Pfeffer in Chicago, Boston's John Morrill, although no longer playing, joined the investors in Beantown. George Wright, a true baseball pioneer who had played professionally even before the National Association formed in 1871, joined Morrill as a Boston stockholder. His old teammate Ross Barnes joined the Chicago investors, while New York's Mayor Hugh Grant bought stock in the proposed New York club.[25] Current players financially involved included Tim Keefe and John Ward in New York, Dan Brouthers and John Clarkson in Boston, Chief Zimmer and Jay Faatz of Cleveland, Jack Rowe, Deacon White, and George Myers for the new Buffalo team, and Fred Dunlap and Ned Hanlon in Pittsburgh. Keefe also was part-owner of a moderately capitalized sporting goods establishment, and to no one's surprise, won the contract to supply baseballs for the Brotherhood's 1890 campaign. They proved somewhat livelier than the baseballs used in previous years.[26]

---

[24] "The Sporting World," *Galveston Daily News*, September 22, 1889, 4.
[25] "The Outlook in Boston," *Chicago Daily Tribune*, September 23, 1889, 3; "What George Wright Says," *Chicago Daily Tribune*, September 23, 1889, 3.
[26] "The Ball Players' Revolt," *New York Times*, September 23, 1889, 2.

The only players hesitant about joining were, ironically, some of the New York players who founded the BPBP. The main reason was their fondness for their owner, John Day. We have mentioned many times that Day, more than any other National League owner, tried to do right by his players. He paid them well, did not try to sell them, opposed the Brush Plan, never issued fines for poor play, and did not send detectives to monitor their after-hours behavior. Even with the storm clouds gathering over Gotham in October, Day maintained, "the players may, of course, have some fault to find with the present rules, and, for my part, I think there can be one or two changes made that would be beneficial to all. The classification rule, if lived up to, would be a good thing, but as it is it can be dropped and never missed." He also said, "In the case of Rowe and White, and similar cases, I don't think that was right. No man should be compelled to play with a club that he did not want to join, and the rule was never made with the idea of sheltering such an evil. It is one of the things that has crept into the rules that were never intended."[27]

What the New York players really hoped was that they might persuade Day to join them in their new venture. Regardless, "The New York players feel badly about jumping from under President John B. Day's management, but they feel that it must be all hands or nobody, and are figuring on President Day's bobbing up in the new league."[28] The saddest part of the whole rebellion, in fact, might be that Day, the man least deserving of the players' enmity, ended up suffering the most from their actions. His financial situation deteriorated so badly in 1890 that other National League owners had to prop up the New York franchise before the season was over. With his tobacco business also struggling, by 1893 he had almost no role in the New York Giants organization, resigning in February. He continued in major league baseball in positions of ever-diminishing

---

[27] "News, Notes and Gossip," *The Sporting Life*, October 16, 1889, 5.
[28] "What George Wright Says," *Chicago Daily Tribune*, September 23, 1889, 3.

importance, falling so far that by 1910, his only source of income was the five dollars per day he made taking tickets at the Polo Grounds for the team he used to own.[29]

The potential of finding more allies outside of the financial world existed as well. Samuel Leffingwell, a prominent leader in the trade union movement, encouraged the Brotherhood to apply for membership in the American Federation of Trades and Labor Unions, the Knights of Labor, or both. He believed that baseball players qualified as skilled workers and mentioned that the players would then "be allied to organizations representing over 1,000,000 of skilled mechanics." He added, "As the Brotherhood will have all the skilled players, and as the main support comes from the workingmen, it will be seen whether mere capital is to rule with despotic sway over the masses of the people in baseball as it would like to do in many other leading industries in the country. Oh, yes, the workingmen are in sympathy with the Brotherhood."[30]

One wildcard was the American Association. In 1889, it had no brotherhood despite occasional rumors of attempts to form one. Yet, all knew that many Association players, those in St. Louis who played for Chris Von der Ahe especially, might well desert if given proper inducements. Although it was probably more by luck than design, the Association had not adopted anything like the Brush Plan, so its players did not have a potential salary limit over which to chafe. The reserve clause and player sales still nettled players, however, providing situations from which Association players might want to escape. Not only that, the nightmare season just concluded in Louisville, the mercurial ownership in St. Louis, the constant worry about which Association team might switch to the National League, and the long train rides to reach Kansas City for

---

[29] For more on Day's tragic career in baseball, see his SABR biography at http://sabr.org/bioproj/person/c281a493, accessed March 22, 2015.
[30] "To Aid the Brotherhood," *New York Times*, November 5, 1889, 8.

games were all reasons that Association players might want to play elsewhere.

The Brotherhood's initial policy toward the American Association was one of noninterference. It made no effort to woo Association stars into its proposed league or to interfere with Association operations. The Brotherhood League's structure, however, made it difficult to imagine the Association would stay neutral forever. If the Brotherhood League proved a success without player reservations sales, it would be more attractive to up-and-coming young players than an Association that did have them, especially if the Brotherhood succeeded in displacing the National League. It was probably unavoidable, therefore, that the Association would line up with the National League against the Brotherhood eventually and that the Brotherhood would respond by raiding Association rosters for more talent.

Although this is what happened, it was no certainty in September and October of 1889. At that time, both an exciting pennant race and the fallout from the recent St. Louis-Brooklyn imbroglio (see chapter thirteen) distracted the American Association, giving its leaders little time to formulate a coherent policy regarding the Brotherhood. In addition, given the unpredictability of the Association's decisions, no one in the Brotherhood could be certain that the Association would become hostile. It seemed best, therefore, to be cautious and wait to see what stance the junior major league would take.

In the last week of September, matters became confused. Some Brotherhood members gave reports to the press about the new league. Other Brothers, including the officers, denied those same reports. The names of various capitalists besides the Johnson brothers circulated as well; some of these men gave details about the scheme, others denied being part of it. Some National League owners started taking precautions while others voiced their disbelief that any plan for secession was afoot. While sportswriters went to immense lengths to dissect the details that they knew about and

The Storm Breaks

raced to interview interested parties whenever the latest rumor reached them, few writers seemed to know anything for certain, either. Even *The Sporting Life* proclaimed its coverage a combination of news, gossip, and rumor.

Part of the reason for the uncertainty was that, sadly for the Brotherhood, details of its plan leaked too early. Writers at the *Chicago Daily Tribune*, including both Harry Palmer and Frank Brunell by this time, learned the details and published them in late September, before the BPBP perfected all its arrangements. The fact that National League owners had such a wide array of responses, from the deep concern of Spalding to the nonchalance of several of his fellows, is a good indication that they were oblivious to the full scope of the Brotherhood's plans, even in late September. It is a good bet that Spalding was most concerned because his hometown newspapermen knew the story, he learned it from them, and then realized how dire things were, especially considering that Brunell ended up heavily involved with the Brotherhood League.[31]

The other reason the BPBP tried to stall was fear. Not fear of their new league's failure, but fear that if National League owners realized how earnest they were, those owners would terminate the contracts of Brotherhood players immediately, thus depriving them of a bit of pay at the end of the season.[32] That is why Ned Williamson remarked, "I understand that the Chicago Club has not as yet settled in full with its players. As soon as that is done I think some facts will be made public that have heretofore been kept quiet."[33]

Spalding and the Boston Triumvirs took the most active approach to fending off a challenge. Spalding began signing players from Western League franchises immediately. Boston tried to do him one better, opening negotiations for the entire franchise of the

---

[31] "Some Corrections," *The Sporting Life*, October 16, 1889, 5.
[32] Ibid.
[33] "Ed Williamson Does Some Talking," *The Sporting News*, October 26, 1889, 1.

Western League's Omaha club. At the very least, Boston hoped to gain up-and-coming pitcher Kid Nichols, but just in case wanted to be ready to import an entire team should any desertions occur.[34]

These developments proved profitable for stronger minor league circuits. With their men suddenly in great demand, visions of greenbacks danced in the heads of minor league executives. Sam Morton, manager of the Western Association's Minneapolis franchise, said: "It will not be long before base-ball managers will be climbing over each other's shoulders in this section to get hold of good Western Association timber for their clubs next year. We may or may not sell. We are like all other people in business, if somebody offers our price we are pretty sure to sell."[35]

The game of bluff between the players and the League continued into the middle of October. On the 11th of that month, Tim Keefe mentioned that the BPBP would hold a meeting and appoint a new committee in one last effort to resolve the "vital grievances" held by the players.[36] Keefe also mentioned, more ominously, that the Brotherhood did not trust the League, especially after the Brush Plan. Queried on what the BPBP wanted, he said, "We want the abolition of the classification of players and want the sale of players entirely done away with. It is not true that we want a share in the purchase money."[37]

In the meantime, however, sources began confirming which Brotherhood players would serve in each city as its key organizers. The men listed, most of whom already played in the city they represented, were as follows:

Philadelphia – Fred Dunlap, Hardie Richardson, Jim Fogarty, and George Wood.

---

[34] "A Confession," *The Sporting Life*, October 9, 1889, 6.
[35] "Sam Morton's Views," *Chicago Daily Inter Ocean*, October 10, 1889, 6.
[36] "League and Brotherhood," *Milwaukee Daily Journal*, October 11, 1889, 6.
[37] "Tim's View of It," *Pittsburgh Dispatch*, October 12, 1889, 6.

New York – John Ward, Tim Keefe, Roger Connor, and Buck Ewing.
Boston – Dan Brouthers, Billy Nash, John Morrill, and Dick Johnston.
Washington – Arthur Irwin, John Irwin, and Sam Wise.
Pittsburgh – Ned Hanlon, Deacon White, Jack Rowe, and Fred Carroll.
Chicago – Fred Pfeffer.
Indianapolis – Jack Glasscock, Jerry Denny, Ed Andrews, and Henry Boyle.
Cleveland – Jay Faatz, Cub Stricker, Paul Radford, and Charles Snyder.[38]

Based on such reports, others continued insisting that the BPBP had no interest in negotiation and that this was a smokescreen to buy time. Fred Pfeffer said as much in one interview. Frank Brunell did, too, stating he had seen many Brotherhood contracts already signed and that one entire team (presumably Cleveland, where he used to cover the team) was already in the fold. Brunell also confirmed the League's intent to fight. Its plan was for its teams to sign as many talented players from the stronger minor leagues as possible, cut prices to undersell the Brotherhood League, pull out all legal strategies to harass the new organization, and, if possible, drive its teams into debt through escalating legal costs. The National League would also try enticing two or three key players from each club back into its ranks through healthy raises or similar methods of bribery.[39]

It was also in mid-October that other League executives finally acknowledged that the players were in earnest. Tom Loftus, the manager who had just finished leading Cleveland to a respectable finish in its first season in the National League, shocked everyone

---

[38] Gotham, "And Here You Are," *The Sporting News*, October 12, 1889, 1.
[39] "Mr. Fred Pfeffer," *The Sporting News*, October 12, 1889, 3; Brunell, "The League's Fighting Plan," *The Sporting News*, October 12, 1889, 3; "George Wright's Views," *The Sporting News*, October 12, 1889, 3.

when he agreed to leave Cleveland and manage in Cincinnati. His reason was that every player on his roster planned to desert the team. The players held no ill will against Loftus, which is why they warned him in advance so that he could find a more promising position while his reputation remained solid. Loftus received $3,500 and 100 shares of Cincinnati stock, and it does not appear he ever reconsidered.[40] Further proof that something was afoot in the Forest City came in late October when Al Johnson purchased a lease on grounds on Wilson Avenue and set men to work on grading the field and constructing a grandstand.[41]

Similarly, John Rogers in Philadelphia started believing the reports. He also hoped for reconciliation, at least in public, and stated his willingness to abandon the Brush Plan, although in exchange he wanted the Brotherhood to agree to requiring players to report in prime condition to play on April 1 each year. He did not like seeing men arrive in April out of shape while paying them as if they were at the peak of their talents. When asked about the Brotherhood's plans, Rogers stated, "I hear that the brotherhood league will surely be organized, and I am ready to believe that it will. I am told that five men in this city have agreed to put in $2,500 each."[42]

Rogers' fellow Philadelphian, Al Reach, also began to see reality by mid-October. When a reporter asked if he believed the BPBP was serious, Reach said,

> Why, of course I do. That is, to this extent: If Ward and others who are the leading spirits in this move can induce enough players to follow them to accomplish their purpose, I believe that the attempt to establish a Brotherhood league will be made. If, on the other hand, enough signatures cannot

---

[40] J. S. McDonald, "Loftus and Schmelz," *The Sporting News*, October 12, 1889, 1; "Stern Talks," *The Sporting Life*, October 30, 1889, 1.
[41] "Brotherhood at Cleveland," *Chicago Daily Inter Ocean*, October 26, 1889, 2.
[42] "Asked of the Brotherhood," *Chicago Daily Tribune*, October 21, 1889, 6.

be secured to warrant success, then the brotherhood men will try to get big concessions from the league."[43]

October 20 was a very important day. That was the first day that League teams could negotiate with players for 1890 and the day on which League teams sent new contracts to their reserved men. If that day passed and the players took no action or returned the contracts unsigned, it was not quite a sign that the revolt had begun, but it did signify a plan to take action. At that point, the only things standing in the way of a baseball rebellion was the Brotherhood meeting scheduled for November 4 and the National League meeting planned for November 13-14. If the two sides could not reconcile by that point, there would be war.

When October 20 came, National League owners sent contracts to their players as usual. At last, baseball observers would find out what the players meant to do. The initial returns were not promising for the League. In Chicago, Spalding received but one signature, that of Cap Anson. Typical of the response of Chicago players was that of outfielder George Van Haltren. When a writer asked him where he would play next year, he answered, "In Chicago." To the inevitable follow-up question, "Under Anson?" Van Haltren replied, "I can't say about that."[44] When a reporter asked Spalding whether he would try court injunctions to retain Chicago's players, he backtracked a bit from earlier statements, claiming, "We may decide to let such of our reserved players as may refuse to sign play their string out as they see fit. I don't say we will enjoin them, and I don't say we will not. At any rate, such action would not be taken before next spring."[45]

In Pittsburgh, meanwhile, team president William Nimick could not muster even one commitment for 1890. When Nimick met

---

[43] "World of Sports," *Milwaukee Sentinel*, October 21, 1889, 8.
[44] "Spalding Says They Will Sign," *The Sporting News*, October 26, 1889, 3.
[45] "Does He Want to Sell," *Chicago Daily Tribune*, October 27, 1889, 3.

outfielder Billy Sunday and asked if he was ready to sign, Sunday answered, "If the Brotherhood matter is settled satisfactorily I will; otherwise I will stick by the Brotherhood." His teammates agreed, stating their intent to abstain from signing anything until the League met with the Brotherhood in November. One unnamed Brother told the press, "If our requests are complied with then I suppose that will end the matter. If not, why, then I guess the League will be shown that the Brotherhood means business."[46] Nimick responded by stating, "Well, the brotherhood has shown its teeth at last. I was expecting it or something similar all along. Sunday was the only man I asked to sign. The rest of them will have to come to me when they are ready to do business."[47]

No other National League presidents reported signing their reserved men, either, although the Indianapolis club did sign a new face, pitcher Ed Eiteljorge, who had turned eighteen years old a few days prior, while Boston signed Bobby Lowe. In the Quaker City, when the fateful day passed and management was bereft of signed contracts, Philadelphia management finally began taking precautions, signing a trio of new men, catcher Jake Virtue, outfielder Eddie Burke, and pitcher Tom Vickery, although Virtue ended up in Cleveland by the time the 1890 season began.[48]

The League's leading men soon suspected that their worst fears might come true. While the Brotherhood's leaders continued to repeat their intentions to meet with the League in November, a few members of the organization struggled to keep the cat in the bag. One Chicago Brother, unable to hold back, stated, "The brotherhood will not make any demands of the league at the league meeting . . . because one week from tomorrow . . . the brotherhood will hold its

---

[46] "Baseball Matters," *New York Times*, October 22, 1889, 3.
[47] Reddy, "The Pittsburg Recalcitrants," *The Sporting News*, October 26, 1889, 3.
[48] H. W. L., "Quaker City Gossip," *The Sporting News*, October 26, 1889, 1; "Just One Contract for Indianapolis," *The Sporting News*, October 26, 1889, 3; "Soden Scores Von Der Ahe," *Chicago Daily Inter Ocean*, October 27, 1889, 2.

meeting at the same hotel, uncover its work, declare its intentions and begin business on its own account. These men will be astonished at the magnitude of the scheme." The unnamed source also confirmed another rumor that had circulated over the last week, saying that while Anson would never join the Brotherhood's league, "It is true that one of the best men in the association is to take Anson's place on first base for the Chicago team next season."[49] Nor was it hard to guess who that man might be. The most highly regarded captain and first baseman in the American Association was Charlie Comiskey of St. Louis. The players in St. Louis disliked their owner, Chris Von der Ahe, intensely. Comiskey was from Chicago. Enough said.

In addition to claims that the Brotherhood might not even open negotiations after all, another unnamed member of the BPBP declared it might up its demands, almost as if it wanted to make sure the League would never agree to a deal. Although the players agreed that the reserve rule should remain, now this source said the Brotherhood wanted the right of reserve to last four years only, at which point the player could either leave his club or negotiate to stay, and at that point the club might reserve him up to four more years. Furthermore, having completed the initial four-year period, any player released by his team in mid-season would still get the pay called for in the rest of the contract, instead of only what he had earned up to that point.[50]

On November 1, just a few days before the Brotherhood's meeting, Tim Keefe announced its program to the baseball world. One writer summed it up by stating, "The League magnates will not be consulted. In other words, the players intend to go it alone."[51] Keefe made an official statement just a couple days later, remarking, "Yes, the players are through with the present owners of the League

---

[49] "No Compromise," *Boston Daily Advertiser*, October 29, 1889, 5.
[50] "This Seems Truthful," *Pittsburgh Dispatch*, October 30, 1889, 6.
[51] "The Brotherhood Plans," *New York Times*, November 2, 1889, 6.

clubs, and will have no further intercourse with them. We have gone too far to retreat now, so we will carry, or at least try to carry, our plans through."[52] Papers also announced the distribution of players for the teams of the new league, and while some individual assignments eventually proved wrong due to defections from the ranks and because some American Association players eventually joined the revolt, for the most part, the lists were on the mark.[53]

The plan required settling a few more details. The players needed to decide on a name. Their choice might not have been very original, but they decided on the Players National League. Brotherhood contracts stated that players would receive their 1889 salary for the next two seasons, plus a percentage of the profits as outlined above. The distribution of players also attempted to equalize the playing strengths of the clubs as much as possible so that all cities might have a chance at a quality team that would draw spectators and make some money.[54] Another departure from the practices of either existing league was that the home and visiting teams would split gate receipts on a fifty-fifty basis, which replaced the previously reported plan to pool all receipts of the entire league and redistribute them. The plans also talked of redistributing the players after each season to make sure the strength of the teams remained equal from one year to the next.[55]

One interesting move was that the BPBP decided to locate a team in Brooklyn. Brooklyn was an Association city (it switched

---

[52] "Keefe's Latest," *Pittsburgh Dispatch*, November 3, 1889, 6.
[53] For the original listings, see "Brotherhood Assignments," *Chicago Daily Inter Ocean*, November 1, 1889, 6.
[54] "The Brotherhood Plans," *New York Times*, November 2, 1889, 6.
[55] "The Sporting World," *Galveston Daily News*, November 2, 1889, 6. This idea, of redistributing players each year, was also a prominent feature of Francis Richter's Millennium Plan. Although not discussed here, Richter was the editor of *The Sporting Life* and offered his plan to try to cure baseball's ills over the 1887-1888 off-season. Part of his plan called for player redistribution to equalize the playing strengths of each team each year. For more on the Millennium Plan, see chapters ten and eleven of Rob Bauer, *Outside the Lines of Gilded Age Baseball: The Finances of 1880s Baseball*.

leagues about two weeks later) at the time. The BPBP reasoned that Brooklyn was big enough to support two teams based on the Bridegrooms drawing more than 350,000 fans in 1889, but in so doing made a powerful enemy of Brooklyn owner Charles Byrne. Still, the BPBP decided it was worth the risk, rather than locating its last franchise in either Washington, D.C., or Indianapolis. Neither of those cities had fared well as National League cities, even without competition, so if the Brotherhood tried to compete with the League in those locations, those teams were almost certain to fail financially.[56]

Even if informed baseball observers knew it would be anticlimactic, the BPBP held its grand conference in New York on November 4 and 5. Imitating the authors of the Declaration of Independence, the Brotherhood issued a statement because "in taking this step we feel that we owe it to the public and to ourselves to explain briefly some of the reasons by which we have been moved." Some observers also noted that the second day of the meeting, November 5, was Guy Fawkes Day, the anniversary of the 1605 plot by English rebels to blow up the House of Lords.[57] Whether the Brotherhood planned the dates to coincide, its statement read:

> There was a time when the league stood for integrity and fair dealing; today it stands for dollars and cents. Once it looked to the elevation of the game and an honest exhibition of the sport; today its eyes are upon the turnstile. Men have come into the business from no other motive than to exploit it for every dollar in sight. Measures originally intended for the good of the game have been perverted to instruments for wrong; the reserve rule and the provisions of the national agreement gave the managers unlimited power, and they

---

[56] "No Use for the League," *Chicago Daily Inter Ocean*, November 2, 1889, 2.
[57] Stevens, *Baseball's Radical for All Seasons*, 105.

have not hesitated to use this in the most arbitrary and incendiary way, and players have been bought, sold, and exchanged as though they were sheep instead of American citizens! "Reservations" became with them another name for property of right in the player, and by a combination among themselves, stronger than the strongest trust, they were able to enforce the most arbitrary measures, and the player had either to submit or get out of the profession in which he had spent years in attaining proficiency.

Even the disbandment and retirement of a club did not force the players from the octopus clutch, for they were then peddled around to the highest bidder. That the player sometimes profited by the sale has nothing to do with the case, but only proves the injustice of his previous restraint. Two years ago we met the league and attempted to remedy some of these evils, but through what has been politely called "league diplomacy" we completely failed. Unwilling longer to submit to such treatment we made a strong effort last spring to reach an understanding with the league.

To our application for a hearing they replied that the matter was not of sufficient importance to warrant a meeting, and suggested that it be put off until fall. Our committee replied that the players felt that the league had broken faith with them; that while the results might be of little importance to the managers they were of importance to the players; that if the league would not concede what was fair we would adopt other means to protect ourselves; that if postponed until fall we would be separated and at the mercy of the league, and that as the only course left us required time and labor to develop, we must therefore insist upon an immediate conference. Then, upon the final refusal to meet us, we began organizing for ourselves and are now in shape to go ahead next year under new management and new auspices.

We believe that it is possible to conduct our national game upon lines which will not infringe upon individual and natural rights. We ask to be judged solely by our work, and, believing that the game can be played more fairly and its business conducted more intelligently under a plan which excludes everything arbitrary and un-American, we look forward with confidence to the support of the public and the future of the national game.[58]

"Orator" Jim O'Rourke, true to his nickname, expressed these feelings with a somewhat more rhetorical flourish. Speaking in his home town of Bridgeport, Connecticut, he told his audience, "We have endeavored to build on a foundation even more substantial than Earth itself. Our ascension from thralldom is positive, uncoupled from all doubts, notwithstanding the warning of the master magnates and the snapping of their whip, which has no more terror for the players as they stand today shorn of all physical strength to use them."[59]

After this, little remains to write. The Brotherhood cleared up a few more details, such as the exact plan for distributing profits, the language of the Brotherhood contract that all league members signed, and things of that nature. They also decided to change course regarding their relationship with the American Association and

---

[58] "Ball-Players' Meeting," *Chicago Daily Tribune*, November 5, 1889, 6. Baseball historian John Thorn believes that the Nationalist Club in Boston might have inspired the wording of the document. The Nationalist Club was an organization recently formed by utopians such as Edward Bellamy, whose utopian novel *Looking Backward* first appeared in 1888, to try to change a society based on competition and individualism. Thorn, *Baseball in the Garden of Eden*, 238.

[59] Lee Lowenfish, *The Imperfect Diamond: A History of Baseball's Labor Wars* (Lincoln: University of Nebraksa Press, 1980): 41.

make a play for some of the elite members of that body because all the press reports concerning the attitude of the Association indicated it would cooperate with the League against the players.[60] Eventually, twenty-six American Association players joined the Brotherhood's league.

With this proclamation, the story shifts from the causes of the Brotherhood War to the history of the war itself. That is a tale for later. It has its heroes and villains. It is a tale of selfishness, greed, lying, cheating, bribery, backstabbing, money, and power, but also heroism, virtue, self-sacrifice, loyalty, and brotherhood. The saga features exciting action on the field coupled with byzantine maneuverings off it. We know that, ultimately, the players lost their battle with the National League. Now, we also know why they felt compelled to fight.

---

[60] "Ball-Players' Meeting," *Chicago Daily Tribune*, November 5, 1889, 6.

The Storm Breaks

Thank you for reading *Outside the Lines of Gilded Age Baseball: The Origins of the 1890 Players League*. If you enjoyed this book, you can find other books in this series, as well as my works of historical fiction, at my website:

robbauerbooks.com

You can also sign up for my Readers Club mailing list to receive notifications about future books and promotions. If you enjoyed reading the book, I would be grateful if you'd leave a short review on whatever website you purchased it from. Favorable reader reviews are very important to authors like me. They help tremendously in attracting new readers and spreading the word about existing books you think others will enjoy. Finally, if you like the book, please consider recommending it to fellow baseball fans so they, too, can learn more about the early years of this exciting sport.

Thank you!

A Few Notes on Statistics

It seems that most baseball fans fall into two classes. One consists of those who enjoy watching the game for the excitement and to enjoy the skill of those who play it. They know the rules and the basic strategies of the game, but what concerns them most is the score at the end of the day. If their favorite team wins 90 or more games in a season, they know they have a good team. Their team will probably end up in the playoffs, which means these fans can enjoy watching their heroes for at least another week, maybe longer, and if things break just right, they can celebrate a World Series title when everything is over.

Then there is the second group, whom I refer to as, for lack of a better term and without meaning to sound pejorative at all, the stat heads. These are the folks who intend to analyze everything about baseball, breaking down every event to its mathematical probabilities and contribution to victory or defeat. These are the people who long ago moved beyond the traditional baseball statistics such as wins, earned run average, batting average, runs batted in, and stolen bases. In place of these traditional measures of skill, the stat heads now swear by new metrics such as wins above replacement (WAR), weighted on base average (wOBA), fielding independent pitching (FIP), or batting average on balls in play (BABIP). They have done so for good reason, too. The traditional stats could be quite misleading in terms of how much they indicated regarding a player's contribution to victory. In real world terms, this means that teams often spend lots of money—millions or tens of millions of dollars—on players who do not help them win that many games. Teams focused on traditional statistics, the stat heads point out, embrace a model that is an inefficient way to win baseball games.

A Few Notes on Statistics

The problem is, of course, that books about baseball that one group finds palatable are not as interesting to the other. Fans who appreciate both equally are hard to find. One reason is that it takes effort and a moderate level of mathematical literacy to understand how some statistics work and what they indicate. Calculating batting average is easy, and the statistic has been around forever, so most observers know what numbers equate to a "good" batting average. Divide the number of hits by the number of at bats, and you have batting average. A .300 average is good, a .200 average is poor, and something between .250 and .275 is average. Figuring BABIP is tougher, and it is also new, so most observers are not sure what a "good" BABIP number looks like, much less how to figure out what someone's BABIP is.

The problem goes the other way as well. Some writers and television commentators never tire of pointing out what a "clutch" hitter some player is, for instance. This drives the stat heads nuts because they know that the "ability" to hit in the clutch is not really an ability at all. Given enough at bats to create a proper sample size, a player's performance in tight situations will be close enough to his performance in all situations that there is almost no difference. Some of the stats heads have dedicated themselves to replacing meaningless or misleading statistics with more meaningful ones, and they do not appreciate it when people perpetuate statistical ignorance.

An admission: I really like statistical analysis, and I think it has done a great deal to advance our collective understanding of baseball. In a perfect (baseball) world, I would like to see all fans take the time to become more statistically literate because it opens new ways of seeing the game and understanding what happens on the field and why it matters.

That being said, there is almost no statistical analysis in this book. The main reason is that the book is not about events on the field; rather, it is about the big issues influencing the game and the habits of various players in the 1880s. Furthermore, the people making decisions about how to run teams and win games in the 1880s had no knowledge of the newer statistics some of us depend on today. It would be unfair to criticize them for not using metrics that did not exist. Therefore, the only times I have used statistics is when I want to give the reader a sense of a player's overall quality as part of a brief biographical sketch, and even then, I have tried to use the same ones for consistency. The only nontraditional statistics requiring elaboration the reader will find in this book are:

Wins Above Replacement, or WAR. This is a number that describes how many wins a player was worth beyond what a replacement player would have produced. Statisticians use the concept of a replacement player, rather than an average player, because a replacement player is a borderline major league player or journeyman veteran who is available at low cost. Teams can find them easily without expending many resources to acquire their services. An average player, in contrast, would require resources to acquire and is not freely available, so a team would have to lose something of value, money or another player, to acquire an average player. WAR can be either positive or negative, with a negative WAR indicating the player performed worse than a replacement player would have and cost his team victories with poor play. A player with a single-season WAR between 2.0 and 3.0 is a quality major league player, a WAR around 5.0 is an all-star level player, and someone with a WAR of 7.0 or more is a Most Valuable Player or Cy Young Award candidate most seasons. A team of only replacement players would win about 30% of the time. Another useful thing about WAR is that it works to compare players from vastly different eras. A player with 3.5 WAR in 1888 contributed the same amount to victory as someone with 3.5 WAR in 1988, even if they made their contributions in different ways.

On-Base Percentage Plus Slugging Percentage Plus, or OPS+. I use this measure because research demonstrates that on-base

A Few Notes on Statistics

percentage and slugging percentage are the two statistics most correlated with scoring runs, with on-base percentage the most important of the two. Putting the two together in one statistic, therefore, is a good measure of a player's offensive contribution to victory. Some other stats are slightly better measures, perhaps, but in this book I want to give readers a general picture of a player's offensive ability, not a precise analysis, so it will do. The plus means that the number reflects how the player compared to the league average for that season. A player with an OPS+ of 100 was exactly average. Numbers above 100 mean the player exceeded the league average, while an OPS+ below 100 means the player hit worse than an average player that year. Every point above or below 100 equals one percent, so a player with an OPS+ of 110 was ten percent better than average, while someone with a score of 90 was ten percent below average. Once again, this has the added benefit of allowing us to compare the contributions of players across eras.

Earned Run Average Plus, or ERA+. This works just like OPS+, except it describes the earned run average of a pitcher compared to what an average pitcher did that season, so the reader will have a general picture of a pitcher's performance for a given season.

I've also used a batter's "slash" numbers in some cases. These are three numbers, separated by slashes, thus the name. The first number is batting average, the second is on-base percentage, and the third is slugging percentage. Like OPS+, I use this to give the reader a feel for the all-around hitting abilities of the player in question.

That's it. If you understand these few concepts, you know what you need to know to understand the statistics used in this book.

The Terminology of the Game in the 1880s

All sports have their own terms and ways of referring to the action, and these terms often differ from the regular usage of the word. These words might also have changed meanings since their use on the baseball fields of the 1880s. Here is a short glossary of words used in this book that fit this description.

Battery – The pitcher and catcher.

Box – In the 1880s, the pitcher delivered the ball from the pitcher's box, rather than standing on the pitcher's mound as they do today. We still have the phrase "knocked out of the box," which refers to hitting a pitcher so hard that his team decides to remove the pitcher from the game, even though the pitcher's box itself is no more.

Bulldoze – To argue angrily with, or otherwise try to intimidate, an umpire. Bulldozing was different from kicking, in that bulldozers did not just whine but often threatened the umpire with his position. In the 1880s, the different leagues sometimes removed their umpires if powerful owners complained about the umpire's work too vigorously.

Championship Season – Games in the championship season were what people today call regular season games. Observers called them championship season games because whoever won the most won the league championship and to differentiate them from the frequent exhibition games teams engaged in before, during, and after the championship season.

The Terminology of the Game in the 1880s

Coaching – When a player engaged in heckling, trash talking, or similar behaviors. Unlike today, coaching generally did not mean trying to improve a player's performance through instruction.

Condition – A general term describing a player's current state of physical well-being.

Crank – A fan or spectator.

Grounds – The playing field.

Hippodroming – Dishonest playing, usually involving one team throwing a game to another to reward gamblers.

Jonah – A player or team that seemed to be bad luck for another player or team.

Kicking – To argue or complain, especially about the umpire's decisions.

Nine – Used as a synonym for a team. Partly because there were nine players on the field at once and partly because some spectators of the 1880s still remembered when teams had nine total players.

Phenomenal – Like it does today, the word signified a player believed to have exceptional talent. However, observers frequently applied it to up-and-coming young players surrounded by a great deal of hype. Writers sometimes changed the word from an adjective to a noun and used it as a blanket term for such men, writing that their team had signed a phenomenal. Baseball writers referred to one pitcher, John Smith, as a phenomenal so often that Phenomenal Smith became his name while he played ball.

Support – On the field, this meant that a team played quality defense to back up its pitcher. If a team played poor defense, people would write that the team did not support its pitcher.

Work – A reference to the quality of a player's performance. For example, writers described a poor or uninspired performance by writing that a player had done indifferent work.

Bibliography

Books

Alexander, Charles. *Turbulent Seasons: Baseball in 1890-1891*. Dallas, SMU Press, 2011.

Bauer, Robert. *Outside the Lines of Gilded Age Baseball: Alcohol, Fitness, and Cheating in 1880s Baseball*. Rob Bauer Books, 2018.

Bauer, Robert. *Outside the Lines of Gilded Age Baseball: Gambling, Umpires, and Racism in 1880s Baseball*. Rob Bauer Books, 2018.

Bauer, Robert. *Outside the Lines of Gilded Age Baseball: The Finances of Gilded Age Baseball*. Rob Bauer Books, 2018.

DiSalvatore, Bryan. *A Clever Base-Ballist: The Life and Times of John Montgomery Ward*. New York, Pantheon Books, 1999.

Jaffe, Chris. *Evaluating Baseball's Managers: A History and Analysis of Performance in the Major Leagues, 1876-2008*. Jefferson, North Carolina, McFarland & Company, 2010.

James, Bill. *The New Bill James Historical Abstract: The Classic, Completely Revised*. New York: The Free Press, 2001.

Lamster, Mark. *Spalding's World Tour: The Epic Adventure That Took Baseball Around the Globe—and Made it America's Game*. New York, Public Affairs, 2006.

Levine, Peter. *AG Spalding and the Rise of Baseball: The Promise of American Sport*. New York, Oxford University Press, 1985.

Lowenfish, Lee. *The Imperfect Diamond: A History of Baseball's Labor Wars*. Lincoln, University of Nebraska Press, 1980.

Nemec, David. *The Beer and Whiskey League: The Illustrated History of the American Association—Baseball's Renegade Major League*. New York, Lyons & Burford, 1994.

Seymour, Harold. *Baseball: The Early Years*. New York, Oxford University Press, 1960.

Spalding, Al. *Spalding's Official Base Ball Guide, 1889*. Chicago and New York: A.G. Spalding & Bros, 1889.

Stevens, David. *Baseball's Radical for All Seasons: A Biography of John Montgomery Ward*. The Scarecrow Press, Lanham, MD, 1998.

Thorn, John. *Baseball in the Garden of Eden: The Secret History of the Early Game*. New York, Simon & Schuster, 2011.

Journals
Nineteenth Century Notes, John Husman, "Toledo and Fleet Walker," Society for American Baseball Research, Spring 2010.

Bibliography

Magazines

Outing, Harry Palmer, "America's National Game," July, 1888.

Newspapers

Boston Daily Advertiser, 1889

Chicago Daily Inter Ocean, 1887, 1889

Chicago Daily Tribune, 1886-1889

Evening Star (Washington D. C.), 1887

Galveston Daily News, 1887, 1889

Los Angeles Daily Herald, 1889

Milwaukee Daily Journal, 1889

Milwaukee Sentinel, 1889

Morning Oregonian, 1887

New York Evening World, 1887, 1889

New York Times, 1885-1889

Omaha Daily Bee, 1887

Pittsburg Dispatch, 1889

Rocky Mountain News (Denver), 1888

St. Louis Daily Globe-Democrat, 1887

San Francisco Evening Bulletin, 1887

The London Times, 1874

The Sporting Life, 1885-1889

The Sporting News, 1886-1889

Websites
Michigan State University History Department, history.msu.edu

Society for American Baseball Research, research.sabr.org and sabr.org.

Index

A

African Americans in Baseball, 15
AG Spalding & Bros., 27-28
AJ Reach Company, 28
Alcoholism and Player Drinking, 12, 60, 70, 91-92, 99, 125-128, 157, 159, 194-195, 202, 243
American Federation of Trades and Labor Unions, 283
Andrews, Ed, 86, 88, 288
Anson, Adrian "Cap", 19, 22-25, 42, 75, 82, 91, 94, 98-99, 107, 109, 163, 169, 172, 174-175, 177, 179, 276, 290, 292

B

Baldwin, Charles, 80-81
Baldwin, Mark, 112, 257-258
Barnes, Ross, 17-18, 21, 282
Barnie, Billy, 133-134, 217, 220-221
Barnum, P. T., 43
Barr, Bob, 58
Bastian, Charlie, 74, 86-88
Beecher, Ed, 143
Beer, 14, 59, 91, 275
Bennett, Charlie, 181-183
Billings, J. B., 28, 113, 149
Blackhurst, James, 50, 52-53, 151, 155
Blacklist, 36, 61-62, 90, 126, 157, 159, 181
Bonaparte, Napoleon, 172
Booth, Fred, 224
Boulanger Affair, 172
Boyle, Henry, 259, 262, 288
Brotherhood of Professional Baseball Players, 6-7, 37-41,

48-49, 66, 73-77, 80, 82, 91, 100-103, 108-109, 120, 169, 186, 215, 233, 251-252,
1888 contract with National League, 157-160
Achieving recognition from NL, 136-160
Formation of Players League, 271-298
Relations with National League in 1889, 254-270
Reaction to Brush Plan, 187-214
Reaction to its formation, 50-64
Stance on player contracts, 121-135
Brouthers, Dan, 74, 152, 155, 257-258, 262, 282, 287
Brown, Bill, 206
Brown, Henry, 154
Brown, John, 29
Browning, Pete, 234, 240-242, 245
Brunell, Frank, 196, 285-286, 288
Brush, John, 10, 33-34, 37, 186, 265
Brush Plan, 10, 161-170, 180, 185-186, 215, 257-262, 264, 268-269, 275, 282, 284, 287, 289,
Impact on 1888 season, 187-214
Brynan, Tod, 112
Buffinton, Charlie, 74
Burdock, Jack, 125, 143
Burke, Eddie, 291
Burns, Tom "Oyster", 35, 222
Bushong, Doc, 35, 68, 249-250
Butler, Benjamin, 110
Byrne, Charles, 6, 34-35, 115, 183, 217, 221-222, 224-226, 253, 294,
Behavior in 1889 pennant race, 245-250

C

Caesar, Julius, 189
Carnegie, Andrew, 28
Carnot, Sadie, 172
Carpenter, Hick, 204
Carroll, Cliff, 52, 57-58, 74, 81-82, 89, 125

Index

Carroll, Fred, 287
Caruthers, Bob, 35, 80, 89-90, 113-116, 119
Caruthers, James, 113
Casey, Dan, 86-88
Casino Rink Co., 28
Caylor, Oliver Perry, 146-147, 203-204, 217-218, 221, 245
Chadwick, Henry, 18, 20, 47, 63, 74, 99, 167-168, 170, 194, 247-248
Chamberlain, Elton, 237
Chinatown (San Francisco), 175-176
Choate, Rufus, 134-135
Clarke, Dad, 112
Clarkson, John, 107-113, 192, 249, 282
Clements, Jack, 86-87
Cleveland, Grover, 171
Collins, Hub, 35, 90, 237
Colosseum, 173
Comiskey, Charlie, 5, 24, 75, 134, 170, 246, 292
Conant, William, 28-29, 113
Connor, Roger, 41, 45, 206, 287
Coogan, James, 276, 279
Cook, Paul, 90, 240
Crane, Sam, 54, 58, 73-74
Cricket, 162-163, 168
Cusick, Andy, 87

D

Dailey, Ed, 87
Dalrymple, Abner, 91, 125, 127, 152
Daly, Tom, 211, 257
Darwin, Charles, 178
Davidson, Mordecai, 35, 234-243, 253
Day, John, 32-33, 37, 43-44, 46-47, 120, 133-134, 141, 145, 155-156, 191-192, 216, 225, 259-260, 263-265, 272, 279, 282-283
Dauvray, Helen, 42

Deasley, Pat, 53
Declaration of Independence, 294
Delahanty, Ed, 267
Delmonico's, 179
Denny, Jerry, 152, 210, 262, 288
Dorgan, Mike, 41
Duffy, Hugh, 208-209
Dunlap, Fred, 56, 69-70, 73, 80, 117-119, 135, 274, 282, 287
Duryea, Jesse, 249
Duval, Clarence, 174-175, 177-178

E

Ebeleard Manufacturing Company, 82
Eclipse Park, 234, 242
Ehret, Red, 237, 240
Eiteljorge, Ed, 291
England Tour of 1874, 23, 42, 162-164, 167-168
Esterbrook, Dude, 46-47, 235-236, 239
Ewing, Buck, 41, 73, 202, 206, 280, 287
Ewing, John, 241

F

Faatz, Jay, 266-267, 282, 288
Farrar, Sid, 87-88, 209
Farren, B. F., 224
Fennelly, Frank, 83
Ferguson, Bob, 277
Ferguson, Charlie, 86-88, 112, 219
Flint, Silver, 91-92, 94, 143
Fogarty, Jim, 86-88, 171, 271, 274, 287
Foley, Curry, 40-41, 105, 157
Force, Davy, 20, 22
Forder, Neville, 168

Fort Missoula, 27
Foutz, Dave, 35, 90

G

Gaffney, John, 59, 277
Galvin, Jim, 84-86
Gambling, 14
George, Will, 206
Gerhardt, Joe, 41, 71, 73
Getzein, Charlie, 55, 208
Gilligan, Barney, 89
Glasscock, Jack, 199, 207-208, 262, 288
Goldsmith, Fred, 246-248, 250
Gore, George, 91, 94, 97, 206
Grant, Hugh, 282
Great Pyramids, 171-172
Great Sphinx, 171-172
Guy Fawkes Day, 294-295

H

Hackett, Mert, 74, 125
Hanlon, Ned, 52, 60, 74, 125-127, 135, 141, 150, 155, 170, 187-188, 258, 262, 265, 271-272, 282, 287
Harrison, Benjamin, 179-180
Hart, Jim, 168, 249, 269
Hatfield, Gil, 206
Haymarket Square Murders, 51
Healy, John, 173, 207, 258
Hecker, Guy, 68, 240, 242, 247
Hecker Supply Company, 68
Heinzel, Emily, 147
Henry Schomberg & Co., 83
Herbert, Harry, 43
Hewitt, Walter, 82

Hines, Paul, 89
Hobert, Bill, 35
Holliday, "Bug", 204
Houck, Sadie, 127
Hulbert, William, 18, 20-22, 25-26

I

Irwin, Arthur, 52, 67, 74, 125-126, 141, 150, 152, 197-198, 274, 287
Irwin, Charlie, 86
Irwin, John, 287

J

James, Bill, 20
Jerusalem, 89
Johnson, Al, 271-276, 285, 289
Johnson, Tom, 274, 285
Johnson, Will, 274, 285
Johnston, Dick, 287
Jones, Charley, 30

K

Kalakaua, King, 166, 177-178
Keefe, Tim, 41, 45-47, 73-74, 125, 152, 192, 254-255, 258, 265-266, 282, 287, 293,
    Reaction to Brush Plan, 196, 198, 206
Keenan, Jim, 249
Kelly, John, 277
Kelly, Mike, 31, 69, 71, 73, 102, 105, 107, 113, 115, 123-124, 152, 176, 192,
    Sale to Boston, 91-100, 127, 132
Kerins, John, 245

Kilroy, Matt, 224
King, Silver, 59
Klumpf, Charlie, 82
Knights of Labor, 149, 154, 283
Knowles, Jimmy, 58
Krock, Gus, 108-109, 112

L

Labor Day, 29
Labor Theory of Value, 132-134
Larner, Bob, 195, 203
Latham, Arlie, 76, 90, 134
Leffingwell, Samuel, 283-284
Leo XIII, Pope, 173
Loftus, Tom, 288-289
Lovett, Tom, 35
Lowe, Bobby, 291

M

MacMillan, Newton, 177-178
Madden, Kid, 30, 107
Manifest Destiny, 180
Manning, Jim, 67, 171
Marr, Lefty, 250
Marx, Karl, 133
Mathews, Bobby, 145-146, 157
Mays, Al, 35
McCarthy, Tommy, 246
McCormick, Jim, 80, 91-92, 94-95, 127
McKinney, Buck, 242-243
McKinnon, Al, 52
McPhee, Bid, 204
McQuaid, John, 277
McVey, Cal, 17-18, 21
Mills, A. G., 179, 268

Morgan, W. J., 167
Morrill, John, 52, 60, 75, 98, 210-211, 281-282, 287
Morton, Sam, 286-287
Mott, Albert, 132-134, 205, 229
Mulford Jr., Ren, 219, 246
Mulvey, Joe, 87-88
Murnane, Tim, 50, 281
Mutrie, Jim, 46-47, 133, 249-250
Myers, Al, 267
Myers, George, 258, 262, 282

N

Naismith, James, 27
Nash, Billy, 287
National Agreement, 47, 66, 74, 104, 122-123, 143, 181, 183-184, 247, 279-280
Nelson, Admiral, 172
Nichols, Kid, 286
Nimick, William, 118-119, 183-184, 291

O

O'Brien, Darby, 35
O'Neill, Tip, 37, 59, 226
O'Rourke, Jim, 17, 31, 33, 41-45, 47-48, 52, 60, 71-73, 143, 163, 206, 297
Orr, Dave, 35, 146-147
Ovens, A. G., 193

P

Palmer, Harry, 20, 61-62, 97, 99, 130-132, 140, 218, 285,
    On Spalding Tour of 1888-1889, 164-180
Peoples, Jimmy, 243

Pettit, Bob, 257
Pfeffer, Fred, 124-125, 143, 152, 258, 271, 276, 281, 287-288
Phelps, Zach, 228-229, 234
Phillips, Horace, 218
Polo Grounds, 275-276, 279, 283
Pottstown Iron Works, 83
Princeton, 88
Pritchard, Joe, 198, 219, 231-232
Purcell, Blondie, 134

R

Racism, 14-15
Radbourn, Charlie, 30, 107, 112, 138, 142-143, 152
Radford, Paul, 35, 288
Ramsey, Tom, 234, 240
Raymond, Harry, 240
Reach, Al, 141, 151-152, 161, 260-261, 289-290
Recreation Park, 153-154
Reilly, John, 204-205
Reserve Rule, 8, 11-12, 32, 51, 62, 65, 72, 76, 80, 100, 103-106, 116, 122, 125, 131, 138, 144, 158, 181-182, 279-280, 284, 295
Richardson, Daniel, 41, 73, 206
Richardson, Hardy, 287
Ridgewood Park, 222, 275
Robinson, Yank, 135, 250
Rogers, John, 32, 148-151, 155-156, 159, 196, 209, 216, 219, 263-264, 272, 279, 289
Roosevelt, Teddy, 179
Rounders, 179
Rowe-White Affair, 180-186, 212, 276, 282
Rowe, Dave, 52, 60, 182
Rowe, Jack, 180-186, 276, 282, 287
Ruth, Babe, 88

Ryan, Jimmy, 169

S

Sabbatarianism, 14
Salary Limit Plan of 1885, 8-9, 65-80, 160, 196, 202, 207, 260
Sanders, Ben, 258
Scandrett, Al, 84
Scanlon, Mike, 57-59, 81
Schomberg, Otto, 83-84
Schomberg Hardwood Lumber Company, 84
Selee, Frank, 227
Shannon, Dan, 240-241
Sharsig, Billy, 146
Shaw, Frederick, 89
Sherman, William, 177
Singer, Nimick, & Co., 154
Slattery, Mike, 206
Smith, Pop, 143
Snyder, Charles, 288
Social Darwinism, 174, 178, 201
Soden, Arthur, 28-33, 36-37, 97-98, 110-113, 115, 138, 149, 159, 183, 191-192, 261, 265, 281, 286
South End Grounds, 31
Spalding, Al, 9-10, 16-19, 21-23, 25-28, 32, 36-37, 42, 50, 60, 70-71, 126, 129-131, 185-186, 209, 211-213, 216, 218, 223, 257-258,
    Formation of Players League, 271-298
    International Tour of 1888-1889, 162-180, 187
    Refusal to meet with Brotherhood in 1889, 264-270
    Role in recognizing Brotherhood, 148-160
    Sale of John Clarkson, 108-112
    Sale of Mike Kelly, 90-94, 96, 98-100
Spalding, James, 17
Spalding, Harriet, 17
Spalding Manufacturing Company, 28

Index

Spalding Tour of 1888-1889, 161-180
Sportsman's Park, 36
Sprague, Charlie, 112
Stackhouse, George, 129, 147, 199, 255
Stern, Aaron, 83, 202, 204, 219, 231-232, 244-245, 251
Stearns, Fred, 55, 109, 117-118, 141, 181, 183
Stovey, Harry, 68, 75
Stratton, Scott, 240
Stricker, Cub, 288
Sullivan, Fred, 67-68
Sullivan, Marty, 257
Sullivan, William "Mugwump", 111, 149, 197
Sunday, Billy, 291
Sutton, Ezra, 19, 22
Swampdoodle Grounds, 81
Swartwood, Ed, 75
Sweeney, Charlie, 127

T

Tammany Hall, 33
Taylor, Billy, 127
Thompson, Sam, 81, 147-148
Titcomb, Ledell, 206
Tomney, Phil, 236, 242
Training by Players, 12-13
Triumvirate, see Soden, Arthur
Twain, Mark, 179
Twitchell, Larry, 259

U

Umpires, 13-14, 24, 75
Union League, 65
United States Congress, 29

V

Van Haltren, George, 112, 290
Vaughn, Farmer, 240
Vickery, Tom, 291
Victorian Grounds, 275
Virtue, Jake, 291
Von Bülow, Hans, 256
Von der Ahe, Chris, 6, 34-37, 59, 67-68, 89-90, 113, 131, 216-217, 221, 226, 243, 253, 284, 292,
    Behavior in 1889 pennant race, 245-250
Vonderhorst, Harry, 223-224

W

Wales, Prince of, 172-173
Walker, Moses, 15, 25
Walker, Welday, 15
Wallace, William, 280
Ward, John, 38-42, 47-48, 72-76, 78, 120, 169-170, 179, 185-188, 197, 199, 213,
    Essay in *Lippincott's*, 103-107
    Formation of Brotherhood, 50-64
    Formation of Players League, 271-298
    Gaining recognition for Brotherhood, 136-160
    Relations with National League in 1889, 254-270
    Stance on player contracts in 1887, 121-135
Washington Park, 245, 248, 275
Watkins, W. H., 55-57, 108
Weaver, Farmer, 240
Webster, Daniel, 134
Welch, Mickey, 41, 73, 206
Western Arms and Cartridge Co., 28
When Clothing Company, 33
Whitaker, W. H., 83
White, Bill, 90

Index

White, Deacon, 17-18, 21, 50, 56-57, 282, 287,
    Role in Rowe-White Affair, 180-186
White, Will, 185
Whitney, Art, 206
Whitney, Jim, 143, 206-207
Wikoff, Wheeler, 64, 228-229, 248, 251
Williamson, Ned, 52, 69, 91, 96-97, 143, 286
Wiman, Erastus, 33, 197, 199, 273, 279
Wise, Sam, 211, 287
Wolf, Chicken, 236-237, 239-241
Wood, George, 87-88, 152, 274, 287
Wood, Robert, 138
Wright, George, 17, 50, 281
Wright, Harry, 20, 23, 87, 209
Wright, Sam, 23

Y

Young, Nick, 10, 45, 60, 64, 73, 106, 182, 184, 188-191, 195, 199, 201-203, 207, 209-211, 262-263, 266-267,
    Role in recognizing Brotherhood, 136-160

Z

Zimmer, Chief, 282
Zulus, 174

ABOUT THE AUTHOR

I'm Rob Bauer, author of historical fiction and nonfiction books and owner of Rob Bauer Books. I hold a PhD in American History and was a Distinguished Doctoral Fellow at the University of Arkansas.

My fiction has two purposes—entertaining readers and explaining historical injustice. Although I enjoy adventure and humorous books as much as the next reader, I'd like my books to stand for something a little bigger. All my studies in history put me in a position to do that. Whether I'm writing about how racism damages the individual psyche, the deportation of the Métis people of Montana, the South's prison labor system, or the utter terror of the Belgian Congo, with my books you'll find yourself in powerful historical stories.

I also write nonfiction about baseball history because I've always loved the game, its history, and its lore. I sometimes joke that baseball may be the one thing in life I truly understand. Although I love the statistical side of the game, if you don't, never fear because my histories go light on the statistics and heavy on what baseball was like in the past. They're stories about baseball, but stories with a point.

When I'm not working on my next story or writing project, I enjoy spending time at the beach. And, oh yeah, I still read a history book or two. When I'm not watching baseball.

ACKNOWLEDGMENTS

I also want to thank the people who helped make this book possible, especially Jim Soular for his help with editing. Ali Holst gets the credit for the cover art and design. Thank you to David Mitchell for his commentary on sample chapters.

I'd also like to thank everyone who purchases *Outside the Lines of Gilded Age Baseball: The Origins of the 1890 Players League* for reading my book. If you enjoyed reading it, I would be grateful if you'd leave a short review of the book on whatever website you purchased it from. Favorable reader reviews are very important to authors like me. They help tremendously in attracting new readers and spreading the word about existing books that you think others will enjoy. Thank you!

Made in the USA
Columbia, SC
26 October 2021